IRREPLACEABLE
Recovering God's Heart for Dads

Greg Austen

ENDORSEMENTS

"This book needs to move to the top of your 'books to read' list. Greg digs deep into the core of God's love for fathers and family and then explores how to apply that amidst a society that, at times, seems opposed to those ideals. What's more, it's balanced with incredible transparency about his personal experiences with his own father, as well as his own journey as a dad. Make no mistake—after reading it, you will walk away inspired."

—Rob Denler, Men's Services Director, Life Network in Colorado Springs, CO

"Greg Austen has been a fierce advocate for fatherhood for decades, whether it was in his own experiences as a father and a son, his graduate research, or his work with CareNet and National Fatherhood Initiative. These experiences and deep understandings shape this book that elicits a renewed commitment to fatherhood as God designed it. As a wounded father myself, I appreciate Greg's candor balanced with his thoughtful research and accentuated with myriad cultural references. This is a book for fathers and sons everywhere. Be prepared to laugh, squirm, and be inspired as you learn to value the role of fatherhood in vibrant ways."

—Timothy Shea, Ph.D.
Education Professor at Lancaster Bible College Capital Seminary and Graduate School

"This book is the perfect blend of heart, vulnerability, and practical advice. I've already integrated Greg's insights into my work nationally with the fatherhood movement and in my own personal journey as a father."

—Erik Vecere
Chief Program Officer at National Fatherhood Initiative

"This book does for fatherhood what Keller's *Meaning of Marriage* does for marriage: it transcends naive formulas and worn-out advice, offering a rare opportunity to build a deeper vision and understanding of God's heart via His institutions. I'm excited for all you will gain from Greg's professional experience, his personal journey as a father, and his humility as a child of our Heavenly Father."

—Alexander Hettinga
Senior Manager of Fatherhood & Family Programming at Care Net

"Greg's book is a much-needed reprieve in a culture that continues on a trajectory that increasingly ignores the importance of the nuclear family and, more specifically, the importance of dads. While maintaining consistent biblical exegesis throughout, his manner is grace-filled and direct. It's my prayer that this book reaches the hearts of men and dads everywhere."

—Andrew Wood
Executive Director of Hope Resource Center in Knoxville, TN

"Dr. Austen's book is important and powerful. Its strength is a three-pronged approach that combines high-level, biblical content; exegetical expertise; and relatable, personal examples. Having just met my real father at the age of 55, I can tell you that this book is needed in today's world. May God bless readers with its healing words."

—Kathleen Patterson, Ph.D.
Professor & Doctoral Program Director at Regent University

"This is a generational anthem for all men with children that proclaims the unique and special purpose that God has for them as fathers. In Irreplaceable, Greg leads you from a biblical perspective both vulnerably and courageously to God's freedom and truth!"

—Amy Ford, President of Embrace Grace, Author of *Help Her Be Brave: Discover Your Place in the Pro-Life Movement*

Published by Greg Austen through Kindle Direct Publishing.

ISBN-13: 9798353485445

To the God and Father of our Lord Jesus Christ: Thank you for your heart and being the source and Spirit of all desire, drive, motivation. You are good, just, and your ways unfathomable. Truly, in you "we live and move and have our being" (Acts 17:28).

To my wife and best friend, Pam: Thank you for your steadfast love, and for being on this journey with me. Your courage, honesty, unconditional love, wisdom, and emotional coaching have made me a better parent and continue to make me a better person. I love you with all my heart.

To my children, Matthew, Tim, and Emily: You have been my inspiration. My greatest joy and contribution to this world is all that you are and will become. Words cannot express how incredibly proud I am of each of you and how honored I am to be your father.

TABLE OF CONTENTS

FOREWORD

I was honored when Greg asked me to provide the foreword for this book. I have known Greg for over 20 years, first as my pastor. I have also worked with him at National Fatherhood Initiative and now at Care Net. He has a heart for fathers, as evident by his efforts to help them be the best dads they can be in a range of settings, including in our nation's prisons. More importantly, I have watched him be a committed and loving father to his children—Matthew, Timothy and Emily. Indeed, Greg is a consistent and inspiring example of a good and Godly father that every dad should seek to emulate.

That said, when I learned the fantastic title of Greg's book, I was reminded of Matthew 3:13-17 through 4:1 because it so clearly illustrates God's heart as a father. This passage is the narrative where Jesus was to be baptized by John the Baptist. After Jesus was baptized, the Bible says, "…he saw the Spirit of God descending like a dove and coming to rest on him; and behold, a voice from heaven said, "This is my beloved Son, with whom I am well pleased." Then Jesus was led up by the Spirit into the wilderness to be tempted by the devil.

As I considered what was happening here, God gave me this notion of "affirmation before temptation." You see, here was Jesus— fully God and fully man—but God the Father knew that in Jesus's humanity, it was so critical that he received his Father's affirmation.

The timing of this affirmation was significant because Jesus was about to set out into the world on the mission for which he came to earth. So, God the Father's words of affirmation confirmed three significant things for his Son: his identity, his purpose and his destiny. Moreover, Jesus was about to face a time of temptation that had significant consequences for his mission and the salvation of mankind. Satan tried to tempt Jesus in three ways: "lust of the flesh," or the desire to enjoy; "lust of the eye," or the desire to obtain; and "the pride of life," or the desire to accomplish. And, as we know, Jesus faced all of these temptations and did not sin.

So, in this passage, God the Father has modeled a key action that every earthly father should emulate. That is, he must love and affirm his children. Why? Because one thing that we know for sure is the tempter will come—in one form or another.

But there is more…

This passage also illustrates clearly an important truth which Greg illuminates excellently in this book. God has a heart for and a unique purpose for earthly fathers. You see, in God's design for family, fathers are irreplaceable in their children's lives in the same way that God the father was irreplaceable in his Son's life. Earthly fathers are called and missioned to be a reflection of a heavenly model. Indeed, children have a "hole in their soul" in the shape of their dad. If a father is unable or unwilling to fill this hole, it can leave a wound that is not easily healed and one, as Greg rightly points out, can have a devastatingly negative impact not only on children but on society at large. So, Greg's book needs to be read, and its concepts and principles embraced both by all fathers and by those who seek to help them connect heart to heart with their children.

Roland C. Warren
President & CEO, Care Net; Author of *Bad Dads of the Bible: 8 Mistakes Every Good Dad Can Avoid* and *Raising Sons of Promise: A Guide for Single Mothers of Boys*

INTRODUCTION: THE FIRE IN OUR STORIES

I wasn't into zombies or *The Walking Dead* franchise as much as my kids were, but I have enjoyed other post-apocalyptic expressions like *The Hunger Games,* and Cormac McCarthy's Pulitzer Prize-winning novel, *The Road.*[1]

Like many post-apocalyptic stories, *The Road* presents readers with a barren, God-forsaken, post-apocalyptic world that offers little hope for humanity. One online forum commented on the savagery of McCarthy's world:

> The remnants of the human species are forced into cannibalizing each other merely to survive or scavenging for tins and other dried goods thanks to some kind of unspecified disaster that has overtaken the planet. As a result, the humans in the book are presented as shadows of their former selves, debased and animalistic in the way that they prey on each other and have lost any sense of moral code.[2]

---

[1] My second son, Timothy, a history major who later got his masters in theology and literature, defines "post-apocalypticism" as "the popular fascination with the aesthetics of post-apocalyptic landscapes, as well as an obsession with the implications of the end of the world on society and human nature." Again, *The Walking Dead, Terminator, Mad Max, The Hunger Games, Divergent, After Earth, The Day the Earth Stood Still, Cloverfield, Elysium, Oblivion,* etc.

[2] https://www.enotes.com/homework-help/explain-what-does-this-quote-means-carrying-fire-424360

In McCarthy's tale, only the main characters—a father and son—carry the seeds of civilized humanity, hope for a better world, and the motivation to thrive. McCarthy communicates this through the concept of "carrying the fire," which comes up in four scenes in *The Road*.

The first is when the boy is afraid and his father has to assure him they'll be okay. The boy asks if it's "because we're carrying the fire." His father nods and says, "Yes. Because we're carrying the fire."

The next comes after an encounter with cannibals. The father promises his son that he and the boy will never become like "those people." He explains that this is because "we're the good guys" and the ones carrying the fire.

The third is when the boy asks whether they might find another father and son like them. He asks, "And they could be carrying the fire too?" Trying not to extinguish hope, the father agrees that it's possible but that they can't be sure.

Finally, at the end of the book (spoiler alert) just before the father dies, he insists his son must continue on:

You have to carry the fire.
I don't know how to.
Yes, you do.
Is it real? The fire?
Yes, it is.
Where is it? I don't know where it is.
Yes, you do. It's inside you. It was always there. I see it.

Friend, you and I have a fire inside of us. It's always been there. And like the boy's experience in the scenes above, it's shaped by our questions, hopes, fears, and even the apocalyptic hurts we've experienced on our journeys. And, yes, it's intimately connected to our fathers—whatever they were or weren't, their powerful presence or haunting absence. Ultimately, as we'll explore in this book, it's also connected to God the Father and Source of All.

Unlike McCarthy's book, *Irreplaceable: Recovering God's Heart for Dads* isn't a work of fiction; it's about reality. And rather than being dark and God-forsaken, it's God-infused and full of light. Like McCarthy's book, however, it is still very much about "carrying the fire," primal relationships, and our human journey along "the road." Moreover, this book is about recognizing and recovering fire *from above* to make better sense of our journeys and pass on an irreplaceable legacy to our children. And it's based on two convictions:

1. "Fire from above"—the foundational desires, drive, motivation, and all that makes humans thrive—comes ultimately from the heart of God.

2. God's perfect design for human relationships includes an irreplaceable role for dads in carrying that fire and passing it on to their children. As biblical scholar N.T. Wright noted: "The God of whom the Bible speaks is, after all, the creator of the world. Part of the point of the whole story is that he loves the world and intends to rescue it, that he's put his plan into operation through a series of concrete events in actual history, and that he intends for this plan to be worked out through the concrete lives and work of his people."[3]

To be even more specific, God, the creator of and giver of all life, carries out his plans through "the concrete lives and work of his people," especially fathers. Or to summarize both points above even more simply for the purposes of this book, God is the source of the fire we carry within us and He has a special heart and purpose for dads.

With that in mind, this book is divided into three sections: Part 1, Essential Foundations, Part 2: Culture Shifts and Challenges, and Part 3: Your Irreplaceable Legacy. By way of analogy, you might think of our road trip together in this book like building a house (essential foundations) that will not only withstand hurricane-force winds and floods (culture shifts and challenges) but remain a thing of shelter and beauty for the next generation (your irreplaceable legacy). And now, before we jump into these sections, I'd like to illustrate and define three key concepts that are central to this book—the father wound, father

---

[3] N. T. Wright, *Simply Christian* (New York: HarperOne, 2006), 195.

5

absence, and fathering well—as well as give some context for my own journey with my dad along "the road."

DEFINITIONS AND DEVASTATIONS

The Father Wound

Michael Jackson was one of the most talented performers who ever lived. His personal life also contributed to his status as a global sensation. He was born on August 29, 1958 and died on June 25, 2009 at just fifty-one years old. Many called him "Wacko Jacko," and whether they were deserved or not, there were many other such nicknames and jokes surrounding the nature of his relationships with children and his many efforts to change his facial appearance. There are two things that he revealed during his life that give a powerful glimpse into the inner motivations of his heart. First, in an interview, he said that when his parents started the Jackson Five, he was about five years old. In the first rehearsal something went wrong and he stopped and said, "Daddy—." However, as Michael described it to the interviewer, "His dad cut him short and said, 'I am NOT your daddy I am your manager.'" Michael said he never forgot that.

Then, several years later, he was speaking in Oxford, England to 800 university students and professors about the foundation he had formed called "Help the Children." About twelve to thirteen minutes into his talk, he started to weep profusely, so much so, that he couldn't talk. As the audience grew uneasy, finally, one young man got up and brought the King of Pop a box of tissues. Once he had gained his composure, he said, "All I ever wanted in life was a father's love . . . all I ever wanted was for my father to call and say, 'Michael, I love you'

7

but he never has."[4]

Any serious consideration of Michael Jackson's driving motivations, discomfort with his appearance, or the associated torment in his soul must take into account "the father wound." Jackson's friend and spiritual mentor, Rabbi Scmuley Boteach, recorded thirty hours of conversations with Jackson in preparation for a book that was intended to let the King of Pop speak directly to the public. Following Michael's untimely death, Boteach reflected on the tragedy:

> What most haunts me is the knowledge that Michael's life could so easily have been saved. What Michael needed was not painkillers but counseling, not the numbing of an inner woundedness through drugs but the awakening of an inner conscience through spiritual guidance... any number of people could have rescued Michael from impending oblivion. [But] most of all, he craved the love and validation of his father. What emerged most strikingly in our recorded conversations... was the hurt he felt toward his father on the one hand, and the extreme affection he harbored for him on the other. Michael had many fans, but he played primarily to an audience of one.[5]

And Michael was by no means alone in this struggle. It has been said that each one of us comes into the world with a hole in our heart the shape of our dad. And when this hole is not filled, the void is often referred to as "the father wound." Here's how I defined the term in a project for the Bureau of Justice Assistance:

> The "father wound" is a phrase often used to refer to the psychological and emotional pain related to one or more of the following: growing up without an involved, responsible, and

---

[4] The details here are from a talk called "The Vital Role of Fathering" that Josh McDowell did at Focus on the Family's headquarters in 2006. The number of the CD I have is 5008595.

[5] Rabbi Shmuley Boteach, "Michael Jackson's Life Could Have Been Saved," Jewish Journal, June 21, 2010, accessed November 14, 2016, http://www.jewishjournal.com/rabbi_shmuley/item/michael_jacksons_life_could _have_been_saved_20100621.

committed father; growing up with a father who was physically present but emotionally absent; growing up with a verbally or physically abusive father; growing up not knowing who your father was.[6]

Here's another excellent definition from Carolyn Custis James' 2015 book, *Malestrom*:

Father wounds…are "wounds caused by a distant, emotionally unavailable, physically absent, or abusive father run deep and leave a gaping hole behind that can, like an unseen congenital defect, diminish the quality of a man's life or escalate over time into something worse. The father wound can be the driving force in a man's life—for good or ill. It can be the making of a man who resolves to do things differently from his dad or morph into a seething rage that transfers the pain to others and repeats the cycle.[7]

I remember being in Atlanta a little over fifteen years ago, preparing to give a conference talk on "Why Dads Matter So Much to God." As I ate my breakfast, I picked up a complimentary issue of *USA Today* and was intrigued by the cover story on former heavyweight boxing champion, Mike Tyson.[8] He was getting ready to turn forty and I was, too. I opened to the article and began reading:[9]

Anything but at peace. Confused and humiliated after a decadent lifestyle left him with broken relationships, shattered finances and a reputation in ruin, the fighter cannot hide his insecurities, stacked as high as his legendary knockouts. He frets about his place in this world—where he comes from, where he's headed and how the life and times of Michael Gerard Tyson will play out. "I'll

---

[6] *Engaging Fathers for Successful Reentry: Research, Tips, Best Practices* (Germantown, MD: National Fatherhood Initiative, 2011), 13.

[7] Carolyn Custis James, *Malestrom* (Grand Rapids: Zondervan, 2015), 78.

[8] Mike Tyson is also famous for biting the ear of his opponent, Evander Holyfield, in 1997.

never be happy," he says. "I believe I'll die alone. I would want it that way. I've been a loner all my life with my secrets and my pain. I'm really lost, but I'm trying to find myself . . . I'm really a sad, pathetic case . . . My whole life has been a waste. I've been a failure."[10]

I continued to read, looking for the one piece of information I knew I would find. There it was: Tyson was a then-divorced father of six who "has doubts and questions beyond legacy. He is angry and still doesn't know the identity of his real father."[11] Now, by all accounts, Mr. Tyson has found some measure of healing since this was written, but this snapshot from his life provides a particularly vivid example of the father wound and its generational impact.

The father wound is a pervasive theme in many of our stories and we'll touch on it often in what follows. I want to reserve our most thorough discussion of it, however, until the last chapter. And there's a reason for this: Healing and personal growth are messy and not easily packaged. For example, we don't miraculously heal from our wounds in chapter one of our stories and then move on to being a good dad in chapter two. As theologian and author Henri Nouwen observed, each of us—even at our best—are still "wounded healers."[12] To say it another way, we don't have the luxury of understanding and eradicating everything wrong with us before we start parenting. And so, it's not that many of us don't need, won't experience, or shouldn't pursue healing, it's just that, as I'll illustrate and make the case for in the last chapter, with God in the picture, often, "the wound is where the light shines through."

Father Absence

There are currently 18.4 million children in the United States growing up in homes without a biological, step, or adoptive father in

---

[10] John Saraceno, "Tyson: 'My Whole Life Has Been a Waste,'" *USA Today*, June 2, 2005, accessed November 14, 2016,
http://usatoday30.usatoday.com/sports/boxing/2005-06-02-tyson-saraceno_x.htm.

[11] Ibid.

[12] See his book with that title.

their home.[13] In other words, 1 in 4 American children have an absent father. Tragically, this disproportionately affects minorities, especially the Black community. Roughly two-thirds of Black children and one-third of Hispanic children live with only one parent, and the research shows this puts children at risk.[14] For instance, father absence increases the chance of a child dropping out of school, and Blacks and Hispanics raised by single moms are 75 percent and 96 percent respectively more likely to drop out of school.[15]

As a busy pastor in the late 90s, I knew little of father absence as a social issue. Typical of most white evangelicals at that time, I thought the biggest issue in our country was "the breakdown of the family," and the two biggest social maladies were abortion and homosexuality (including the threat, then, of the legalization of gay marriage).

One of my congregants, Roland Warren (who later became the president of the National Fatherhood Initiative and then Care Net), recommended I read *Fatherless America* by David Blankenhorn. In it, I came across this provocative statement by the late anthropologist, Margaret Meade, which altered the course of my life: "The supreme test of any civilization is whether it can socialize men by teaching them to be fathers."[16] Blankenhorn corroborates her assertion and makes the case for why father absence is our most damaging and consequential social trend. What I learned, and what he meant by quoting that statement, is not that it is the only important social issue, but that it has a unique consequential relationship to many other social issues. For example, like father absence, poverty is also a critical social issue to address. But the strategic, consequential nature of the relationship between father absence and poverty is clearly seen by the fact that in 2011, children living in female-headed homes with no spouse present had a poverty rate of 47.6 percent, four times the rate

---

[13] U.S. Census Bureau, 2021.
[14] "My Brother's Keeper Task Force Report to the President," May 2014, accessed October 25, 2016,
https://www.whitehouse.gov/sites/default/files/docs/053014_mbk_report.pdf.
[15] Ibid., 5.
[16] David Blankenhorn, *Fatherless America: Confronting Our Most Urgent Social Problem* (New York: Harper Collins, 1996), 3.

for children living in married-couple families.[17]

It is because of those kinds of statistics that father absence is rightly seen by many as a primary cause behind "the breakdown of the family." Again, my vocational course was altered by learning that for many of the most intractable social ills affecting children, father absence is to blame.[18] Even if we take a seemingly unrelated hot topic like gun violence, the unique consequences of father absence can be seen: Individuals from homes without a father are 279 percent more likely to carry guns and deal drugs than their peers who live with their fathers.[19] Rarely has a Marvel character said something as profound as the hero in Netflix's Luke Cage in commenting on the violence in his own community: "Everyone has a gun. No one has a father."

There is no place, however, where father absence shows up more vividly than behind bars. Ninety-two percent of parents in prison are fathers.[20] Children in father-absent households have significantly higher odds of incarceration than those in mother-father families. Youths who never had a father in the household experienced the highest odds.[21] Again, minorities are affected disproportionately: In 2012, Black males were six times more likely to be imprisoned than White males. Hispanic males were two and a half times more likely.[22]

Fathering Well

Whether we have wounds from our father, or whether they were

---

[17] "Information on Poverty and Income Statistics: A Summary of 2012 Current Population Survey Data," U.S. Department of Health & Human Services, accessed November 14, 2016, http://aspe.hhs.gov/hsp/12/PovertyAndIncomeEst/ib.cfm.

[18] Sara McLanahan, Laura Tach, and Daniel Schneider, "The Causal Effects of Father Absence," *Annual Review of Sociology*, 39 (2013): 399–427.

[19] Andrea N. Allen and Cecilia Lo, "Drugs, Guns, and Disadvantaged Youths: Co-occurring Behavior and the Code of the Street," *Crime & Delinquency* 58 (2012): 932-953.

[20] Lauren E. Glaze and Laura M. Maruschak, "Parents in Prison and Their Minor Children," *Bureau of Justice Statistics Special Report* (2010): 2, accessed November 14, 2016, https://www.bjs.gov/content/pub/pdf/pptmc.pdf.

[21] Cynthia C. Harper and Sara S. McLanahan, "Father Absence and Youth Incarceration," *Journal of Research on Adolescence* 14 (September 2004): 369–397.

[22] E. Ann Carson and Daniela Golinelli, "Prisoners in 2012: Trends in Admissions and Releases, 1991–2012." *Bureau of Justice Statistics* 25 (2013): 25, accessed November 14, 2016, http://www.bjs.gov/content/pub/pdf/p12tar9112.pdf.

absent or not, we all know that a good dad protects, provides, nurtures, and guides. Moreover, few questions loom larger for good parents than, "How do I give my kid(s) my best and what they will need to succeed?" For the purposes of this book, success will be defined as raising kids who are wise, self-aware, empathetic, culturally literate, pure, and God-fearing; who have their vocational direction and self-worth rooted in the cross; who enjoy relationships and are prepared for healthy marriage (whether they'll marry or not); who care about beauty, justice, and—to the extent they have the capacity—are able to make a positive impact on their world. It's extremely important to give this nuanced definition at the outset as, sadly, not every father or potential father shares the same definition of success. Linda Hamilton, for instance, says that when she wanted to get married to Canadian filmmaker James Cameron and have kids, "he used to say to me, 'Anybody can be a father or a husband. There are only five people in the world who can do what I do, and I'm going for that.'"

Thankfully, we can still learn powerful lessons from Cameron and others about how *not* to be. That's one of the reasons I've always loved the story of Sampson, the greatest of the judges and God's Terminator, if you will, in Judges 13-16. It's a wild ride where incarceration, surprisingly, ends up being a saving grace in this "hero's" train-wreck of a life. For most of his days, Sampson lacked self-awareness and, more often than not, misused the fire he was given. When we're not self-aware, we're blind to our weaknesses and the baggage we carry, have trouble with self-control, as well as connecting the dots between our passions and behavior. In the Bible, blindness is the theological term for a lack of self-awareness. And in Sampson's story, we see his blindness repeatedly, especially in how he allows his last girlfriend, Delilah, to dupe him.[23] Again, it's not until the end of his life when he's in prison and has his eyes gouged out that, ironically, he's finally able to see spiritually.[24] That's when he cries out to God[25] and truly comes to understand his story in the larger context of God's story: that is, his unique and irreplaceable role in God's larger purpose, ideal, and design.

---

[23] 16:1-20.
[24] 16:21.
[25] 16:28.

My Dad and Me

Understanding our own stories is essential for all of us, especially if we want to avoid causing "a train-wreck" in the lives of others, and instead, pass on a life-giving legacy to our children. That being said and in order to set the context for what follows, I need to tell you a little bit about my dad's story and what shaped him (and me). Especially that latter task is a tall order since we are "fearfully and wonderfully made," and our life stories are attached to family systems and cultural waters that are amazingly complex. As Eugene Peterson observed, the danger in these kinds of scenarios is thinking that "simplification is achieved by amputation. For reality is, in fact, complex and diverse."[26] Indeed, one of the hardest parts of writing this book has been summarizing my dad's story. Do I tell it through the lens of a series of devastations or graces? We've all known people who've gone through similar circumstances and some come out bitter and some better. Some take their identity as heroes, some as victims. One of the foundational principles of this book is that the painful parts of our story matter to God and can become windows of grace in our healing. And so, for this reason, I'm going to use the devastations' lens in summarizing my dad's story.

Unlike the father and son in *The Road*, my dad and I never had to fight off flesh-eating humans. We did, however, barely survive a church apocalypse. Indeed, we spent 1973–1981, in a toxic church environment that was not far from a Kool-Aid-drinking cult– a place where it came out later that the pastor and his despotic wife terrorized and abused their foster children, as well as others.[27] Moreover, you can't understand my dad's story or mine without knowing some of what happened during that destructive decade. And so, in the remainder of this extended introductory section, I'll give an extremely brief sketch of his life (and our life together) through the lens of three devastations: the father wound, spiritual abuse (the church apocalypse), and divorce. Then in the last chapter, I'll pick up on the

---

[26] Eugene H. Peterson, *As Kingfishers Catch Fire* (New York: WaterBrook, 2017), 281.

[27] You can read the full story in *How I Became a Christian Despite the Church* available through Amazon.

14

story of our last two years together.

Wild at Heart, Yet Wounded

In many ways and especially in his younger years, my dad was "man's man;" that is, a man admired for traditionally masculine interests and activities. As a boy, he loved to swim, fish, and camp. As a young adult, he became proficient on the trampoline and was a skilled gymnast, scuba diver, and canoeist. In his early thirties, in true *Deliverance* fashion, he almost lost his life running a wing-dam into white water with some of his buddies. He was part of a generation where women were the primary nurturers and men were the providers. Among other things, he taught me to fish, split wood, and work hard. He believed in doing things well and would often say, "It's easier to do something right the first time than explain why you didn't."

Despite feeling at retirement that he had worked too hard for too little for too long, my dad really was an involved, responsible, and committed father. I have many pleasant memories of him. The earliest, from ages five to eight, are watching TV with him, especially shows like *Mod Squad, UFO, Adam 12*, and *Emergency*. I remember being with him when Muhammad Ali won fight after fight, Richard Petty and Mario Andretti won race after race, Evel Knievel attempted his jump of the Snake River Canyon, and the gymnast Nadia Comaneci earned her perfect tens.

He was an interesting, creative, albeit wounded soul, who loved magazines like Popular Science and Popular Mechanics and, like MacGyver, could make amazing things out of a few discarded materials. Ingenuity was his specialty. When I was in second and third grade, he helped me win first place in the school's science fair. We made a water drop microscope one year, and a working telegraph the other.

One of our biggest points of connection as I entered later adolescence was reading The Hardy Boys books together. I shared a couple of my favorite Hardy Boys books with my dad: *House on a Cliff, While the Clock Ticked*, and *The Shore Road Mystery*. He read them, thoroughly enjoyed the experience, and then joined me in these adventures.

15

Although my dad wasn't a big sports guy, we played catch and Frisbee in the backyard on many occasions. We also got seriously into ping-pong when I was eleven or twelve, often playing as soon as he got home from work. The closeness we shared during this season is one reason I love the 2013 film *About Time*. Several times throughout the movie, the father and son are seen talking together while playing ping-pong. This simple setting provides cohesiveness for one of the movie's central themes: delight in the father-son relationship, something we enjoyed in my later teens and early twenties.

The closeness we shared was quite the contrast to my dad's experience with his own father. My dad carries deep, unhealed wounds from a father who originally didn't want him—my grandfather reportedly struck my grandmother when she told him she was pregnant. My grandfather rarely took the time to understand my dad and largely viewed him as a big disappointment. For example, when my dad was young and still living at home, he got into a serious relationship with an attractive, well-to-do girl who his parents hoped he would marry. When she broke things off one evening, he was devastated. After telling his parents what happened, he left the house abruptly and stayed out all night, driving around the Pine Barrens of South Jersey. Worried he might be suicidal, his parents also stayed up most of the night. The next morning, when my dad finally came home, his dad came out to greet him. Instead of asking how he was or trying to comfort him, the first thing out of his mouth was, "Boy, you sure know how to lose the good ones, don't you?!"

The fact that my dad vividly remembers this as an 82-year-old man as if it just happened yesterday (he only recently told me this story!) shows the truth of Proverbs 18:21: "death and life are in the power of the tongue."

Spiritual Abuse & Its Aftermath

The unhealed wounds my dad carried from a father who never affirmed him are, I believe, the primary reason he was vulnerable to and threw himself—and his family—into a lethal church environment. His uniqueness, entrepreneurial spirit, energy, and competencies were recognized by the church, which rewarded him with the three essentials for a healthy self-worth: I am accepted, I am valuable, and I am important.[28] Further, his hunger for belonging and a better relationship with my mom made him even more susceptible.

Did this church help our family in any way? That's a tough question that's unfortunately lost among the ruins. My dad "came to faith" in an environment where fear, shame, busyness, performance, and control masked and kept the deepest wounds of his heart and a troubled marriage from ever being addressed. He ended up sacrificing one of the choicest decades of his life for what? For God? The reality is that my dad became a star player for a perverse pastor and his ambitious wife's agenda, all at the expense of a genuine relationship with God, time with his family, and the pursuit of his own interests.

Bottomline, he was had and used.

That is the reality for which he may never forgive himself or, sadly, God. As his son, it seemed that during these years he genuinely loved God and tried to live the Christian life. Later he abandoned God and eventually returned to his agnostic roots. He lives now with great bitterness and believes the church robbed him of many things, including a lot of the color, fun, and adventure in life; time for himself; and time with his children.

What was my experience of him during those years? During much of my early adolescence he was often too busy with church commitments and a new business to spend much time with me. I remember wanting so bad for him to take me on the yearly church canoe trip. I knew he loved to canoe but every year he said no. I knew he loved camping too, but he never could find time to take me.

The song, "Ships" by Barry Manilow describes our relationship during those years. I used to listen to it over and over:

> We walked to the sea just my father and me
> And the dogs played around by the sand.
> Winter cold cut the air hanging still everywhere,

---

[28] Sometimes the message, "I am capable," is included here. It is related to the question, "Do I have what it takes?" As John Eldredge points out in his writings, a message that all fathers should make sure they pass on to their children, especially sons, is "You have what it takes."

Dressed in gray did he say, "Hold my hand?"
We're just ships that pass in the night
And we smile and we say it's alright
We're still here it's just that we're out of sight
Like those ships that pass in night.[29]

Something huge happened when I was 15 though: My father opened up to me in a way he never had before. While my mom was at choir practice every Sunday night, we would go to the local *Mister Donuts*, each get a coffee and pastry, and then come back to the church parking lot to talk.

At this time, the church's manipulation was getting more and more evident. I wanted to go to a certain college in Springfield, Missouri, but the pastor and his wife had their own ideas about my future and wanted me to go to a school close to home. I felt it was none of their business, only my parents' and mine. My dad, who was normally passive and preferred the role of the silent victim, suddenly spoke up: "If I were you, when you turn eighteen, I'd get as far away from this place as possible."

I was stunned. It was the first time he treated me as a peer or adult, and it was the beginning of a trusted friendship that grew and grew. So much so, that five years later, in 1986, when I was preparing to marry, I had a hard time deciding who would be my best man, my dad or my best friend. I ended up choosing my best friend, but the difficulty I had deciding shows just how close we were. Regrettably, we lost the treasure of this friendship in the aftermath of my father's next devastation.

Divorce & Its Aftershocks

In September 1990, my dad invited me out for breakfast and dropped a bomb while we were eating: "Your mother wants a divorce." I tried everything I knew to talk them out of it, but their hearts were hardened toward each other. The issues between them went far deeper and had a greater history than I understood at the time. My mother

---

[29] Manilow, Barry. 1979. "Ships," by Ian Hunter.

initiated the process by leaving the house and my dad stepped even more firmly into his passive victim role. Three months later, they were divorced. I had been aware of difficulties in their communication, but never thought these would end in divorce. For years, even as a married adult, I took this severing of legacy very hard, and dealt with significant bitterness over their refusal to work things out.

Though I've since grown in empathy and compassion toward those who've suffered divorce, I spent most of my early adulthood grieving the loss of the friendship my dad and I once shared. The drift in our relationship began with the events leading up to my mom's request for the divorce. She wanted him to enter her world and go to the gym with her. Despite my urging and encouragement, he refused to go outside his routine and pursue my mother's heart. Then, when my mom threatened to leave and began to pursue a divorce, I watched as my dad did nothing to stop her; instead, playing the martyr with his friends in the church, and then beginning to pursue other women in a way that seemed desperate. In short, my dad became an embarrassment to me and I lost respect for him. I ended up confronting him about all of this one day and it didn't go well. We ended up not speaking for several months.

It didn't help when my dad remarried a seriously wounded and embittered woman whose last words to my wife and me were, "Go to hell." But it was my dad's gradual deconversion that affected our closeness most severely. We no longer shared our faith—something that had once seemed precious to both of us. I was now an ordained pastor, who at thirty-one had just spent six years in Louisville, KY completing a seminary degree. It was a big slight when my dad made it clear he had no interest in coming to my graduation. For many years after, I struggled with a lack of respect and bitterness toward him. Visiting him and his wife, while she was alive, was mostly a duty and something that stirred up painful emotions.

In the last ten years, our relationship has improved. I pray for him often and am learning to love and accept him—to just be a son. I still feel sad about what we lost—what we could have had. He was a good man in his prime who encouraged and influenced many. Today, my children know little of him, and he seems content with that. Once caught up in a cult-like church where he sacrificed more than he wished he had, he now lives only for himself and avoids anything that makes him uncomfortable. Regrettably, his consistent choices to pursue comfort over courage these last ten years, including proactively checking himself into an assisted living facility, have led to an irreversible decline in health and mobility.

Hope and God's Heart for All

Few things can desensitize us more to God than when the father wound is fused together with spiritual abuse. Sadly, on this side of spirituality wrongly pursued, my dad seems unable to feel the father heart of God, and his abusive church experience left him with many reasons not to trust any expressions of love associated with a church. Indeed, his father wound remains open and unhealed, functioning as an additional barrier to experiencing friendship and peace with God. As N.T. Wright has observed:

It was—with the distressing predictability that clergy and counselors know only too well—that deep down in his memory and imagination [the man who cannot believe in or feel the love of God] there was a sense of unlovedness; of family and teachers telling him that he was no good; of never being praised or cherished or celebrated. No doubt there was praise and celebration at various times. But the abiding life-forming memories are of condemnation, criticisms, put-downs. Being made to feel inferior, stupid, weak. So the capacity to receive love, had been covered over as though with a thick, calloused, leathery skin… There's a glorious, beautiful world out there, but some people turn in on themselves, bundling themselves up in darkness to avoid being dazzled.[30]

So where is hope? How can anyone know or find God, let alone feel His love or be "dazzled"? Further, where does the fire come from to be the best dads we can be? Who gives or holds it; that is, who is

---

[30] N.T. Wright, *Lent for Everyone: Mark, Year B* (Louisville, KY: Westminster John Knox Press, 2012) 85-87.

the ultimate source of desire, motivation, and all that makes humans thrive? And what if you feel more like a dying ember in this season of your life than one who "carries the fire"? Listen carefully to God's heart toward you: "A bruised reed he will not break, and a dimly burning wick he will not quench..."[31] What's more, here's some more really good news as we get started: God's heart for dads is in one sense his desire for everyone. And in what follows, I pray you'll find plenty of reasons to be dazzled in ways that inspire, give insight, and heal, helping you not only make better sense of your journey and the world we live in, but also find joy as you pass on an irreplaceable legacy.

---

[31] Isaiah 42:3a, NRSV.

PART ONE: ESSENTIAL FOUNDATIONS

"All candles are lighted by his torch."

—Thomas Manton

CHAPTER ONE: EPISTEMOLOGY AND IPAS

The journey toward recovering God's heart for dads begins with epistemology, the study of how we know things. Our epistemology determines where we start when we answer questions like, "How do I know God exists?" and "What is God like?" The French philosopher René Descartes said, "I think; therefore, I am." Do we, like Descartes, start with our own existence and what we're able to think or observe? Or do we start with God since the first verse in the Bible starts out: "In the beginning, God..."?

The late teacher Dr. R.C. Sproul helpfully pointed out that a person can't start with God unless they *are* God. We have to start, rather, with *self-consciousness*.[32] As the song "Chasing Shadows" by Kansas says, "All of us are just an audience looking for evidence to help it all make sense."[33] In other words, it's natural and human to struggle with life's questions. Part of life on planet earth is seeking to understand what we experience. Again, we start with self-consciousness, because that is the only place we can start. We are not

---

[32] *Self-consciousness* is different than *self-autonomy*, the idea that we are alone in this universe and the sole masters of our own destiny. The Bible teaches, rather, that we need God's initiative and assistance to seek or even care about him (John 6:44a; Acts 16:14). Further, God is supreme, not us, and that's why the autonomous self is an arrogant delusion. But, as R.C. Sproul pointed out, the existence of God is "first in the way of being, not first in the order of knowing." That is, God is the beginning, first cause, and source of all things; however, our experience of this begins with ourselves, not God. For more, see R.C. Sproul, "Presuppositional Apologetics" (video of lecture, 2010), accessed May 8, 2015, http://www.youtube.com/watch?v=a4xyK1t6eyQ.

[33] Kansas, "Chasing Shadows," by John and Dino Elefante on *Vinyl Confessions*, Epic, 1982, compact disc.

God; we are creatures!

How a Guy Named Bob Helped Me Care About Epistemology

When I was a sophomore at Lancaster Bible College, I had the privilege of taking a philosophy class from the school's most gifted and popular professor at the time, who I'll call Bob. He had a gift for making difficult subjects like epistemology clear, exciting, and extremely relevant. I'll never forget the provocative question he asked my class one spring day in 1985:

"Why do you believe that Jesus is the way, the truth, and the life?"

For my classmates and me, this was an important question. Most of us had grown up in Christian homes and reflexively believed John 14:6: "Jesus told him, 'I am the way, the truth, and the life. No one can come to the Father except through me.'" Bob knew this, and he wanted us to explore *why*. Further, he wanted us to consider how we knew we weren't self-deluded.

Bob went on to lay out six ways humans know things:

1. **Reason**—This is the Mr. Spock of Star Trek lens: "I believe it because it is logical." For example, if harsh words stir up anger or can crush one's spirit and I don't want to do either of those things, then I should not use harsh words.

2. **Nature**—This means I see evidence in the physical world that something is true. For example, Psalm 19:1 is an epistemological argument from nature regarding God's existence: "The heavens declare the glory of God and the sky above proclaims his handiwork." (ESV)

3. **First-Hand Witness**—This means I know it because I was there. For example, I know the birthdays of my three biological children because I was there when they were born. I was a first-hand witness to these events.

4. **Second-Hand Witness**—This means I know it because someone I trust was there or experienced it. This is the big reason why we believe most of what we believe: 9/11, JFK or Lincoln's assassination, the fall of Rome, etc.

5. **Authority**—This is closely related to second-hand witness

and means that an authority I respect said it's true. It could be our parents, the Bible, the Koran, a famous person from the past or a celebrity, or a news outlet.

6. **Intuition**—This means I believe it because it feels right, resonates with or rings true for me. For example, a line in the old Easter hymn "He Arose" states, "You ask me how I know he lives – He lives within my heart." That would be an intuitive answer to Bob's "Why do you believe…" question.

Now let's return to Bob's challenging question to my class: "Why do you believe that Jesus is the way, the truth, and the life?"

As I pondered his question over the next several months, I realized my answer—in sync with the New Testament's primary way of handling Bob's question—was based largely on second-hand witnesses. In other words, I didn't believe Jesus was who He claimed to be just because, "that's what the Bible says" or because it's what my parents taught me. Nor were my beliefs just some blind "leap of faith." Rather, I believed because I had come to trust that the gospel writers and the apostle Paul were credible witnesses. Indeed, I placed a lot of weight on the confession of "Doubting Thomas" and similar-minded passages (bold added for emphasis):

- So the other disciples told him [Doubting Thomas], 'We have seen the Lord." But he said to them, "Unless I see in his hands the mark of the nails, and place my finger into the mark of the nails, and place my hand into his side, **I will never believe.**" (John 20:25, ESV)

- We proclaim to you the one who existed from the beginning, whom we have heard and seen. **We saw him with our own eyes and touched him with our own hands.** He is the Word of life. This one who is life itself was revealed to us, and we have seen him. And now we testify and proclaim to you that he is the one who is eternal life. He was with the Father, and then he was revealed to us. We proclaim to you what we ourselves have **actually seen and heard** so that you may have fellowship with us. And our fellowship is with the Father and with his Son, Jesus Christ. We are writing these things so that you may fully share our joy." (1 John 1:1-4, NLT)

- "Many people have set out to write accounts about the events that have been fulfilled among us. They used the eyewitness reports circulating among us from the early disciples. Having carefully investigated everything from the beginning, I also have decided to write an accurate account for you, most honorable Theophilus, so you can be certain of the truth of everything you were taught. (Luke 1:1-4, NLT)

- "Let me now remind you, dear brothers and sisters, of the Good News I preached to you before. You welcomed it then, and you still stand firm in it. It is this Good News that saves you if you continue to believe the message I told you—unless, of course, you believed something that was never true in the first place. I passed on to you what was most important and what had also been passed on to me. Christ died for our sins, just as the Scriptures said. He was buried, and he was raised from the dead on the third day, just as the Scriptures said. He was seen by Peter and then by the Twelve. After that, he was seen by more than 500 of his followers at one time, most of whom are still alive, though some have died. Then he was seen by James and later by all the apostles. Last of all, as though I had been born at the wrong time, I also saw him. For I am the least of all the apostles. In fact, I'm not even worthy to be called an apostle after the way I persecuted God's church." (1 Corinthians 15:1-9, NLT)

But as valuable as second-hand witness proof is, it's not the only "way of knowing" supporting the Christian faith. As I've grown older and experienced life—especially as a dad—I now have a much greater respect for the supreme importance of intuition when it comes to discerning what is true and recovering God's heart. Before diving into that discussion, however, I want to first illustrate five of the six ways of knowing above by looking at the Resurrection of Jesus Christ. Not only is Christ's Resurrection intimately connected to Professor Bob's "Why do you believe…" question, it is the linchpin for determining whether the Christian faith is true. Indeed, the veracity of much of what follows in recovering God's heart for dads stands or falls on an empty tomb.

Why the Resurrection Matters

French scholar Ernest Renan, in critiquing Christians for what he perceived as the lack of hard evidence for their faith, reportedly said, "You Christians are living on the fragrance of an empty vase." He was referring, of course, to the empty tomb. But the apostolic witnesses never appealed to the empty tomb as the primary proof of Christ's resurrection. They appealed instead to Christ's appearances, to the fact that He ate with them, and to His ever-present power and love. What these early followers of Christ saw led to their believing.

Of course, it takes more than evidence to believe in the resurrection of Christ. It also takes the Spirit of God working in a person's heart (Acts 16:14). But that doesn't mean belief in the resurrection should be held apart from strong evidence. As theologian Greg Boyd observed, "When it comes to truth the mind and the Spirit work in harmony."

A healthy skepticism is good but Thomas suffered with a problem that is common to all of us to one degree or another: unbelief and a lack of faith in God's promises. And really there are only two questions that have ultimate relevance regarding Jesus' resurrection:

- Did Jesus really rise from the dead?
- So what?

We will look at the "so what question" below, but first let's look at the strong and compelling evidence that Jesus really did rise from the dead [Note: After each bolded heading, I have indicated which of Professor Bob's six ways is illustrated in parentheses]:[34]

- **Over 10 Post-Resurrection Appearances by Jesus and Lots of Witnesses (second-hand witness)**
  Five independent sources—Matthew, Mark, Luke, John, and Paul–testify to the Resurrection. John Stott notes, "an investigation of the ten appearances reveals an almost studied variety in the circumstances of person, place and mood in which they occurred. He was seen by individuals alone (Mary Magdalene, Peter, and James), by small groups and by more

---

[34] My favorite writings defending the Resurrection of Christ are *Surprised by Hope* by N.T. Wright (especially chapter four), *Loving God* by Chuck Colson (chapter six), and *The Case for Christ* by Lee Strobel (chapters 11-14).

than 500 people together. He appeared in the garden of the tomb, near Jerusalem, in the upper room, on the road to Emmaus, by the lake of Galilee, on a Galilee mountain and on the Mount of Olives."[35] Additionally, Paul's account in 1 Corinthians 15 was written 15-20 years after the Resurrection. The idea was if anyone had doubts about the certainty of the event, they could ask around. As Billy Graham observed, "there is more evidence that Jesus rose from the dead than there is that Julius Caesar ever lived or that Alexander the Great died at the age of thirty-three."[36]

- **The Humble Beginnings of the Disciples Themselves (reason)**
  Who started this resurrection story, anyway? Were the disciples just 12 gullible guys with a weakness for ghost stories? Were they shrewd conspirators who started the resurrection plot as a way to jumpstart their new religion? Neither. One day the disciples are fearful and hiding and the next day they are facing hostile crowds. Paul is eventually beheaded for his beliefs and Peter is crucified upside-down—avoidable ends for gullible ghost story fans and fake-religion masterminds alike. The growth of the church itself also points to something beyond the imaginations of twelve men. The Christian church is the largest institution to exist in the history of the world, yet its origin is far humbler than any other institution, movement, or code of law. As someone has said, "the Grand Canyon was not formed by someone dragging a stick." Similarly, the evidence is stacked against anyone who would claim the church was brought into existence by the lies or hallucinations of twelve men.

- **How the Biblical Account Has Stood Up to Careful Study (authority)**
  Arguably the resurrection of Christ has been studied more carefully than any other event in history. Consider these few examples from just the last 250 years:

---

[35] John Stott, *Basic Christianity* (London: IVP, 1978) 57.
[36] https://billygraham.org/devotion/evidence-of-jesus/

- Simon Greenleaf (1782–1853) was an American lawyer and devout Episcopalian who contributed extensively to the development of Harvard Law School. He has been hailed by many as one of the greatest legal scholars of all time. He emphatically declared that anyone who carefully examined the evidence for the resurrection would find it convincing.[37]
- Albert Henry Ross (1888–1950), the British freelance journalist, wrote *Who Moved the Stone?* under the pseudonym Frank Morison, but it was not the book he set out to write. He began his work to discredit the resurrection, but became convinced of its truthfulness as he wrote. The apologetic classic has influenced many including T.S. Eliot, G.K. Chesterton, Dorothy Sayers, Josh McDowell, James Warwick Montgomery, and Lee Strobel.[38]
- Lew Wallace (1807–1905) was an American lawyer, Union General, governor of New Mexico Territory, and author of *Ben Hur*.[39] Although Wallace never became a regular churchgoer, his research nurtured his faith and brought him to a place of greater respect for Jesus as the Son of God.[40]
- Anne Rice (1941–2021), the brilliant and famed writer of *The Vampire Chronicles*, who has had quite an eclectic faith journey wrote in 2016, "Jesus changed the world in many different ways. For believers, He is the Son of God. But anyone can recognize that historically Jesus' Life and Death and Resurrection changed Western Civilization forever. Jesus brought monotheism out of the Middle East and into the West. And within three

---

[37] https://www.famous-trials.com/jesustrial/1051-evangeliststestimony
[38] https://en.wikipedia.org/wiki/Albert_Henry_Ross
[39] Most know this as a classic movie with Charlton Heston and a cool chariot race, but most don't know that it was also the best-selling novel and most influential Christian book of the 19th century!
[40] https://www.guideposts.org/better-living/entertainment/books/ben-hur-how-lew-wallace-found-faith-in-epic-fiction

hundred years paganism in the West was dead and Christianity had replaced it."[41]

   o   Francis Collins (1950–), the esteemed leader of The Human Genome Project and the former Director of the National Institutes of Health came to embrace the resurrection as true.[42] In doing this, he joined a legacy of world-renowned scientists like Pascal, Copernicus, Galileo, Newton, and others.[43]

- **The Alternative Doesn't Ring True and is Existentially Unsatisfying (intuitive)**

   In 1 Cor. 15, Paul essentially says, "Try this on for size. See how plausible it feels. Here are a few realities you need to face if there is no resurrection from the dead:"

   o   Christian preaching amounts to nothing. (verse 14)
   o   If you're a Christian, your belief system is devoid of truth. It is fruitless—without effect, empty, imaginary, and unfounded. (verses 14,17)
   o   Paul and billions of others of like faith have misrepresented or are misrepresenting God. (verse 15)
   o   Humanity is still under the control and penalty of sin. (verse 17)
   o   Those who have died as Christians are lost. (verse 18)
   o   All of us face the miserable and pitiful fact that we have no hope beyond this life. (verse 19) (Eugene Peterson, in *The Message*, puts it this way: "If all we get out of Christ is a little inspiration for a few short years, we're a pretty sorry lot.")
   o   We should all "eat, drink, and be merry" with no concern for eternity. (verse 32) And finally…
   o   We must come up with a better explanation for why Paul continually risked his life. (verse 32)

---

[41] https://www.hollywoodreporter.com/news/general-news/why-novelist-anne-rice-went-873286/
[42] See his talk on "How I Became a Christian" at https://www.youtube.com/watch?v=HaEQyNeaFZs
[43] https://scottsauls.com/blog/2018/04/04/resurrection-not-for-dummies/

- **Examples of the Concept of Resurrection in the Physical World (nature)**
Nearly every denial of Jesus' resurrection rests solely on the contention that resurrection itself is not possible. Many believe something like this: "I don't know why the disciples thought Jesus rose from the dead, but it seems to me that any explanation is better than the one which assumes he actually rose from the dead." The Apostle Paul anticipated this response and addressed this objection head-on in 1 Corinthians 15:

  o The resurrection is truly miraculous, Paul agrees, but is it any more miraculous than the birthing process (45-49)? Blaise Pascal poses the same question this way: "What reason have atheists for saying that we cannot rise again? Which is the more difficult—to be born or to rise again? Is it more difficult to come into being than to return to it?"

  o Life often comes out of death. Take a seed for instance (36). "What you sow does not come to life unless it dies," Paul reminds his readers. Right there in the simplicity of a seed is the phenomenon of life being brought about in death.

  o Finally, Paul says, look at "the variety of bodies" around you (39-44). Notice that your flesh is different than the flesh of animals, birds, or fish. Is it really so unreasonable to imagine a heavenly existence that is imperishable, glorious, and powerful? To say it another way, take a walk around an animal shelter or a zoo. Now, look up at the sun, the moon, and the stars. With such a mind-numbing variety of life forms and natural phenomena around us (and many more to yet be discovered!), who are we to unilaterally declare resurrection is impossible? C.S. Lewis says it well:

> At present we are on the outside of the world, the wrong side of the door. We discern the

freshness and purity of morning, but they do not make us fresh and pure. We cannot mingle with the splendors we see. But all of the leaves of the New Testament are rustling with the rumor that it will not always be so. Someday, God willing, we shall get in.[44]

An Epistemology of Love

We've seen above that the evidence for Christ's resurrection is compelling. And Paul concludes 1 Corinthians 15—the great resurrection chapter—with this answer to the "so what" question:

> With all of this going for us, my dear friends, stand your ground. And don't hold back. Throw yourself into the work of the Master, confident that nothing you do for him is a waste of time or effort.[45]

Make no mistake, recovering God's heart for dads is central to "the work of the Master." And when it comes to loving our families well, N.T. Wright's additional insights on the "so what" question are profound:

> The resurrection is… the defining event of the new creation, the world that is being born with Jesus. If we are even to glimpse this new world, let alone enter it, we will need a different kind of knowing, a knowing that involves us in new ways, an epistemology that draws out from us not just the cool appraisal of detached quasi-scientific research but also the whole-person engagement and involvement for which the best shorthand is "love"….[46]

Again:

> *Love is the deepest mode of knowing* [italics mine] because it is love that,

[44] C.S. Lewis, *The Weight of Glory* (San Francisco: Harper, 1980), 41-45.
[45] 1 Corinthians 15:18, The Message.
[46] N.T. Wright, *Surprised by Hope* (New York: HarperOne, 2008), 73.

while completely engaging with reality other than itself, affirms and celebrates the other-than-self reality. This is the point at which much modernist epistemology breaks down. The sterile antithesis of "objective" and "subjective"... is overcome by the epistemology of love, which is called into being as the necessary mode of knowing for those who will live in the new public world, the world launched at Easter, the world in which Jesus Christ is Lord and Caesar isn't.[47]

Wright's insights are worth reading a few times and pondering. Not only does he tie together our topics of resurrection and epistemology, he takes us beyond reason and into the world of relationships. It is in this world of relationships, guided by an "epistemology of love," that we discover God's heart for dads and the irreplaceable role He has for them in their children's lives. But before going on to explore how God teaches us about himself through loving family relationships, let's take another look at intuitive knowing and what I learned from Bob.

Intuition & Matters of the Heart

One of the things I pride myself in is I can still beat most people I know—including my kids—in ping-pong. Now, admittedly, only two of my biological children and their spouses care much about the game or beating me. But two of my sons—my oldest, Matthew, and son-in-law, Josh—care about it very much! And don't get me wrong, they're good but not as good as me. My secret? Certainly, some of it has to do with learned skills and practice but there's something else at play when I'm at my best: intuition. I get into this place that many craftsmen, artists, and musicians do where they work, paint, dance, play, etc. from their heart. It's like I'm concentrating less and feeling more. Truth be told, sometimes a good IPA can intensify my enjoyment and help me relax. Once I get into my groove, my sons, as MC Hammer says, "can't touch this!"

Intuition is that way of knowing that helps us experience the hazy

---

[47] Ibid.

dreaminess of an impressionistic painting. You don't appreciate a Monet or a Van Gogh by logically thinking through it. You feel it. You let the colors and impressions wash over you. Let's return to Ernest Renan's quote above that "Christians are living on the fragrance of an empty vase." Although his perspective reflects a lack of awareness of the significant testimony that undergirds the Christian faith, there's some truth to what he says. Indeed, there is a "fragrance" to the empty tomb just like that of flowers or perfume. The Resurrection of Jesus Christ permeates the world with traces of joy and hope. And these aromas are something you experience (not unlike marriage or parenting) rather than just reason out. It's like how you appreciate a symphony or music by your favorite artist, or a cool breeze and rustling leaves, fireflies lighting up your backyard, or the warmth of the sun. Yes, you can observe or study these things but how do you appreciate them for all they are? You feel, immerse yourself, get caught up in, or bask in them.

When I first heard and considered Bob's six ways of knowing, intuition (#6 above) seemed the weakest way of knowing. And, from an intellectual point of view, the intuitive answer to Bob's question "he lives within my heart" seemed just plain goofy. As I mentioned earlier, 35 years later and on the other side of close friendships, romance, sex, marriage, being a dad, a grandfather, and seeking joy in life, my views have changed. What my heart says now matters more than it once did. What's more, I'm more in touch with my heart.[48] All of this is because I've learned something about love… love—that thing that's so powerful but impossible to quantify or dissect scientifically. As the French mathematician and philosopher Blaise Pascal famously put it:

"The heart has its reasons, which reason does not know. We feel it in a thousand things. It is the heart which experiences God, and not the reason."

What Pascal is saying is that the heart—that intangible core of who we are, has eyes. And these eyes, connected with our deepest loves

---

[48] I'm using heart here in the way the Bible does as a person's inner control center—the seat of one's mind, will, and emotions. Or as Dane Ortlund describes it in *Gentle and Lowly*, it's "our motivational headquarters" or "the central animating center of all we do." (18) An older synonym that's also helpful is "affections."

and longings, tell us powerful things about reality. This is intuitive and, although it, again, can't be quantified scientifically, it is absolutely a valid lens by which we see and experience reality. This being the case, as Roman Catholic apologist Peter Kreeft advises regarding the heart, "Instead of looking *at* it and explaining it or explaining it away, let us look *with* it."[49]

Learning to look with the heart is a spiritual endeavor and part of the faith journey. And one place in Scripture where you can vividly see the transformative effect of intuitive knowing and an epistemology of love is in the story of Job. As part of the wisdom books in the Bible, Job wrestles with the heady and emotionally charged topic of unjust suffering. Through a series of tragedies, Job loses his wealth, his children, and his health. Most of the book is a series of dialogues where his wife and his friends bring him little comfort. Toward the end of the story, God questions Job at length in a way that humbles and changes him. Finally, Job responds and note carefully what he says: "My ears had *heard of* you but now my eyes have *seen* you."[50]

What Loving Family Relationships Teach Us About God

Returning to where we started in this chapter, when it comes to thinking about God, self-conscious experience is not only the starting point, it's also often the gateway to "seeing" or finding God. When it comes to epistemology or our knowledge of God, there is head knowledge and there is heart knowledge. Head knowledge deals with logic and cold, hard facts. Heart knowledge deals with intuition, passions, and love.

All this being said, one of the most powerful evidences of the existence of a loving Creator is the beauty of human love, seen especially within the context of a healthy family: the emotional and sexual union within marriage and the deep trust and interdependency between spouses, parents, and children. Even when we've experienced brokenness in these relationships, we retain an awareness of what things could be or should be. This capacity to love and be loved is not

---

[49] https://www.memoriapress.com/articles/reasons-heart/
[50] Italics mine. Job 42:5, NIV.

simply an evolutionary necessity—some kind of survival of the fittest. It's, as we'll see in the next two chapters, a reflection of the character of the One who made us.

CHAPTER TWO: JAMES BOND AND THE TRINITY

It was 1993 and my wife and son were traveling back home with me to Southern Seminary in Louisville. On our way, we stopped at a McDonald's for dinner. While Pam ordered our food, I took point on getting our two-year-old, Matthew Gregory, settled. Having been stuck in his car seat for hours, he immediately started using the orange plastic table and seats as a jungle gym. Pam arrived with our food and as I helped Matthew get some fries, he suddenly looked up, full of wonder and dependence, and said, "I love you, Daddy." It was the first time I heard those words as a father. My soul leapt, my heart smiled, and I immediately went over to the other side of the bench, embraced him and with tears in my eyes said, "I love you too, Bud."

Moments like these are some of the most precious on earth. Why? Because in them we discover what life is all about—we learn first-hand that love and relationships are the core of our existence and purpose. In those moments, God, *The* Irreplaceable Father, is teaching us about himself. Sadly, such simple, relational truths have become not only undervalued but largely forgotten.

In this chapter, I'd like to illustrate what has been lost relationally about God's heart by unpacking a few big theological words or concepts: anthropomorphic language, theophanies, and especially the Trinity.

Anthropomorphic or Theomorphic?

Sorry for the big words, but I actually want to use them to make a simple, life-changing point about God's brilliance and heart toward us. First let's look at the words themselves:

- Both share the root word "morph," which means to transform.
- The prefixes give these words their distinct meanings: "Anthropo" means man or humankind and "Theo" means God.

In the Bible, statements about God often use what theologians call anthropomorphic language; that is, language that speaks of God in human terms.[51] For example, we might talk about "the *eyes* of the Lord" or "the *long arm* of the Lord." Other places in Scripture where God actually appeared in human or earthly form are called "theophanies;" that is, temporary appearances that represented his presence but weren't actually his true essence (e.g. the burning bush). Old Testament Scholar Bruce Waltke gives the following fresh perspective on anthropomorphic language, showing God's kindness and desire for us to know Him:

It is often said that the Bible represents God anthropomorphically (i.e., as a human being). More accurately, *a human being is theomorphic, made like God so that God can communicate himself to people.* He gave people ears to show that he hears the cry of the afflicted and eyes to show that he sees the plight of the pitiful (Ps. 94:9).[52][emphasis mine]

I believe Waltke's observation can be taken further: God created the family structure not just because it's useful to humans, but to reflect His relationship with us. He gave us parents who provide, nurture, and guide us to help us better understand how God provides for, nurtures, and guides us. Similarly, one of the reasons God gave me the experience of hearing Matthew say "I love you" for the first time is so I could better understand what God the Father must have felt when he said of Jesus, "This is my beloved Son in whom I am well pleased." That experience also let me further feel some of the great love involved

---

[51] For example, see Ex. 33:20, 23; Deut. 33:10; Isa 59:1, 63:9; Job 11:5; Ps. 16:11, 11:4, 55:1; Rev. 22:4; Ps. 11:4; Heb. 4:13.
[52] Bruce K. Waltke, *Genesis: A Commentary* (Grand Rapids, MI: Zondervan, 2001), 65.

in the Father sending his one and only son Jesus into a hostile world to save us: "For God so loved the world that he gave his only begotten son, that whosoever believes in him would not perish but have everlasting life."

In summary, Waltke is pointing out that God designed humans and the family structure to be theomorphic in order to teach us about Himself—especially His loving and intimate nature, and the relationship He desires to have with us.

Life's About Love and Relationships

Let's think more about our cherished connections on planet earth. The Beatles got it mostly right when they said, "love is all there is," as did Abraham Lincoln when he said, "The better part of a man's life consists of his friendships." Living is about intimacy, "knowing and being known." Regina Spektor captures the experience well in her song, "The Visit:"

I'm so glad that you stopped by
And I will not ask you why
It's just good to see you
You always make me smile
And you always make me sigh

Artistic expressions like this, whether the artist is aware of it or not, are infused with the sacred, teaching us deep truths about human nature and ultimately the relational heart of God.

Let's look at another example from the arts—this time a classic series of films—which offers unexpected insight into the source of all realities, The Triune God.

The movie franchise or his name? Bond... James Bond.

Let me say at the outset that my intent in exploring some of the appeal of the Bond films isn't to pooh-pooh them as a source of entertainment. The truth is many of them are favorites and I've gotten a lot of enjoyment out of them over the years.

My purpose is rather to use the 25 movies spanning six decades for reflective and illustrative purposes. Indeed, these films provide many snapshots of the engine of motivation and desire firing on all cylinders; pictures that are a mix of both holy and disordered desire. These films also provide us with a fun and accessible gateway into the more difficult—yet far more important—task of better understanding and appreciating the loving and relational heart of God and His designs for family and human flourishing.

Gadgets, Girls, and God?

Bond movies incorporate all the best in the world: the most exotic locations, the most elaborate stage sets, world-class stuntmen, the hottest gadgets, and, admittedly, the most beautiful women.

I will not skirt the issue (excuse the pun): there are a lot of scantily clad women in Bond movies and James Bond is a philanderer. Everyone who knows him knows he will visually indulge in, use, and sleep with any woman he chooses–without a second thought. In real life, there are many damaging effects from such wayward sexual habits.

But Bond movies are clearly fantasy and the lack of negative sexual repercussions isn't the only indicator. Bond also never gets seriously hurt or dies[53] in any one of his thousands of altercations, fights, chases, etc. In fiction, *Diehard* can be surpassed by Dieharder and even Diehardest, but real human bodies can't endure all those things without severe, likely permanent consequences.

Let's be honest: the idea of unlimited sexual pleasure with unlimited beautiful partners in a world where you never get hurt or contract a sexually transmitted infection has a certain appeal. But it's fantasy—a lie. Uncommitted sex outside the context of marriage leaves spiritual and emotional pain in its wake. As Dr. Armand Nicholi of Harvard Medical School observed:

> Sexual permissiveness has not led to greater pleasure, freedom and openness, more meaningful relationships between the sexes, or exhilarating relief from stifling inhibition but has often led to empty relationships, feelings of self-contempt and worthlessness.[54]

---

[53] SPOILER ALERT - except in *No Time To Die, again, a*fter six decades and 25 films.

[54] *Quoted in The Journal (published by Summit Ministries), Nov. 2003.*

Along with this emptiness comes physical limitations as well. God didn't design the human body for unlimited sex that would be painful, not pleasurable. Added to this, few women look like Bond women and, unfortunately for most of us men, few of us look like Bond!

So being aware of these unrealistic plot features, what else is there in these movies that could appeal to people – and especially dads – who love God and believe sex belongs within marriage?

There's actually plenty. For starters, Bond has a number of admirable qualities: Strength; courage; tenaciousness; sacrifice; being fully engaged and present; living a life of consequence—one that matters and makes a difference; being skilled and committed to excellence—that is, doing the best you can with what you have. Candidly, even the desire for beauty, justice, sex, and saving the world are created by God and can be holy in the right context. It's only when they're severed from God and his purposes in marriage and parenting that they become disordered.

Lest we think this is a Bond problem or an "unbeliever" problem, do Christians ever live lives that separate their relationship with God, their marriages, or parental responsibilities from an existence that is fully alive? Or to ask it differently, do we always live lives that are courageous, tenacious, sacrificial, wide awake, and consequential? Are any of us ever tempted to live as if God's design for family is something different from pursuing what's beautiful or saving the world? A "yes" answer to any of these questions indicates we have areas in which we need to grow, too. With that in view, let's further unpack what Bond's appeal can teach us.

James Bond lives life to the fullest and has plenty of passion, drive, and fire. He's not just sharp, he also consistently makes the best decisions, immediately or exactly when they need to be made. We can only dream of having this kind of focus in life, to consistently "nail it" in a way that every one of our acts of heroism saves the world. Often as men we question just how valuable our contribution is to the world. We switch into autopilot as we get up, grab our coffee, and go to work.

Our routine is often not demanding and for many not even challenging. And when it is challenging, The Killers's 2021 song "Pressure Machine" captures our experience well:

> Keep the debt cloud off the kids
> Only sunshine on their lids
> Jimmy Cricket and Power Wheels

And memories of Happy Meals
Sometimes I look at the stars
I think about how small we are
Sweating it out in the pressure machine…
And every year goes by faster than the one before[55]

Buried in the recesses of our soul is a quiet desperation for adventure, a hunger for more than our current experience. James Bond speaks to that "wild at heart" part of us and stirs and soothes those fantasies. Are those fantasies all bad? Things we need to eradicate or repress? Or are they mixed with image-of-God stardust that the Creator has put in our hearts?

Bond movies speak to something that wants to be more than we are. A part of us that wants to save the world, to experience life to its fullest—to live with passion and fire for…what? Who?? For God? Mother England? Beauty? Sex? Family?

You see, rather than simply being a temptation to trade modesty for immodesty, holiness for disordered desire, or virtue for vice, Bond movies help us ask deep spiritual questions and can even awaken something good and wholesome inside of us. Indeed, they can be counter-intuitive reminders of holy and God-sized dreams, as well as what lies look like. These well-crafted spy thrillers can even be an invitation to switch from a closely guarded and inhibited life to an open-hearted, courageous one in which we more fully express the image of God within us.

In many ways, the best movies in the Bond series offer an interesting contrast and comparison to what Christianity teaches about God as the source of all good things, including purpose, love and relationships.[56] And despite the spirit of our age that continues to aggressively de-link marriage, sex, and parenting (more on that in chapter six), God still intends for these components of loving family relationships to be connected, bring humanity joy, and provide knowledge of who he is. And this brings us to Christianity's biggest and most mysterious concept of all: the Trinity.

---

[55] Brandon Flowers / Dave Keuning / Jonathan Rado © Kobalt Music Publishing Ltd., Universal Music Publishing Group.
[56] James 1:17.

The Trinity: The Doctrine That's at the Heart of All Reality

In his classic *On God and Christ*, St. Gregory of Nazianzus (329-390), captured our challenge in recovering God's heart well: "To know God is hard, to describe him impossible..."[57] No doubt, this is a big contributor as to why modern expressions of worship often lack theological depth when talking about God. A 2020 Christianity Today article reported: "[The Trinity] almost never comes up in the songs sung by American Christians, according to a new study of the 30 most popular hymns and the 30 most popular worship songs over the past five years. Evangelical churches mostly sing about Jesus, with only occasional references to the Father and few (if any) mentions of the Holy Spirit. Songs that mention the relationships within the Godhead are even rarer..."[58]

Yet for two thousand years, belief in the Trinity and salvation by grace through faith have been two of the most essential doctrines of Christianity. Herman Bavinck, in his classic book *The Doctrine of God*, said, "The confession of the Trinity throbs at the heart of the Christian religion: every error results from, or upon deeper reflection may be traced to, a wrong view of this doctrine."[59]

The twentieth-century Russian theologian Vladimir Lossky states this even more strongly:

> If we reject the Trinity as the sole ground of all reality and all thought, we are committed to a road that leads nowhere; we end in an aphoria [despair], in folly, in the disintegration of our being, in spiritual death. Between the Trinity and hell there lies no other choice.[60]

Donald Bloesch, in his *Essentials of Evangelical Theology*, notes, "to bypass the Trinity is to end either in deism or pantheism. In the first, God becomes remote and distant, and in the second, indistinguishable

---

[57] St. Gregory of Nazianzus, *On God and Christ* (Crestwood, NY: St. Vladimir's Seminary Press, 2002), 39.
[58] https://www.christianitytoday.com/ct/2020/july-august/trinity-worship-music-hymns-father-son-holy-spirit.html
[59] Herman Bavinck, The Doctrine of God, trans. William Hendricksen (Grand Rapids, Mich.: Baker, 1977), 285.
[60] Michael Reeves, *Delighting in the Trinity* (Downers Grove, IL; IVP Academic, 2012), 130.

from the depth or core of the world."[61] God is not part of some nebulous Force, as in *Star Wars*, or the Borg, as in *Star Trek*. He is triune yet relationally one.

Christianity, in its embrace of God's relational oneness, is passionately monotheistic: "Hear O Israel: the LORD our God, the LORD is one!" (Deuteronomy 6:4, ESV) How do we then make sense of the concept of the Trinity then? The late theologian R.C. Sproul gives this simple explanation for the *formula* doctrine of the Trinity:

The formula of the Trinity is this: "God is one in essence, three in person.

The formula seeks to protect Christianity from serious combat on two fronts. On the one hand, the church wants to maintain its strict adherence to monotheism. Hence the first part of the formula—"God is one in essence." This means simply that there is only one Being we call *God*.

On the other hand, the church seeks to be faithful to the clear biblical revelation of the deity of Christ and the deity of the Holy Spirit. Therefore the church distinguishes between three persons in the Godhead—Father, son, and Holy spirit. This accounts for the second part of the formula—"Three in person."[62]

But formulas—often helpful in bringing clarity—don't move hearts and they tell us little about love. It's only as we explore more of God in *relationship*—the Father, Son, and Holy Spirit together—that we can begin to recover His heart. As theologian Fred Sanders puts it, "God's way of being God is to be Father, Son, and Holy Spirit simultaneously from all eternity, perfectly complete in a triune fellowship of love."[63]

We learn from Jesus's high-priestly prayer that there was eternal love between the persons of the Trinity even before the world was created: "Father, I desire that they also, whom you have given me, may be with me where I am, to see my glory that you have given me because

---

[61] Ibid., 37.
[62] R.C. Sproul, *The Mystery of the Holy Spirit* (Wheaton, IL: Tyndale, 1990) 37.
[63] Fred Sanders, *The Deep Things of God: How the Trinity Changes Everything* (Wheaton, IL: Crossway, 2017), 68.

you loved me before the foundation of the world."[64] We will talk more in chapter four about why God has revealed himself as "Our Father" and not "Our Mother." But for our purposes here, St. Gregory of Nazianzus explains what this prayer teaches us about God: "'Father' designates neither the substance nor the activity, but *the relationship*, the manner of being, which holds good between the Father and the Son...'the Only-Begotten Son' who is in the bosom of the Father..."[65] [Emphasis mine]

God's Triune nature gives powerful evidence that He is a personal and loving Creator, and reveals how important fatherhood is to Him. As John Eldredge eloquently points out:

> The story that is the Sacred Romance begins not with God alone, the Author at his desk, but God in relationship, intimacy beyond our wildest imagination, heroic intimacy. The Trinity is at the center of the universe; perfect relationship is at the center of all reality... One early mystic says we were created out of the laughter of the Trinity.[66]

Any and all loving or nurturing images we associate with human fatherhood have their roots in the intimacy and perfect relationship that exists within God himself.

In the Bond movies, the transcendent experiences of beauty, sex, justice, and saving the world are consistently delinked from marriage and parenting. In God's economy, however, these concepts are inseparable. Let's briefly review what marriage, sex, and parenting teach us about God in relationship, and finish out the chapter by looking at one of the most important passages in the Bible. For the more we become connected to the relational heart of God, the more we can live out our full humanity with fiery strength and passion.

Marriage

Marriage is an experience where two become one.[67] Although, as St. Gregory of Nazianzus said, "To know God is hard, to describe him impossible," a healthy marriage does give us a glimpse into the perfect

---

[64] John 17:24, ESV.
[65] St. Gregory of Nazianzus, *On God and Christ* (Crestwood, NY: St. Vladimir's Seminary Press, 2002), 84.
[66] Brent Curtis and John Eldredge, *The Sacred Romance* (Nashville: Nelson, 1997), 73.
[67] Genesis 2:24.

relationship that is at the center of all reality. The best marriages enjoy something that is ageless and evergreen. Theological advisor Michael Reeves, in his highly-accessible *Delighting in the Trinity*, observes this about the first couple:

> There is something about the relationship and difference between the man and the woman, Adam and Eve, that images the being of God... that reflects a personal God, a Son who is distinct from his Father, and yet who is of the very being of the Father, and who is eternally one with him in the Spirit.[68]

Sex

In Scripture, the word "know" often implies intimate personal relationship, not merely awareness of facts and circumstances. We can see this clearly in how the King James version uses "know" or "knew" in place of sexual intercourse:

- "And Adam knew Eve his wife; and she conceived, and bare Cain, and said, I have gotten a man from the LORD."[69]
- "And knew her not till she had brought forth her firstborn son: and he called his name Jesus."[70]

Although it's rare, we still use "know" or "knew" this way today. For example, in one episode of the old classic TV show, *The Rockford Files*, Jim asks a young lady how well a certain gentleman knew the victim in his investigation. She replied, "Oh, he knew her well... He knew her in the biblical sense of the word, if you know what I mean."

Is this word usage just a funky 17th-century linguistic carryover? No, it's actually tied to the original meaning of the Hebrew word, and this tells us a ton about how God created sex and what He thinks about it. In other words, describing sex as "knowing" injects the idea of relationship right into the word itself, which is the antithesis of much of what we see in Bond and those who might delude themselves or others that sex is "just physical."

It is also important to note that, although "intimate personal relationship" plays out differently when it comes to God, "know" is also used to express his special covenant love:

---

[68] Michael Reeves, *Delighting in the Trinity* (Downers Grove, IL: IVP, 2012), 37.
[69] Genesis 4:1.
[70] Matthew 1:25.

- "Before I formed you in the womb I knew you... I appointed you a prophet to the nations."[71]
- "You only have I known of all the families of the earth..."[72]
- "And then will I profess unto them, I never knew you: depart from me, ye that work iniquity."[73]

Parenting

Being connected heart-to-heart with our kids is also at the center of being a good parent. As many of us are well aware, each child is different, with unique passions, abilities, personalities, strengths, and weaknesses. Good moms and dads love their children unconditionally, and often all the more in their struggles. These very experiences help us take great encouragement when God tells us He "is like a father to his children, tender and compassionate to those who fear him. For he know how weak we are, he remembers we are only dust."[74]

In a similar way, empathizing with the temptations our kids face because we once were in their shoes helps us more deeply appreciate Jesus' heart toward us in our struggles against sin: "For we do not have a high priest who is unable to empathize with our weaknesses, but we have one who has been tempted in every way, just as we are—yet he did not sin."[75]

Maybe you don't have any children yet, or maybe you can't have children. Maybe you've had a bad or nonexistent experience with your father. Whatever the case, these passages reveal God's heart to you. *This* is what He is like. *This* is what he desires from earthly fathers. For those of us with wounds, these verses can also be stepping stones in our healing as we learn that what happened to us wasn't God, but was rather a serious distortion of His design.

One of the Most Important Passages in the Bible

All that we've been saying in this chapter has been building to one point: God created us to be like Him—especially in areas related to biological family relationships—so that we would get to know him. Indeed, God designed these theomorphic ways in us to give us a

---

71 Jeremiah 1:5, ESV.
72 Amos 3:2, ESV.
73 Matthew 7:22, KJV.
74 Psalm 103:13-14, NLT.
75 Hebrews 4:5, NIV.

glimpse of who he is. He then gave us his Word, the Bible, to further guide our way.

The Apostle John sums up the loving, fiery, dazzling, relational nature of the Triune God:

> God is love, and whoever abides in love abides in God, and God abides in him. By this is love <u>perfected</u> with us, so that we may have *confidence* for the day of judgment, because as he is so also are we in this world. There is no *fear* in love, but perfect love casts out fear. For fear has to do with punishment, and whoever fears has not been <u>perfected</u> in love.[76] [Emphasis mine]

In this beautiful passage, notice the unbelievably precious positional statement (in bold). It's sandwiched right between the themes of perfecting or maturing in love (underlined), and not being afraid of judgment and punishment (italicized). What does "because as he is so also are we in the world" mean?

It means that in Christ, our standing with God is secure. Because we are viewed positionally in him, "we enjoy the same privileged place with the Father" as Jesus did when he was on earth![77] Eugene Peterson's translation in *The Message* nails it: "Our standing in the world is identical with Christ's."[78]

The father heart of God was central to John's understanding, as demonstrated by what he wrote just a few verses before: "In this the love of God was made manifest among us, that God [the Father] sent his only son into the world, so that we might live through him."[79] The apostle Paul enlarges John's thought here by pointing out "that God" (again, the Father) was "in Christ . . . reconciling the world to himself, not counting their trespasses against them."[80] No wonder John exclaims in the middle of his letter, "What marvelous love the Father has extended to us! Just look at it—we're called children of God! That's who we really are."[81]

---

[76] 1 John 4:16-18, ESV.
[77] Gary Burge, *NIV Application Commentary* (Grand Rapids, Zondervan).
[78] 1 John 4:17b, MSG.
[79] 1 John 4:9, ESV.
[80] 2 Cor 5:19, ESV.
[81] 1 John 3:1, MSG.

🔥 Going Deeper: Please take a moment to pause and allow the powerful truths in 1 John to sink in. Without question, these few verses—maybe more than in any other place in the Bible—clearly teach that the essence of God is holy love. What you believe about Christ's sacrifice and the Father's heart toward you will largely determine whether you live in confidence or fear. Friend, do you believe your standing in the world is identical with Christ's? If you did, just think how strong you'd be!

CHAPTER THREE: KNOWING GOD AS FATHER

In his classic *Knowing God*, J.I. Packer wrote:

> If you want to judge how well a person understands Christianity, find out how much he makes of the thought of being God's child, and having God as his Father. If this is not the thought that prompts and controls his worship and prayers and his whole outlook on life, it means he does not understand Christianity very well at all.[82]

This provocative statement, especially in light of how Jesus taught us to pray,[83] underscores the importance of exploring two doctrines that are often pitted against each other: the Universal Fatherhood of God and the Redemptive Fatherhood of God.

Here are quick definitions and scriptural support for both:

- **A Doctrine for Everyone**: the Universal Fatherhood of God:
  - God as Father = Creator of *all*
  - "But now, O LORD, you are our Father; we are the clay, and you are our potter; we are all the work of your hand."[84]
  - "Have we not all one Father? Has not one God created us?"[85]

---

[82] J.I. Packer, *Knowing God* (London: Hodder & Stroughton, 1973), 224.
[83] Matthew 6:9. We will discuss the "Lord's" or "Our Father" prayer" in depth in chapter four.
[84] Isaiah 64:8, ESV.
[85] Malachi 2:10a, ESV.

- **A Doctrine for Believers Only**: the Redemptive Fatherhood of God:
  - o God as Father = Adoptive Parent of *some*
  - o "Yet to all who did receive him, to those who believed in his name, he gave the right to become children of God..."[86]
  - o "You parents—if your children ask for a loaf of bread, do you give them a stone instead? Or if they ask for a fish, do you give them a snake? Of course not! So if you sinful people know how to give good gifts to your children, how much more will your heavenly Father give good gifts to those who ask him."[87]

Referring to God as father is not unique to Christianity or Judaism. The Greek god Zeus was addressed as "father," indicating that he was the "supreme patriarch and ruler of the cosmos, the same way the emperor could be hailed as 'father' of the Roman state."[88] Further, Greek references to the chief deity as "father" in a number of cases meant "creator" or "progenitor," and applied to the deity's power rather than his intimacy.[89] Even in the Old Testament, "references to God as father, occurring first in Deuteronomy...relate particularly to God's being the creator and provider...":[90]

Deuteronomy 32:6 is a perfect example: "Is this the way you repay the LORD, you foolish and senseless people? Isn't he your Father who created you? Has he not made you and established you?"[91]

In this verse, God is the father who "created," "made," and "established" His people. Because of this, there's honor and respect that every person on the planet, and especially His people, should give Him. These last two sentences capture the essence of the universal

---

[86] John 1:12, NIV.
[87] Matthew 7:9-11, NLT. As part of the Sermon on the Mount, this verse is limited in application to "disciples" (5:1). Further, as part of that context, Jesus' words are limited to those who have embraced his rule, not all "the Gentiles" (6:32).
[88] Craig S. Keener, *A Commentary on the Gospel of Matthew* (Grand Rapids, MI: Eerdmans, 1999), 217.
[89] Ibid., 217, footnotes 165 and 165.
[90] *Dictionary of Biblical Imagery*, ed. Ryken, Leland and Wilhoit, James C. and Longman, Tremper III (Downers Grove, IL: IVP, 1998), 333.
[91] Deuteronomy 32:6, NLT.

Fatherhood of God as and may seem pretty straightforward to most readers. So why has it been so controversial for many Christians?

An Unnecessary Cage Match & What the Bible Teaches

George Eldon Ladd, one of the most influential evangelical scholars of the last century,[92] was not a fan of the universal Fatherhood of God. In his time-honored textbook, he spends two pages refuting a certain version of it, seeking to make the case that Jesus never taught people are "by nature children of God."[93] What Ladd meant is that Jesus never taught that all humans have *the same inherent desires* as God. In other words, Ladd believed that all humans on this side of the Fall have distorted desires and hearts that are estranged from their Creator; they are lost and don't seek God. As Jesus told the religious leaders who rejected him, "If God were your Father, you would love me for I came from God and am here...You are of your father the devil, and your will [nature] is to do your fathers desires...."[94]

Though I'm in agreement with Ladd that all humans are *not* "by nature" children of God in this sense, I believe he went too far in rejecting the universal Fatherhood of God altogether. In other words, there is a legitimate sense in which all humans, created in His image, are the children of God.

Here are a few vivid examples in Paul's writings:

- "For 'In him we live and move and have our being'; as some of your poets have said, 'For we are indeed his offspring.'"[95]

---

[92] In a poll conducted by Mark Noll in 1986, this work ranked as the second most influential book among evangelical scholars, second only to Calvin's *Institutes*. See Mark Noll, *Between Faith and Criticism: Evangelicals, Scholarship, and the Bible in America* (1986), 212.

[93] 2 Peter 1:4 reserves this gift for those who have received the redemptive Fatherhood of God. This rich teaching, discussed below, is related to our adoption as sons and daughters, and should be distinguished from the apostolic doctrine of the universal Fatherhood of God described here.

[94] John 8:42-44, ESV. See also Ephesians 2:3.

[95] Acts 17:28, ESV. Interestingly, Ladd admits in a footnote that "Paul has a doctrine of God's universal Fatherhood resting upon the fact of creation (Acts 17:28–29)," although he believes that this "represents a different line of thought" from Jesus. See Ladd, *A Theology of the New Testament*, 83.

- "For this reason I bow my knees before the Father, from whom every family in heaven and on earth is named…"[96]
- "…one God and Father of all, who is over all and through all and in all."[97]

Regarding these last two examples, New Testament Scholar, Klyne Snodgrass observes:

> Paul refers to God as Father forty-two times in his letters, of which eight are in Ephesians. No other description of God is used so frequently in the New Testament… God is the Father of believers, but both a narrower and broader use of "Father" also occurs. More narrowly, God is viewed as the Father of our Lord Jesus Christ, which marks out the uniqueness of Jesus' relation to the Father. In 3:15 (and 4:6) the broader sense occurs: God as the Father of all humanity….[98]

And what about Jesus' teachings? In the parable of the prodigal son[99] that we'll unpack below is a classic text where Jesus clearly teaches the universal Fatherhood of God. Regarding this passage, Ladd acknowledges, "humankind's place is in the house of the Father,"[100] but his complete rejection of the universal Fatherhood of God steals beauty from the story. And his approach, unlike Snodgrass' above, is reactionary. In the end, it has the practical effect of dismantling an important bridge for the gospel that Paul uses in Acts 17:28, diminishing something all humans share in common, and weakening important doctrines that Jesus and Paul actually shared.

Fred Sanders, professor of theology at Biola University, does a better job at capturing the essence of Ladd and others' concerns (mine included) without being reactionary:

---

[96] Ephesians 3:14-15, ESV.
[97] Ephesians 4:6, ESV.
[98] Klyne Snodgrass, *The NIV Application Commentary: Ephesians* (Grand Rapids: Zondervan, 1996), 179. Snodgrass also notes that Paul references God's universal fatherhood in 1 Cor 8:6.
[99] Luke 15:11–24.
[100] Ladd, *A Theology of the New Testament*, 85.

56

Turned into a system, this idea of universal fatherhood was theologically disastrous. Classic FOGBOM (Fatherhood of God, Brotherhood of Man) liberalism made the gospel seem like a description of the general state of affairs rather than an announcement of what God has done in Christ; it was never able to account for sin or recognize the need for a costly redemption; and it quickly lost its grip on the doctrine of the Trinity.[101]

The problem then is not with a belief in the universal Fatherhood of God itself. It's when the universal Fatherhood of God is "turned into a system," and divorced from the redemptive Fatherhood of God—that second doctrine we'll discuss more in the later part of this chapter.

Practical Implications & Why the Universal Fatherhood of God Matters

Jesus said to his disciples in the Sermon on the Mount, "Love your enemies and pray for those who persecute you, so that you may be sons of your Father who is in heaven. For he makes his sun rise on the evil and on the good, and sends rain on the just and on the unjust."[102] This bolded statement is what many call "common grace," and reminds us that the "Father of lights" is the source of "every good and perfect gift."[103] American Commentator David French recently noted that "common grace" explains why conservatives and progressives, whether religious or irreligious, can often still work together for the good of mankind: "God's grace elevates us, and so do functioning institutions like healthy families, churches, and communities."[104]

As the Maker, Creator, and the Establisher of humanity's very existence on this planet, God is the universal Father. The early church scholar J.N.D. Kelly notes that in pre-Nicene theology, "'Father'

---

[101] Fred Sanders, *The Deep Things of God: How the Trinity Changes Everything* (Wheaton, IL: Crossway, 2017), 93.
[102] Matthew 5:44–45.
[103] James 1:17.
[104] https://frenchpress.thedispatch.com/p/the-question-that-dictates-how-christians

referred primarily to His role as creator and author of all things."[105] And it is this sense that is "probably the original meaning in the Apostle's Creed," when it states, "I believe in *God the Father, Maker of heaven and earth*."[106] God's universal Fatherhood is real and an important part of our apologetic to all people, whether or not they will ever experience God as Redemptive Father. In taking His universal Fatherhood seriously, Christians are reminded of the common heritage and human "sameness" we all share. Lost prodigal humanity does matter to God! That includes you and me. It includes our favorite political candidates, and their bitterest rivals. It includes our dearest friends, and those who have hurt us so deeply, we wonder whether we'll ever fully heal. Everyone is loved—more than they know—by their Creator.[107]

When we truly believe we're all children of God, created in his image, it's easier to follow Paul's exhortation to the Philippians: "Do nothing out of selfish ambition or vain conceit. Rather, in humility value others above yourselves, not looking to your own interests but each of you to the interests of the others."[108] Wearing an uncomfortable mask during a global pandemic can become a way of honoring God's children around you. George Floyd's death grieves us deeply and, no matter our skin color, we yearn for institutions which protect the sacred image of God in every person. Regarding any issue, it becomes less about *our* personal take, freedom, or rights, and more about the second greatest commandment—"Love thy neighbor."

The universal Fatherhood of God also reminds us to love and accept others (sometimes even our parents or children) even if they reject our faith or fall away from beliefs they once held precious. Loving and accepting others doesn't mean that, in embracing them, we must accept all their ideas and behaviors. It does mean, however, that we must acknowledge that choice is the gift of adulthood. It also means that, as filmmaker Phil Vischer tweeted:

---

[105] J.N.D. Kelly, *Early Christian Doctrines* (New York: HarperOne, 1978), 83.
[106] Cameron, "Fatherhood of God," 254.
[107] John 3:16; 1 Timothy 2:3-4.
[108] Philippians 2:3-4, NIV.

We've got to get rid of the "us" vs. "them" mentality that pervades so much of evangelicalism. How can we love "them" if we are so focused on how 'them' is against "us?"...that one of "us" could become "them" is so threatening, that we cannot love. We can only oppose. For fear that others of "us" could become "them" if we don't take a stand against the "them-ness" of the one that once was "us"... not saying doctrine does not matter. Just saying love over all.[109]

While wrestling with the meaning of difficult descriptors like "objects of his wrath" or "vessels fit for destruction"[110] for those outside of Christ, Christians cannot lose sight of the true brotherhood of man. The Bible teaches that all human life is sacred and we're our brother's keeper. All human offspring on this planet—whatever "kindred, tongue, tribe, or nation" they may be from—share a frailty, a common dust, and are "fearfully and wonderfully made."[111] In fact, the universal Fatherhood of God is intimately tied to and undergirds a full-orbed belief in the sanctity of human life that's rooted in the *Imago Dei*– from womb to the tomb. Indeed, it's in part because we've come to undervalue simple truths like the universal Fatherhood of God that listening conversations and diverse friendships are rarer and rarer.

Listening Conversations and Diverse Friendships

Listening is rudimentary to being a good human; it's one of the most fundamental forms of respect. Further, it's a basic signifier of our humility. And our wisdom: Proverbs tells us it's only the fool that utters all his mind[112] and "He that answers a matter before listening it is a folly and shame to him."[113]

The fundamental loss of human children of God, created in His image, listening to one another is a primary contributor to America's polarization. As musician Michael W. Smith observes in his

---

[109] Posted on 4.24.21. Since his *Veggie Tales* fame, Phil Vischer has successfully reinvented himself as a helpful cultural analyst and Christian apologist.
[110] Romans 9:22.
[111] Psalm 139:14.
[112] 29:11, KJV.
[113] 18:13.

autobiographical *The Way of the Father: Lessons from My Dad, Truths About God*:

> So much of the conversation today is *not* conversation at all, but more confrontation, manipulation, sensation, dictation, litigation, and even damnation. No matter our politics or personal beliefs, we have to listen once again and be open to having some uncomfortable dialogue, even within our own hearts.[114]

We can learn a lot about listening conversations, as well as fostering friendships that transcend polarization, from the late Supreme Court Justices Ruth Bader Ginsburg and Antonin Scalia, as well as from current Justices Sonia Sotomayor and Clarence Thomas.

Andrew MacDonald, Associate Director of the Wheaton College, Billy Graham Center shared this story about Ginsburg and Scalia's relationship:

> Revered by liberals, Ginsburg was the ideological opposite of Scalia in nearly every respect. Despite these differences, the two were 'the best of friends,' dating back to their time on the U.S. Court of Appeals for the D.C. Circuit...

> When asked how they were able to maintain a friendship despite profound differences, Ginsburg answered:

> We know that even though we have sharp disagreements on what the Constitution means, we have trust. We revere the Constitution and the Court, and we want to make sure that when we leave it, it will be in as good a shape as it was when we joined the Court.

> [Some have noted that unlike the friendship that Ginsberg and Scalia modeled, we are] "saturated with polarization, tribalism,

---

[114] Michael W. Smith with Robert Noland, *The Way of the Father* (Franklin, TN: KLove, 2021), 142.

power, and selfishness, we are habituated to believe the lie that the highest good is to win."

Scalia's son recently tweeted a story about how his father would buy roses for Ginsburg for her birthday. Seeing him with the roses, Judge Jeffrey Sutton once asked, 'So what good have all these roses done for you? Name one five-four case of any significance where you got Justice Ginsburg's vote.' Scalia replied, 'Some things are more important than votes.'[115]

And here is Justice Sonia Sotomayor on her friendship with her ideological opposite, Justice Clarence Thomas:

I have probably disagreed with him more than any other justice… and yet… he is a man who cares deeply about the court as an institution… about people… He has a very different vision than I do… but I think we share a common understanding about people and kindness towards them. That's why I can be friends with him and still continue our daily battle over our differences of opinion in cases. But you really can't begin to understand an adversary unless you step away from looking at their views as motivated in bad faith… until you can look at their views and think about what the human reaction is that's motivating those views. What are they afraid of? What is it inside of them that moves them to be seeing the world in this way? You can't begin to engage them unless you can do something about that conversation.[116]

Making Sense of "The Fear of the LORD"

Another reason to acknowledge and retain the doctrines of both the universal and redemptive Fatherhood of God is that doing so

---

[115] I found this story originally at
https://www.christianitytoday.com/edstetzer/2020/september/some-thing-more-friendship-of-ginsburg-scalia.html but is no longer available at that link.
[116] Sotomayor made these remarks on June 17, 2022:
https://www.instagram.com/tv/Ce61ZmGF9TA/?igshid=YmMyMTA2M2Y=

brings clarity to our understanding of the fear of God. The late philosopher Dallas Willard provides an excellent full-orbed definition of "the fear of the Lord":

> [It is] more than "reverential awe" . . . fear is the anticipation of harm. The intelligent person recognizes that his or her well-being lies in being in harmony with God and what God is doing in the "kingdom." God is not mean, but he is dangerous. It is the same with other great forces he has placed in reality. Electricity and nuclear power, for example, are not mean, but they are dangerous. One who does not, in a certain sense, "worry" about God, simply isn't smart.[117]

Many question how the fear of the Lord can be the beginning of wisdom,[118] when we are also told, "perfect love casts out fear."[119] This is easily answered when both the universal and redemptive Fatherhood of God are considered: God as the Maker, Creator, and Establisher of all humans—the universal Father—should be feared. He is the Potter with authority over the clay. He gives life, and He can take it. He has the power to create and destroy both body and soul in hell. These are sobering facts for all, and whoever does not fear God at some level, as Willard observes, is just not smart. On the other hand, in Christ, believers come to know "*Abba*," their Father God, according to His special redemptive love.[120] Here, blood-washed saints learn that God's wrath is fully satisfied,[121] that they have been given the robe of Christ's righteousness, and that they can boldly come to His throne of grace. Now, as recipients of the extravagant redemption of the Father, we experience His perfect love which casts out fear. The fear of the Lord was a beginning, but now more and more it is our Heavenly Father's goodness that leads us to repentance.[122]

---

[117] Dallas Willard, *Renovation of the Heart* (Colorado Springs, CO: Navpress, 2002), 51.
[118] Proverbs 1:7.
[119] 1 John 4:18.
[120] John 1:12–13.
[121] 1 John 1:2.
[122] Earlier in my ministry, an artist friend gave me a painting she had done of the hands of the divine Potter molding the clay. In it, she brought the concepts of the

In summary, it's better to retain the doctrine of the *universal* Fatherhood of God taught clearly by Paul[123] and Jesus,[124] while plainly distinguishing it from the *redemptive* Fatherhood of God that applies only to believers. So, rather than say as one of evangelicalism's premier leaders John Stott did that, "The universal fatherhood of God . . . is potential, not actual," it is better to say that the universal Fatherhood of God is actual and part of the powerful invitation to all persons to know and return to God as *Abba*, in His redemptive Fatherhood through Christ.[125] It's to this rich topic—seen most clearly in the doctrine of adoption—that we'll now turn.

Aiden's Story & What It Means to Be Adopted by God

Long before ABBA was associated with a Swedish pop group, songs like *Dancing Queen*, and movies like *Mama Mia*, it was a Greek term akin to "Papa" or "Dad," connoting "affectionate respect."[126] Many of us understand this concept intuitively as when we've called our father to share our heart, we begin by saying, "Dad..." Or when our kids come to us for advice, they warmly address us as "Dad" or "Daddy." In the same way. Scripture uses "Abba" to describe the relationship we have with God through adoption. This term of "affectionate respect" teaches us that in Christ we should have no reticence in coming to God.[127]

Earlier this year, some dear friends invited Pam and me to be part of a very special day in the life of their family. It was the conclusion of a stressful, challenging two-and-a-half-year process of fostering and working toward the adoption of their now two-and-a-half-year-old son, Aiden.[128] Due to the pandemic, we gathered on Zoom with the Judge; essential court and social service personnel; our friends, their

---

universal and redemptive fatherhood beautifully together by entitling her painting "Caress."
123 Acts 17:28–29; Ephesians 3:15; 4:6.
124 Luke 15:11–24.
125 *Authentic Christianity,* ed. Timothy Dudley-Smith (Downers Grove, IL: IVP, 1995), 24.
126 Cameron, "Fatherhood of God," 254.
127 Mark 14:36; Romans 8:15; Galatians 4:6.
128 They had also spent three years prior to his birth in an arduous process of getting their home licensed for foster care!

three biological children, and Aiden; and a few other of their family members and friends.

Although there were formalities, the Judge kept things surprisingly light, humorous, and celebratory. The whole thing took less than a half-hour and was a truly joyous occasion. There were lots of tears and smiles—all focused on the rosy-cheeked, ruddy little guy who would now be protected and surrounded by love for a lifetime.

In reflecting on what it means to be adopted by the Creator of the Universe, I found some of the official adoption language the Judge read especially meaningful:

It is on [date redacted] ordered and adjudged, that said child is be adopted by the Plaintiffs and that the name of the said child shall be changed to Aiden [last name redacted] and from the entry of this Judgment, all relationships between the child and his natural parents shall be terminated as well as all rights, duties, privileges, and obligations of any person founded upon such relationships, including the rights of inheritance under interstate laws of this State except such rights which may have been vested prior to the entry of this judgment and the entry of this Judgment of Adoption shall establish the same relationships, rights, duties, and obligations between the child and the adopting parents as if such child were born to such adopting parents in lawful wedlock, including the rights of inheritance under the interstate laws of this state.

Modern adoption, like our friend's real-life experience, sheds light on what it means to be adopted by God. But there are also differences. Jerry Bridges, in his helpful book *The Gospel for Real Life*, notes "the adoption that Paul refers to is not that of an infant or small child, as is typical in our culture today. In Jewish culture it would refer to the status of those who have advanced from minors to full-grown sons . . . In Roman culture adoption would refer to the practice of wealthy but childless couples' adopting a worthy young man to be their heir and carry on the family name."[129]

---

[129] Bridges, *The Gospel for Real Life*, 143.

Paul's letters to Romans and Galatians both vividly describe what adoption into God's family is like.

- "For all that are led by the Spirit of God are sons of God. For you did not receive the spirit of slavery to fall back into fear, but you have received the Spirit of adoption as sons, by whom we cry, 'Abba! Father!' The Spirit himself bears witness with our spirit that we are the children of God, and if children then heirs—heirs of God and fellow heirs with Christ."[130]
- "So that we might receive the adoption as sons. And because you are sons, God has sent the spirit of his Son into our hearts, crying, 'Abba! Father!' So you are no longer a slave, but a son, and if a son, then an heir through God."[131]

Bridges notes that these verses on adoption detail three precious truths for the Christian:[132]

- We have been brought into close personal relationship with God.
- We have confident and ready access to Him.
- We receive the full rights of sons.

Bringing Everything Together in the Tale of Two Sons

The story of the prodigal son illustrates these three truths well. It's actually the story of two sons[133] and perhaps a better title is "the parable of the Father's Love."[134] This story is one of Jesus' most treasured and important parables, where the doctrines of the universal Fatherhood and the redemptive Fatherhood of God are brought together and pictured clearly.[135] The father in this story is the source, maker, and establisher of both the prodigal and the obedient older son—all of the roles associated with the universal fatherhood of God. The redemptive

---

130 Romans 8:14–17a.
131 Galatians 4:5b–7.
132 Bridges, *The Gospel for Real Life*, 144.
133 Luke 15:11.
134 Joachim Jeremias, *Rediscovering the Parables* (New York: Charles Scribner's Sons, 1966), 101.
135 Another example of this being done is in my friend Janice Freytag's painting of the divine Potter molding the clay. She brought the concepts of the universal and redemptive fatherhood together by entitling her painting "Caress."

fatherhood is seen later in the story when the prodigal comes to his senses,[136] repents, experiences the *Abba* embrace of the father, and—amazingly—is restored to the full rights of a son.

In this parable, we learn about "the yearning God" and His heart for the lost.[137] And it's actually the story of two sons, not just the prodigal. These sons represent two common paths to God, both of which miss His heart.[138] The younger son, the prodigal, represents "the tax collectors and sinners" or the path of irreligious free expression and experimentation. We might think of this son as "Oscar Goes Wild." The elder brother represents "the Pharisees and scribes"—the path of religion intoxicated with its own goodness. We might think of this second son as "Manny Moralist." This kind of religion can't get excited about God's scandalous love or extravagant parties for sinners. Tim Keller, in his wonderful little book *The Prodigal God,* lays out how both prodigals and elder brothers equally need God. He says:

> Jesus does not divide the world into the moral "good guys" and the immoral "bad guys." He shows us that everyone is dedicated to a project of self-salvation, to using God and others to get power and control for themselves. We are just going about it in different ways…The gospel of Jesus is not religion or irreligion, morality or immorality, moralism or relativism, conservatism or liberalism… In the gospel's view, everyone is wrong, everyone is loved, and everyone is called to recognize this and change.[139]

Bridges' third truth about biblical adoption—receiving the full rights of sons—is especially illustrated in the restoration of the prodigal son. The father gives three commands to give him gifts, including a robe, a ring, shoes, and a fatted calf. In his classic book,

---

[136] Coming to ones' senses is akin to regeneration, or being dead and then made alive, as in Eph 2:1-5.

[137] Ladd, *A Theology of the New Testament,* 84. Of note, there are three stories about something that's lost in Luke 15: a lost coin, a lost sheep, and a lost son.

[138] See 15:1-2 for the two audiences.

[139] Tim Keller, *The Prodigal God: Recovering the Heart of the Christian Faith* (New York: Dutton, 2008), 44-45.

Rediscovering the Parables, the late German theologian Joachim Jeremias helps us appreciate the culture behind these symbols:[140]

- **Robe**: This was "a mark of high distinction," and, "when a king wants to honor a deserving official, he presents him with a costly robe . . . the son is treated as a guest of honor."

- **Ring**: This is "a signet-ring"—a gift which "signified the bestowal of authority."

- **Shoes**: In the setting of this story, these "are a luxury, worn by free men," meaning that "the son is no longer to go about barefoot like a slave." [Again, this ties in well with Rom. 8:15 and Gal 4:7 cited above, giving us a perfect picture of what it looks like to be released from a spirit of slavery. To use an image from Harry Potter, we are not Dobby the house elf, reticent to ask for anything and constantly cowering in craven fear, lest we are beaten again. No, again, we have confident and ready access to God. It's like the image of Jack Kennedy's son playing under his desk. There is no need to think that we are taxing God, or that He does not want us around, for he "has a big house with plenty of room to spare (John 14:1–6; cf. Jer 3:19). There is no need to be fearful, for God will run to us, throw his arms around us, and kiss us when we return from our prodigal wanderings (Luke 15:20)."][141]

- **Fatted calf**: The father's last order is to kill the fatted calf. Jeremias notes that culturally "as a rule meat is rarely eaten." It is only "for special occasions [that] a fatted calf is prepared. Its killing means a feast . . . the festal reception of the returning son to the family table"![142]

This moving, precious response helps us see and feel what it means to be God's son or daughter in the fullest sense. Indeed, and to Packer's point that we began this chapter with, keeping the truth of what it means to be God's child close to our hearts will change the way

---

[140] Joachim Jeremias, *Rediscovering the Parables*, 102-103.
[141] "Father, Fatherhood" in *Dictionary of Biblical Imagery*, ed. Ryken, Leland and Wilhoit, James C. and Longman, Tremper III (Downers Grove, IL: IVP, 1998), 276.
[142] Op. Cit., 103.

we worship, pray (more on that in the next chapter), and, in truth, our whole outlook on life. Undeniably, this parable touches on something very deep in all of us. And Phillip Yancy, in his book *Vanishing Grace*, helps us understand why the gospel makes the most sense of what that "something" is:

> Mark Rutland whimsically recalls a survey in which Americans were asked which words they would most like to hear. He predicted the first choice: "I love you." Number two was "I forgive you." The third choice took him by surprise: "Supper's ready." It dawned on Rutland that these three statements provide a neat summary of the gospel story. We are loved by God, forgiven by God, and invited to the banquet table.[143]

Being adopted by the Father and calling Him *Abba* as Jesus himself did (Mark 14:36) means we go from being a rebel, an object of God's wrath, a hireling, a slave, one who longs for the pig trough, to a place of "dignity, honor, and full acceptance . . . the guest of honor at a feast of celebration . . . clothed in the robe of the perfect righteousness of Christ."[144] Moreover, "the Spirit of adoption"[145] makes us joint heirs, friends of God (John 15:15), and people who no longer serve out of fear or to get a reward, but instead now serve primarily out of deep gratitude and love for a Father who has lavished His love on us in Christ!

Michael Reeves' reflections provide a fitting conclusion for this chapter:

> Knowing God as our Father not only wonderfully gladdens our view of him; it gives the deepest comfort and joy. The honor of it is stupefying. To be the child of some rich king would be nice; but to be the beloved of the emperor of the universe is beyond words. Clearly the salvation of this God is better even than forgiveness, and certainly more secure. Other gods might offer forgiveness, but this God welcomes and embraces us as his

---

[143] Phillip Yancy, *Vanishing Grace* (Grand Rapids: Zondervan, 2014), 71.
[144] Bridges, *The Gospel for Real Life*, 145.
[145] Romans 8:15.

children, never to send us away. (For children do not get disowned for being naughty.) He does not offer some kind of 'he loves me, he loves me not' relationship whereby I have to try and keep myself in his favor by behaving impeccably. No, 'to all who received him, to those who believed in his name, he gave the right to become children of God' (Jn 1:12)—and so with security to enjoy his love forever.[146]

[146] Michael Reeves, *Delighting in the Trinity* (Downers Grove, IL: IVP, 2012), 76.

CHAPTER FOUR: THE "OUR FATHER" PRAYER

Pastor Steve Brown tells a story[147] in his book *Approaching God: How to Pray* about a time a young woman named Sarah came into his study. Steve looked up from his reading and she said, "I went to a Bible study last night and I learned some really good stuff. I learned that you can't hug a stiff kid."

Steve rolled his eyes internally, thinking she was stating the obvious—hugging teenagers sometimes felt like hugging a telephone pole. "That's a good illustration. I'll use it sometime," he responded, then he went back to his reading, hoping she would leave.

But she just stood there. Finally, Steve asked, "What is it, Sarah?" "I learned something else last night," she said, "I went to babysit after the Bible study for a two-year-old. He had played in the mud all day and was the dirtiest kid I have ever seen. I walked into his room and he lifted up his arms to be hugged. I found out that it's easier to hug a dirty kid than it is to hug a stiff kid."

What Sarah said is so true, isn't it? Steve then gives this application:

I'm not worried about your dirt. Jesus already took care of that on the cross. When Jesus said, "It is finished," it really was. He took your sin to the cross. And not only that, Paul talks a lot about what theologians call imputation. That means that he took your sin and gave you the goodness, the obedience, the perfection of Christ. Whenever you stand before God, you are clothed in the

---

[147] Adapted here for brevity from Steve Brown, *Approaching God: How to Pray* (Nashville: Moorings, 1996), 19-20.

71

righteousness of Christ. Your sin is covered, but the stiffness (e.g., "I'll do it my way," "I am my own master," "I'll control this situation, thank you") will kill you.[148]

Steve's story connects with us so well because it gets right at the heart of the gospel and helps us come to God as a child.[149] It teaches us something powerful about how to approach the One who welcomes and embraces us, never to send us away. In this chapter, we'll take a detailed look at two phrases in The Lord's Prayer or the "Our Father" as our Roman Catholic siblings call it. And since the Catholic name for the prayer resonates so uniquely with the theme of this book, we'll use the "Our Father" prayer as our primary designation. This important prayer teaches us 1) *who God is*, 2) *the theme of the Bible*, and 3) *what it means to be a Christian.*

We'll begin our discussion of who God is where most Christians would start with their own children.

Who Is God, and Is He Male?

Most children's catechisms answer the question, "Who is God?" with some version of the statement, "He is a spirit and has no body as we do." A study guide commenting on the Westminster Shorter Catechism's version of this question explains, "When we say that God is *a* Spirit we make clear the fact that He is distinct from all things . . . , but the important thing is that when we confess God is a Spirit we *deny* that God has any material substance."[150] In his commentary on the Westminster Confession of Faith, R.C. Sproul expands on these ideas further:

The confession affirms that, as Jesus himself taught (John 4:24), God is a spirit. That is, God is immaterial in his being. He has no extension that can be measured with a ruler or weighed on a scale.

---

[148] Although I can no longer find the exact source for *this* version of his quote that he follows up his "hugging a dirty kid" story, a similar version can be found in his *Feeling Guilty? Grace for Your Mistakes* 2016 eBook.
[149] Mark 10:14.
[150] G.I. Williamson, *The Westminster Shorter Catechism for Study Classes* (Phillipsburg, NJ: P&R, 1970), 17.

Because his being is… immaterial, and spiritual, God is invisible. We cannot see him unless he manifests himself through some physical medium. For this reason, Paul says that the invisible things are clearly seen through the things that are made (Rom 1:20)… but God himself, a spirit with no physical body, is invisible.[151]

Simply put, God is incomprehensibly beyond us. We can't fathom His essence despite our attempts to humanize Him. We can't stand God up against the wall and keep a record of His growth or height. We can't capture the weightiness of His glory or immensity on a scale.

Directly related to this is the fact that God is asexual. This means it is improper to view God as male, female, or both. Yes, God did make us male and female to teach us important things about Himself, but those things are about who he is as a person, not his anatomy. That being so, whatever virtues are associated with being male or female, God has them all!

Nevertheless, although God isn't male, Christians are to pray:

Our Father in heaven,
hallowed be your name.
Your kingdom come,
your will be done,
on earth as it is in heaven.
Give us this day our daily bread,
and forgive us our debts,
as we also have forgiven our debtors.
And lead us not into temptation,
but deliver us from evil.[152]

Why Christians Pray to "Our Father"

The "Our Father" prayer is the key text on how to approach and address God. It's also one of the "three great summaries" that has

---

151 R.C. Sproul, *Truths We Confess: A Layman's Guide to the Westminster Confession of Faith, Volume 1: The Triune God* (Phillipsburg, NJ: P&R, 2006), 36.
152 Matthew 6:9-13, ESV.

"been at the heart of historical catechetical practice:"[153] "[T]he late first or early second century treatise *The Didache of the Apostles* includes . . . the command that the believers should pray the Lord's Prayer three times daily."[154]

N.T. Wright summarizes the meaning of the prayer well:

The prayer is... a way of saying to the Father: Jesus... caught me in the net of his good news... I want to be part of his kingdom movement. I find myself drawn into his heaven-on-earth way of living. I want to be part of his bread-for-the-world agenda, for myself and for others. I need forgiveness for myself... and I intend to live with forgiveness in my heart in my own dealings with others. (Notice how remarkable it is, at the heart of the prayer, we commit ourselves to live in a particular way, a way we find difficult.) And because I live in the real world where evil is still powerful, I need protecting and rescuing. And, in and through it all, I acknowledge and celebrate the Father's kingdom, power, and glory.[155]

Let's look more deeply at what it means to pray the words, "Our Father."

The word "father" (Greek *pater*) in Matt 6:9 and Luke 11:2 probably translates the Aramaic *abba*, an intimate term we've already touched on. New Testament scholar Craig Blomberg describes this concept of intimate relationship with God as "virtually unparalleled in first-century Judaism."[156] "Father" (*pater*) pervades Matthew's longer introduction to the "Our Father,"[157] appearing five times before the "Our Father" begins in Matt 6:9. Christians "should consider God as accessible as the most loving human parent,"[158] Blomberg states.

---

[153] J.I. Packer and Gary A. Parrett, *Grounded in the Gospel: Building Believers the Old Fashioned Way* (Grand Rapids: Baker, 2010), 123.

[154] Ibid., 63.

[155] N.T. Wright, *Simply Christian: Why Christianity Makes Sense* (New York: HarperOne, 2006), 160.

[156] Craig Blomberg, *The New American Commentary,* Vol. 22, Matthew, ed. David Dockery (Nashville: Broadman, 1992), 119.

[157] Matthew 6:1-8.

[158] Ibid.

Although this is true, Blomberg's observation is not precise enough. The prayer does not begin, "Our Mother" or "Our Parent," but specifically "Our Father." Why?

Why Call God Father and Not Mother or Parent?

Fuller Seminary professor Scott Sunquist notes:

"Why not Mother?" The simple answer is that we are not given "Mother" as a name for God. The deeper reason may be that "mother" or "mother earth" were designations for a goddess who brought forth creation from her own being. She "birthed" creation from her womb. God the Father creates *ex nililo* [out of nothing]. A mother god points to a creation that shares her essence. This is not the biblical story. The biblical account... protects... the absolute holiness or separateness of God. Many adjectives can describe God (a lion, a strong tower, shepherd, king, fortress, and even a bird), but only one name is appropriate: Father.[159]

Additionally, in a patriarchal ("father-rule") culture, God also relates to us as Father and in masculine ways to demonstrate His power and authority. But we must be careful here. This need not mean that God has more of a masculine nature than a feminine one as theologian John Frame asserts: "There is no reason to assume that the proportions of male and female imagery are not part of the revelation of his nature."[160] In other words, what Frame is saying is that since "the pronouns and verbs referring to God in Scripture are always masculine, and the images of him (Lord, King, Father, husband, etc.) are typically masculine"[161] it is proper to view God as more masculine than feminine in his nature. But in a world where women have been viewed as property with no legal status for most of history, this kind of thinking can easily translate into oppressive views of women even in

---

[159] Sunquist, *Understanding Christian Mission,* 189–190.
[160] John M. Frame, *Systematic Theology: An Introduction to Christian Belief* (Phillipsburg, NJ: Presbyterian & Reformed, 2013), 112.
[161] Ibid., 109.

the Church. Consider this example from the twelfth-century Scottish monk Richard of Saint Victor in his *On the Trinity*:

We must observe that there are two [different] sexes in the human nature, and for this reason, the terms defining relationships are different according to the difference of sexes. We call one who is a parent either "father" or "mother" [according to their] sex. In case of progeny, [we say] in one case "sons" and in another "daughters." In the divine nature instead, as we all know, there is absolutely no sex. *It was convenient, then, to associate terms referring to the more worthy sex— as it is recognized— to the most worthy being in the universe. This is the reason why the custom of indicating one as Father and one as Son in the Trinity has suitably come into habit.*[162] [emphasis mine]

And here is my big concern as it relates to essential foundations in recovering God's heart for dads—specifically here in calling God "Father," not "Mother," yet *not* viewing him as a male: As a man, if you view God as male, it will affect how you view women—especially your wife and daughter(s). In thinking of yourself as more "God-like" than the females, you will invariably—even if subconsciously—treat them as inferior or, as Richard of Saint Victor says, less "worthy." Further, you will be deceived into thinking that God sees them that way too. And as a woman, if you view God as male, it will affect your understanding of your worth and that of others, as well as your experience of His love.

Admittedly, there is much mystery here, especially when we consider Christ's identity in the Incarnation as the man, Jesus of Nazareth. As Frame says, "Only in the case of Jesus did God become flesh permanently…"[163] Although some of the reasons for this are intimately tied to the Son's fulfillment of the roles of the second Adam and prophet, priest, and king, we are definitely into the realm of God's "secret things" (Deut. 29:29) and exploring them further is beyond our capacity, as well as the scope of this book. When it comes to our

---

[162] Ruben Angelici, *Richard of Saint Victor, On the Trinity* (Eugene, OR: 2011), 207.
[163] John M. Frame, *Systematic Theology: An Introduction to Christian Belief* (Phillipsburg, NJ: Presbyterian & Reformed, 2013), 391.

questions—especially about God—and we've exhausted our mental capacities, it's time to rest, bow before "Our Father," and pursue the simplicity of childlike trust.

The Simple Heart of What It Means to Pray to "Our Father"

When a human is taught to think of God as Father, "a familial intimacy is immediately introduced into the divine-human relationship…. Familial intimacy means that 'the merely formal—as also the merely fearful—can have no place.' [Indeed,] it is his love that is supremely evident in our invitation to call him our Father."[164]

Craig Keener helps us further understand what God's "Fatherhood" would have meant to most of Jesus' hearers:

This is a relationship that denotes both respectful dependence and affectionate intimacy as well as obedience . . . In first century Jewish Palestine, children were powerless social dependents and fathers were viewed as strong providers and examples on whom their children could depend… *Perhaps more significantly, the context (6:7–8) indicates that intimate communion is implicit in "our Father"*; effective prayer is not a complex ritual but a simple cry of faith predicated on an assured relationship (7:7–11).[165]

One of the early church fathers, whose identity is unknown, wrote a welcoming thought as part of a homily in an incomplete work on Matthew: "He wishes himself to be called Father rather than Lord, so that he may give us great confidence in seeking him and great hope in beseeching him."[166]

Another amazing aspect of the Father's affection is that it does not change, as some human fathers' affection does. As He said in Malachi, "I have loved you" (1:2) and "I the LORD do not change."

---

164 Cameron, "Fatherhood of God," 254.
165 Craig S. Keener, *A Commentary on the Gospel of Matthew* (Grand Rapids, MI: Eerdmans, 1999), 216–218.
166 *Ancient Christian Commentary on Scripture*, New Testament 1a, Matthew 1-13 (Downers Grove, IL: IVP, 2001), 132.

And as we are reminded in the Psalms, "even if my father and mother abandon me [emotionally or physically], the LORD will hold me close."[167] Unfortunately, this constancy has not always been true in my relationship with my father, and I know you or someone you love can relate.

Throughout my childhood, my dad loved to pick out thoughtful, practical gifts. Early on, when I was six or seven years old, I came down with chickenpox and had to miss fun, end-of-the-school-year events with my friends. My dad surprised and cheered me up by bringing home something I loved: coloring books with a box of large, fresh crayons. As I got older, his gifts continued to reflect how well he knew me. For example, one Christmas when I was twenty and beginning to do my own carpentry jobs, my dad bought me a portable aluminum ladder that could be adjusted many ways to fit whatever job I was doing.

As mentioned in the introduction, our relationship changed soon after my parents divorced, my dad got a new wife and family, and he left the church. Rather than learn from his mistakes, my dad seemed to blame everything on God and religion. I, a young minister who stood squarely in the Christian tradition he'd rejected, became collateral damage. Distance grew like the thistles and thorns around *Sleeping Beauty*'s castle. Forgiveness came years later in my late forties, but, even then, I missed his delight—evidence that I was a priority, as was often expressed in his thoughtful gifts described above.

Even three years ago, at fifty-three, I found myself still longing for my dad to ask the simple question, "Can I treat you to breakfast?" It seemed I was worth no more than a phone call every other month, despite the hours he spent with nothing to do but read or watch TV. No more helpful gifts or even a card on my birthday. No more holidays spent together—even if all he had to do was let me give him a ride. Occasionally he would say, "I love you," the words did not lead to anything that would require any cost or effort on his part. It felt as if I was no longer worth it. Over time, he had changed in his relationship toward me, and—if I'm honest—I toward him.

---

[167] Psalm 27:10, NLT.

We will never experience this with "Our Father in heaven." He does not change. He is the ideal, ultimate, faithful (Ps 27:10) and "everlasting Father" (Isa 9:6). He is the "one Father," over all his children (Mal 2:10; Matt 22:9; 1 Cor 8:6; Eph 4:6). He is the "Father of mercies" (2 Cor 1:3) who has compassion on his children and those that fear Him (Ps 103:13). He created them (Deut 32:6), and carries them in His arms (Deut 1:31). He provides for what they need (Matt 6:25-34). He gives them good gifts (Matt 7:7–11; Luke 11:11–13). He "disciplines those he loves, as a father the son he delights in" (Prov 3:12 NIV; see also Heb 12:5–11).[168]

"Your Kingdom Come": Pausing to Get the Theme of the Bible Right

In his thought-provoking book, *Desiring the Kingdom*, Calvin College professor Jamie Smith gives a helpful description of the kingdom that can apply to all people, not just Christians:

To be human is to desire "the kingdom," *some* version of the kingdom, which is the aim of our quest. Every one of us is on a kind of Arthurian quest for "the Holy Grail," that hoped-for, longed-for, dreamed-of picture of the good life—the realm of human flourishing—that we pursue without ceasing.[169]

The kingdom, then, is that "hoped-for, longed-for, dreamed-of picture of the good life" that gets us up in the morning. It could be God, His description of human flourishing, His dream for our lives, or some substitute, an idol of choice—something that seems right in our own eyes.

Recognizing that all people pursue some "kingdom"—some big picture that orients their lives, Graeme Goldsworthy, the highly respected Old Testament teacher, helpfully defines the "kingdom of

---

[168] Some of the structure and references for this paragraph were informed by "Father, Fatherhood" in *Dictionary of Biblical Imagery*, ed. Ryken, Leland and Wilhoit, James C. and Longman, Tremper III (Downers Grove, IL: IVP, 1998), 275.
[169] James K. A. Smith, *Desiring the Kingdom* (Grand Rapids, MI: Baker Academic, 2009), 54–55.

God" as the "the hope or expectation of Israel" that finds its fulfillment in Jesus.[170]

He then details how the theme of the Bible—from Old Testament through New Testament—is the kingdom of God, and how "every... unfolding of the revelation leads to the Person of Jesus Christ come in the flesh."[171]

The kingdom, then, that we pray will come in the "Our Father" prayer is the Father's recipe for the "good life"—the only Hope with a capital "H" that will not disappoint—Jesus.[172] In light of this, how appropriate are these wise words of St. Augustine, which echo throughout the last 1600 years of church history: "Thou hast made us for thyself and our hearts are restless until they find their rest in Thee."[173] Or more recently, Dallas Willard said it like this: "The condition of life sought for by human beings through the ages is attained in the quietly transforming friendship of Jesus."[174]

The Close Relationship Between the Kingdom of God and His Fatherhood

In returning to our topic of the Fatherhood of God, George Eldon Ladd observed, "an inseparable relationship exists between the Kingdom of God and His Fatherhood."[175] There are numerous examples of this close relationship (Matt 6:9–10, 13:43, 25:34, 26:29; Luke 12:32), and Ladd sees all of these passages as pointing to the fact that "God is seeking out sinners and inviting them to submit themselves to his reign [kingdom] so he might be their Father."[176]

Or better yet, God, the universal Father, Source, Creator, Maker, and Establisher of every person, is seeking sinners and inviting them

---

[170] Graeme Goldsworthy, "The Kingdom of God and the Old Testament" *Present Truth* 22, accessed November 14, 2016, http://www.presenttruthmag.com/archive/XXII/22-4.htm. Ibid.

[171] Ibid.

[172] Romans 5:5, NLT.

[173] Augustine, *Confessions* (Indianapolis: Hackett, 2006), 3.

[174] Dallas Willard, *The Divine Conspiracy* (New York: Harper Collins, 1998), 124.

[175] Ladd, *A Theology of the New Testament*, 83.

[176] Ibid., 82.

to submit themselves to His reign so He might be their "*Abba*, Father." What is exciting, humbling, and mind-blowing is that Jesus Christ "loves us and has freed us from our sins by his blood and has made us a kingdom, priests to his God and Father" (Rev 1:5b–6a). We have the privilege in Christ of reigning with God and carrying out His will in this world.

Going back to creation, "Humanity is given a twofold cultural mandate: to fill the earth and to rule the creation as benevolent kings (Gen 9:2; Ps 8:5-8; Heb 2:5–9)."[177] Despite the fall, this kingly mandate includes the "enduring command for humanity to develop the potential endowed in creation [especially our children!]"[178] as service to God."[179] All humanity, even irreligious people, do this without even being aware of it. They produce great art, beautiful music, amazing inventions, astounding innovations, and other unbelievable creative feats that stretch human potential. Think of Van Gogh, Elton John, Bill Gates, Steve Jobs, Albert Einstein, Frank Lloyd Wright, and others. Made in the image of God, they cannot help themselves from doing great things and interacting with the world in astounding ways. But Christians especially, the ones who have experienced the great love of "*Abba* Father," should be excited about the "potential endowed in creation" and have an ever-expanding view of kingdom work. As Abraham Kuyper famously said, "There is not a square inch in the whole domain of our human existence over which Christ, who is Sovereign over all, does not cry: 'Mine.'" It is to the practical implications of this every "square inch" view of Christ's Lordship— especially as it applies to the "Your Kingdom come" petition in the "Our Father" prayer—that we now turn.

God's Kingdom is a Lot Bigger Than Your Church

Some church leaders—even full-time pastors supported by families—can feel angry or frustrated with moms or dads who they feel are not involved and committed enough to the local church due to family commitments. A few years ago, one pastor shared with me over

---

[177] Bruce Waltke, *Genesis, A Commentary* (Grand Rapids, MI: Zondervan, 2001), 67.
[178] Words in brackets, mine.
[179] Ibid.

breakfast how certain young dads in his church—who I knew personally and thought should be commended—needed to "grow up, address their idols of family, and roll up their sleeves to make this church… work." Much of his anger was misplaced. Although part of his frustrations might have been partially addressed by members "leaning in" to their church commitments, the true source of this frustration comes from impatience; unbiblical and unrealistic expectations (I speak from experience!); lack of awareness of how championing moms and dads is part of the church's most strategic mission; and ignorance (or rejection of) "sphere sovereignty."

Dutch theologian and statesman Abraham Kuyper (1837-1920) is credited with the helpful theological concept of "sphere sovereignty." It was a favorite concept of the late Chuck Colson, and has contributed to changes in my own thinking in the last twenty years. One of the most accessible summaries of the concept is in Richard Mouw's book, *Abraham Kuyper: A Short and Personal Introduction*. Sphere Sovereignty, Mouw explains, is Kuyper's term for the idea of "each sphere [domain] having its own unique or separate character . . . its own place in God's plan for creation, and each is directly under the divine rule."[180] Another Kuyperian scholar put it this way: "Each sphere has its own identity, its own unique task, its own God-given prerogatives. On each God has conferred its own peculiar right of existence and reason for existence."[181]

Families led by parents are an example of one sphere of God's kingdom.[182] The family is not only a legitimate sovereign sphere of God's kingdom, it is the oldest—established long before churches, governments, and business.

James Bratt, in his recent biography of Kuyper, underscores the place families held in Kuyper's thought:

[It was] first in every sense of the term. It was the first institution

---

[180] Richard J. Mouw, *Abraham Kuyper: A Short and Personal Introduction* (Grand Rapids, MI: Eerdmans, 2011), 23.
[181] Ibid., 24.
[182] In his work, Kuyper wrote especially about the spheres or separate domains of the church, education, the family, the state, the arts, and the sciences. Business or the marketplace would certainly be added to this.

to appear in history and seeded all the rest. Its health was the foundation and surest barometer of society's wellbeing. It grew from nature, prospered by nurture, and properly taught its members how to balance personal autonomy, mutual dependence, and due responsibility—that is, it was society in a miniature. Likewise, its authority was the source of, model for, and limit upon the state. Properly functioning, it also exhibited church-like qualities in being crowned with love and becoming a school for morals.[183]

Each sphere has its own separate domains of authority and legitimacy and needs to respect the other spheres. Governments, for example—another of Kuyper's spheres—do not grant rights to families, which are another sphere. They recognize rights. Churches also—another separate sphere—need to recognize the unique and separate sphere of families. Families do not exist to make the church's vision and programs work. Although this last sentence may sound strong, I used to believe, at some level, that they did, and I was often frustrated that families were not more committed to the "kingdom work" of the church. I used to think of "kingdom work" as primarily something the church did related to evangelism and discipleship. My view here was intertwined with a phrase often used by influential and now disgraced former megachurch pastor, Bill Hybels: "The church is the hope of the world." I now believe only Jesus is the hope of the world, although I freely admit and appreciate how He uses families, churches, and other spheres, to bring about his will.

Mouw clarifies exactly why Christians need to have a more expansive view of God's kingdom work:

Kuyper makes much of the fact that the Kingdom of Christ is much bigger than the institutional church. The Kingdom is the broad range of reality over which Christ rules. Actually, Christ's Kingdom is the whole cosmos—remember Kuyper's manifesto about every square inch of creation belonging to Jesus. But in a

---

[183] James Bratt, *Abraham Kuyper: Modern Calvinist, Christian Democrat* (Grand Rapids, IL: Eerdmans, 2013), 144–145.

more focused sense—the sense we will be assuming here—the Kingdom covers all of those areas of reality where Christ's rule is acknowledged by those who work to make that rule visible.

The institutional church is certainly an important part of Christ's Kingdom. It is where we as believers gather to worship—where we are shaped by the preaching of the Word, by participation in sacraments, by instruction in the church's instructions and teachings, and by less formal patterns of fellowship. In the life of the institutional church, believers regularly acknowledge the authority of Jesus Christ over their daily lives.

But the church is only one part of the Kingdom. And it is no trivial thing to point that out. I once heard a prominent pastor complain from the pulpit about lay people—he used the example of Christians in the business community—who don't give enough of their time to church activities. This is how he put it: "These folks work all day at their marketplace jobs, and then they go home and watch television. Other than coming to Sunday services," he said, "they don't seem to care about Kingdom activities!"

Kuyper would have been horrified at that statement—as I was. The pastor was equating church and Kingdom, as if the two terms were interchangeable. Kuyper would urge business people to see their places of work [or their families] as providing important opportunities for Kingdom service.[184]

Bringing it All Together

We've covered a lot of territory in this chapter looking especially at two key phrases from the "Our Father" prayer. We first looked at the phrase "Our Father in heaven" and discussed why, despite God being neither male nor female, we are to address Him as "Our Father." Whatever virtues are associated with being male or female, God has all of them in spades, as both men *and women* reflect the image of God.

---

[184] Mouw, *Abraham Kuyper*, 57.

We noted that God relating to us as Father and Son may have to do with distinguishing true worship from the polytheism associated with pagan goddess worship; demonstrating His power and authority; and the Son's fulfillment of the roles of second Adam, prophet, priest, and king. We especially highlighted that the primary reason for God's relating to us as Father is to communicate intimate family relationship; that is, so that we might have great confidence and hope in approaching Him.

Second, we looked at the phrase "Your kingdom come," identifying it as the major theme of the Bible, and defining kingdom broadly as that "hoped-for, longed-for, dreamed-of picture of the good life" that gets us up in the morning.[185] We then noted that God is seeking the lost and inviting them to submit to his kingdom so he might be their Redemptive Father. Amazingly, for those of us who know God in this way, he's set things up so we get to join him as partners in carrying out His agenda for the world![186] Indeed, all humanity—whether they know it or not—are part of God's twofold cultural mandate of 1) filling the earth and 2) ruling the creation as benevolent kings.[187] Humans do this in many ways, one of the most obvious being developing the potential of our children as primary service to God. In wrapping things up, we introduced the concept of sphere sovereignty and ended with this critically important point: The institutional church, although an important part of Christ's kingdom, is not the center of things and should respect, champion, and support the legitimacy of family as foundational and the oldest sovereign sphere of Christ's kingdom.

---

[185] James K. A. Smith, *Desiring the Kingdom* (Grand Rapids, MI: Baker Academic, 2009), 54–55.
[186] Matthew 28:18-20; 2 Corinthians 5:18-20.
[187] Genesis 9:2; Psalm 8:5-8; Hebrews 2:5–9.

CHAPTER FIVE: THE MOTHER OF ALL
FATHERHOOD PASSAGES

Although not important to him now, my dad's story of how he "came to Christ" is interesting. In 1973, he and my mom went to the theater to see the movie *Lost Horizon*, one of the bigger '70s box office bombs (it is credited as one of the fifty worst films of all time).[188] The production cost more than seven million and returned only half of that to Columbia Pictures.[189] This ill-fated musical opens with a group of Europeans being evacuated by plane from war-torn China, only to later crash in the Himalayas. There they find Shangri-La, an imaginary, remote paradise on earth—utopia.[190] For my dad, the film paralleled the spiritual search he was undergoing. He wanted to be a good person, to be different inside and out, but he didn't know how. He came out of the theater determined to live like the people in Shangri-La, where everyone loved one another and got along. Within five minutes of leaving the theater, however, he got into an argument with my mom! Clearly he couldn't be a better person on his own. Shortly after, he listened to a pastor on the radio speak from Matthew 5 about how "Those who hunger and thirst for righteousness shall be filled." My dad bowed his head that night and asked God for a righteousness only God can give.

---

[188] https://en.wikipedia.org/wiki/Lost_Horizon_(1973_film).
[189] Jarrott, Charles, dir. 1973. *Lost Horizon*. Columbia Pictures.
[190] Excerpted from *The American Heritage Dictionary of the English Language, Third Edition* Copyright © 1992 by Houghton Mifflin Company. Electronic version licensed from Lernout & Hauspie Speech Products N.V., further reproduction and distribution restricted in accordance with the Copyright Law of the United States. All rights reserved.

Although my dad no longer considers himself a Christian, his account evidences one of the major themes of the last chapter: All of us, whether we're religious or not, are looking for some kingdom, Shangri-La, Bond-like "save the world" experience, or "best life now." But what is *God's* kingdom, *his* design for "the good life"? And how are parents, and especially dads, intimately tied to it?

In this chapter, we'll answer these questions by taking an in-depth look at Malachi 4:6a: "And he will turn the hearts of fathers to their children and the hearts of children to their fathers." Although Malachi 4:6a's context is only six verses, this critically important passage is the hinge between the Old and New Testaments. In a similar way, this chapter too serves as a hinge between the first foundational half of this book and the second more practical half. Finally, we'll give precision to the unique and irreplaceable role parents–especially dads–have in recovering God's heart and passing it on.

Properly Understanding Malachi 4:6a

In my eleven years working at National Fatherhood Initiative, this passage was the most oft-quoted verse by faith-based practitioners: "And he will turn the hearts of fathers to their children and the hearts of children to their fathers…"

Unfortunately, as often as it was quoted, it was just as often poorly understood and applied. And it still is. The common conception goes something like this: "400 years before Jesus came to this earth, the Scriptures spoke about a central expression of love that would characterize the ministry of Jesus: reconciling fathers and families heart to heart."

Upon closer investigation of the context of Mal 4:6, however, the "he" of this passage refers first to John the Baptist, not Jesus, and "the fathers" to the Jewish forefathers, not biological fathers. Further, the verse is in a context of impending judgment, not heart-warming reconciliation. It's no wonder the second half of the verse (Mal 4:6b)— "lest I come and destroy the land with a decree of utter destruction"— is never included when 4:6a is displayed on marketing flyers, websites, or merch!

Here's the passage in full:

"For behold, the day is coming, burning like an oven, when all the arrogant and all evildoers will be stubble. The day that is coming shall set them ablaze," says the LORD of hosts, "so that it will leave them neither root nor branch. But for you who fear my name, the sun of righteousness shall rise with healing in its wings. You shall go out leaping like calves from the stall. And you shall tread down the wicked, for they will be ashes under the soles of your feet, on the day when I act," says the LORD of hosts.

"Remember the law of my servant Moses, the statutes and rules that I commanded him at Horeb for all Israel.

Behold, I will send you Elijah the prophet before the great and awesome day of the LORD comes. And he will turn the hearts of fathers to their children and the hearts of children to their fathers, lest I come and strike the land with a decree of utter destruction" (Malachi 4:1-6, ESV).

Resetting Malachi 4:6 in Context

Prior to the time the prophet Malachi was writing, the Mesopotamian kingdoms of Assyria and Babylon had taken Israel in 722 B.C. and Judah in 586 B.C. into exile. Old Testament scholar David Baker notes that these overlords had a different approach to their captives than Israel's later Persian rulers:

[Assyria and Babylon focused on] displacing major parts of captured populations, resettling them in various parts of far-flung territories and importing others to take their place (e.g., 2 Kings 17:23-24; 25:7, 11–21).... Persia, however, reversed this policy... when they conquered the Babylonian empire. It allowed subject people to return to their ancestral lands and reestablish their religious practices (e.g., 2 Chron. 36:22–23; Ezra 1:1–4). This the Judeans did, rebuilding the temple and the city walls and establishing their own province under Persian rule (Ezra,

Nehemiah, Esther). It is within this setting that Malachi prophesies.[191]

Identifying "the Fathers" of Malachi 4:6: Parents, Biological Fathers, or Jewish Forefathers?

Correctly handling the bible involves first understanding what the first writers intended as "the true meaning of a biblical text for us is what God originally intended it to mean when it was first spoken. This is the starting point."[192] In determining the original intent, then, we will examine three possibilities:

First, let us consider whether less literal translations, like the New Living Translation (NLT), are correct in translating or replacing the Hebrew word for "the fathers" in 4:6a (also in 4:6b) with "parents." Evidence for this more inclusive choice can be clearly seen earlier where the term "son" is used to describe both male and females.[193] God is metaphorically the Father of Israel, and the nation is collectively designated as "sons." Although Malachi 4:6 certainly has significance or application for "parents," substituting "fathers" with "parents" does injustice—as we shall see shortly—to the context and original intent of this passage.

A second approach—probably the most popular—is to retain "fathers," but understand them as specifically biological fathers that are M.I.A. (missing in action), physically, emotionally, or spiritually. Although not the original intent of this passage, this interpretation has merit as it picks up on an estrangement between the older and younger generations, probably not unconnected with the laxity around the marriage bond (2:14–16). And this is seen as a primary cause for the subsequent weakening of family life evidenced by broken biological family relationships.

The third approach, which captures the original meaning of Mal 4:6, recognizes "the fathers" as the great Jewish ancestors (Abraham,

---

[191] David W. Baker, *The NIV Application Commentary: Joel, Amos, Malachi* (Grand Rapids: Zondervan, 2006), 209.
[192] Gordon D. Fee and Douglas Stuart, *How to Read the Bible for All Its Worth* (Grand Rapids, MI: Zondervan, 2003), 29–30.
[193] Malachi 2:10, 3:17.

Isaac, Jacob, Moses, etc.) who earlier entered into covenant with God.[194] This usage is consistent with how "the covenant of our fathers" is used in Malachi 2:10. Further, Old Testament scholar and Wheaton College professor, Andrew Hill, notes that Malachi's "postscript specifically mentions two of the prominent patriarchal figures of earlier Israelite history"—Moses and Elijah. He also notes that the "fathers" as "Jewish ancestors" interpretation "accords better than... the 'family discord' approach because the prophet consistently appeals to the past."[195] He concludes that Malachi is about "covenant renewal" and the "bonding of the current generation of postexilic Israelites to the Mosaic covenant of their ancestors."[196] The reconciliation of fathers to sons is a reconciliation between ancestors and descendants, "the 'resolution of opposites' at the macro level in the sense of faithful ancestors versus faithless descendants."[197] It is not primarily about "a reform of the contemporary social order (especially at the microlevel of the family)."[198]

The late British evangelist G. Campbell Morgan's commentary on Malachi 4:6 agrees with Hill above and gives further clarity that "the fathers" are the Jewish patriarchs—not simply parents or biological fathers:

This final word then, being a warning, not a sentence, is a Gospel of Love, and is closely connected with a declaration of the possibility of escape from the threatened curse, and a statement of the condition of such an escape.... the turning of the heart marks the condition upon which the curse may be averted. The mission of Elijah, as here indicated, is not social, but spiritual. It is not that he will come to bring about reconciliation in the families of the people. "The fathers" are the patriarchs Abraham, Isaac, and Israel, from whose ideals of life and state of heart these children have so sadly wandered, and the mission of Elijah shall

---

194 Zechariah 1:2–4.
195 Andrew Hill, *The Anchor Yale Bible: Malachi* (New Haven, CT: Yale UP, 1998), 388.
196 Ibid.
197 Ibid.
198 Ibid., 387–388.

be that of turning these wandering hearts back to those ideals, and to that state of heart.[199]

Although Malachi 4:6a is not about resolving family discord, family discord is often a symptom of the greater problem this verse is addressing, namely the need for "motion back to the point of departure" from the living God.[200] Why is correcting our interpretation of this verse important? Because the original outcome sought is primarily spiritual, not social. Efforts to promote involved, responsible, and committed fathers fall short of the call of *this* passage when they do not include strategies that intentionally call hearts back to a reconciled relationship with their redemptive Father through Christ:

> This is what the LORD says: "Stand at the crossroads and look; ask for the ancient paths, ask where the good way is, and walk in it, and you will find rest for your souls." But you said, "We will not walk in it."[201]

Malachi's Version of the Good Life

In the last chapter we described "the Kingdom" as the "hoped-for, longed-for, dreamed-of picture of the good life" that gets us up in the morning–whether God's vision for our lives, or some cheap substitute—an idol of choice, something that seems right in our eyes. Malachi's version of the "good life," found in 4:2–3, uses three images:

- "the sun of righteousness will rise with healing in its wings,"
- "you shall go out leaping like calves from the stall," and
- "you shall tread down the wicked, for they will be ashes under the soles of your feet."

The first image refers to "the dawning of a new day ushering in an era of righteousness in which . . . [Israel] will experience the

---

[199] G. Campbell Morgan, *Wherein?: Malachi's Message to the Men of Today* (New York: Revell, 1898), 115–116.
[200] Hill, *The Anchor Yale Bible,* 387.
[201] Jeremiah 6:16, NIV.

complete reversal of current circumstances."[202] One scholar noted that light and salvation are synonymous in the Old Testament, "light being the sacramental sign of God's love."[203] Calvin and Luther further saw "sun of righteousness" as a reference to Jesus, and his interpretation is also reflected in the KJV's translation where it capitalizes the title, "Sun of righteousness."[204] Goldsworthy's definition of "the kingdom of God" as "the hope or expectation of Israel that finds its fulfillment in Jesus"—discussed in the last chapter—is consistent with seeing Christ as the "sun of righteousness."

The second image, "you shall go out leaping like calves from the stall," refers to "a sense of carefree and energetic playfulness characteristic of tethered calves released to pasture."[205] The Hebrew word translated here as "leaping" literally means to "frisk, paw the ground."[206] It reminds me of a time when my family owned two well-fed black labs, Oliver and Sydney. Peaceful and secure inside their master's house, they would suddenly start racing around like banshees in a spirit of carefree playfulness until my wife or I let them out to play.

The third image of the good life, "you shall tread down the wicked, for they will be ashes under the soles of your feet," is meant to convey the total conquest and eradication of evil. The enemy's head is not only under the foot of the victor, symbolizing subjugation, but is "ashes," denoting total destruction.

Together, Malachi's three descriptions of the "good life" paint a picture of being so healed internally and secure in the love of God that we live with a carefree playfulness, fearing nothing but God, courageously joining Him in the battle to overcome evil with good (a battle that cannot be lost!).[207] This is the life any good, spiritually motivated dad desires for himself, his children, and his children's children.

---

[202] Ibid., 349-350.
[203] Ibid., 350.
[204] Ibid., 349.
[205] Ibid., 353.
[206] Ibid., 352.
[207] Romans 8:31.

Who is the "he" of 4:6a?

Malachi 4:4-5 summarize the role of the law and the prophets symbolized by Moses and Elijah, and we have here a prophecy of the coming of another Elijah (called Yahweh's messenger in 3:1) whose ministry would be characterized by reconciliation and the hope of escaping the curse.[208]

Luke 1:16–17 (also Matt. 11:14) identifies this Elijah as John the Baptist. According to the prophecy given by an angel in Luke, John was the one to bring Malachi's prophecy to completion by getting things ready for Jesus.[209] So this is a prophecy about John and by extension—in an even greater way—the ministry of Jesus (remember John the Baptist was, according to John 1:23, only "the voice of one crying out in the wilderness, 'Make straight the way of the Lord [the Word]'"). Jesus is the culmination of all that the law (e.g. Moses) and the prophets (e.g. Elijah) pointed to, as well as the ultimate reconciler of hearts. It is only "in Him" and through the cross that we have the hope of the forgiveness of sins and restoration to "Our Father" and His ways (i.e. "the ancient paths" of Jer. 6:16).

As mentioned above, the whole context that surrounds Mal 4:6a is one impending judgment, "the day of the LORD." However, if one understands that "the fear of the LORD is the beginning of wisdom,"[210] even Malachi's warning can be seen as an expression of love and common grace from the universal Father. This "day of the LORD" is coming like a coin that has two faces, like "burning" fire that has two sides: it can be destructive (4:1), or it also can give warmth ("*sun* of righteousness" in 4:2). "Evildoers" will receive the former, and those who "fear" God the latter.

---

[208] "Most of Elijah's recorded ministry involved standing against this departure from Israel's covenant with God . . . Because of his courageous stand, even in the face of death (1 Kings 19:2), he stemmed the tide of encroaching paganism, protecting Israelite religion and culture." (Baker, 304.) His heroic stand plus his possible return due to the mysterious nature of his death (2 Kings 2:11-12) led to his mention by Malachi.

[209] Luke 1:17; Mal. 4:6.

[210] Proverbs 1:7.

Malachi's Vision of Hope: Remember, Return, and Rest

It's our heart attitude that determines how we will receive "the day of the Lord," not our pedigree or ethnicity. However, it's also a heart attitude that shows up in how we live. Intellectual assent or association with correct doctrine is not enough. As Abraham Kuyper has well said, "Purely intellectual knowledge of God is a frozen crust of ice from which the stream of life has run dry."[211] Or to say it differently, right behavior rooted in a right attitude toward God trumps correct theology disconnected from a heart for God. So how do wandering hearts get recaptured? And how does Malachi point to hope in the midst of impending judgment? It starts with the call to "remember" in verse 4. But not just cognition or recall—this biblical remembering requires faithful obedience.

The return to obedience for wandering hearts often comes through remembering significant events that are connected to historical people and places. That is one of the purposes of a wedding day, baptism, or communion—these events are important not only when they are happening, but as future reminders of how participants and observers should act. That is one of the reasons we began this book on recovering God's heart by recalling and reexamining the Resurrection of Christ, the linchpin for determining whether the Christian faith is true.

One might recall Simba's "remembering" in Disney's *The Lion King*. Influenced by the lies of his Uncle Scar, Simba left his blessed life associated with Pride Rock to wander the jungle and wastelands. Later confronted by the wise, albeit eccentric, baboon named Rafiki (meaning "friend"), Simba comes to a riverbank where he looks down and sees his reflection alongside his late father's reflection in the water. He then looks up in the sky and sees a vision in which his father, who loved him dearly, says, "Remember, you are more than what you have become." At this place of repentance, Simba turns from his shadow self, rejects the lies of his Uncle Scar, and returns to Pride Rock to embrace his destiny as the Lion King.

---

[211] Abraham Kuyper, *To Be Near Unto God* (Grand Rapids: Eerdmans, 1918), 173.

This passage in Malachi asks us to recall Moses at Mount Horeb. Baker notes:

> "Horeb" is an alternative name for Mount Sinai.... the place where Israel became a nation, since there they received their "constitution," the law of Moses (Ex 19–24), as well as various other instructions on how to live as a people under the authority of God (Ex 25–Num. 10:10).[212]

Israel had an amazing identity, but they had forgotten it. And this forgetfulness is part of what led to their wandering and disobedience.

Israel is similarly commanded to "remember" in Joshua 1:13. There, the command is associated with rest and land in a positive sense: "Remember the word that Moses the servant of the LORD commanded you, saying 'The LORD your God is providing you a place of rest and will give you this land.'"[213] This same rest and land are threatened in Malachi 4:6 if Israel does not return to covenant obedience. "Land" in both Joshua 1:13 and Malachi 4:6b is the territory of God's covenant people.[214] Land can also have a broader meaning and refer to the whole earth, a meaning that is certainly included in Malachi 4:6b.[215] There, at the conclusion of the Old Testament and before Christ's advent, the text is pregnant with apocalyptic warning and expectation.

When humanity (and especially God's covenant people) wander from God's law, it affects the earth.[216] Sin spoiled Eden and continues to bring destruction to the "land." In our day, protecting and honoring God's creation in nature and the environment—that is, "keeping the earth,"—is an undervalued priority among many Christians. But as Old Testament scholar Iain Provan noted:

> We are simply tenants, tasked with serving the garden (and its creatures) and keeping it—or, in more modern language,

---

[212] Ibid., 206.
[213] Joshua 1:3 ESV.
[214] Genesis 15:18–21.
[215] Genesis 1:1.
[216] Genesis 3:17–18; Romans 8:19–22.

"conserving" it… I am to view myself as an earth keeper, working and taking care of God's garden.[217]

Or as Anglican priest Tish Harrison Warren recently wrote on why environmental destruction is bad for our worship:

Every disappearance of plant and animal species is a loss of something made with infinite love and creativity. Nature is an icon—a window into heaven. When we destroy the icon, we can no longer hear its call to worship.[218]

Sin has been appropriately defined in theologian Cornelius Plantinga Jr.'s work *Not the Way It's Supposed to Be: A Breviary of Sin* as "vandalism" of His Shalom (or "place of rest").[219] Our wandering hearts often make friends with the lie that God is detached and unconcerned about the details of our lives or our physical planet. Upon "remembering" the covenant, however, one sees an expression of God's love that is worthy of tattooing on our hearts, something that communicates His delight in us, as well as His protection and provision. That same "law" also has the purpose of showing us our inability to please God. Indeed, it shows us our desperate need for a Savior.

The answer for all humanity is to "remember" and look to God's promise to help us "turn". For Israel, Malachi 4:1-6 was a prophetic call to "shift their allegiance back to Yahweh and the demands of his covenant."[220] This meant "unconditional surrender" and "complete reorientation of their worldview."[221]

Southern Baptist theologian Russell Moore uses a helpful New Testament analogy to demonstrate the simplicity of this turning:

---

[217] Iain Provan, *Seriously Dangerous Religion* (Waco, TX: Baylor University Press, 2014), 224-239.

[218] "Even the Apples Call His Name," Christianity Today, September 2021, 32.

[219] Cornelius Plantinga, Jr., *Not the Way It's Supposed to Be: A Breviary of Sin* (Grand Rapids: MI, 1995), 16.

[220] Andrew Hill, *The Anchor Yale Bible: Malachi* (New Haven, CT: Yale University Press, 1998), 387.

[221] Ibid., 387.

A drowning Simon Peter did not need a nautical map or the foreknowledge of nuclear submarine technology. He needed to cry out "Lord, save me," and to grab hold of the hand that could pull him up again (Matt. 14:30-31).[222]

The good news of the gospel and the real hope of this Malachi passage, however, does not come through our efforts to remember or turn, but in God's initiative. It is *he* who sends the one that "will turn," and because of this "he *will* turn." In other words, real Hope with a capital H arrives on the day that God acts through the coming of "Elijah the prophet" –that is, John the Baptist and in a greater way Christ, as John was only "the voice" preparing the way for "The Word." This is incredibly significant. The close of Malachi—indeed, the last words of the entire Old Testament—focus on the initiative and sovereign love of God. It is only because of the amazing and intimate love of "Our Father" that the "utter destruction" of 4:6b, which first came to Eden at the fall, is reversed in Christ. It is Christ alone that can bring healing to the nations (Rev. 22:2) and reconcile hearts to the ultimate Father! That's what we need to rest in as we recover God's heart and turn our attention to the practical task of being irreplaceable fathers ourselves.

Practical Implications

Properly understood, Malachi 4:6a is a call to courageously keep the Triune God and his ancient ways at the center of our efforts. This is important even for Christians who serve in secular settings, like Daniel or Esther, and must carry out their work more covertly or creatively. As authors Corbett and Fikkert point out in *When Helping Hurts*, if we work to change individuals' behaviors using means that are devoid of Christ or without biblical teaching, the result is "people who put their faith in middle-class values and in their ability to adopt those values. We . . . [will] have replaced their own worldview with that of the modern worldview, which believes that humans achieve progress

---

[222] "Integrity and the Future of the Church," Plough Quarterly, Autumn 2021, 109.

through their own strength."[223] In other words, if God is left out of the conversation, we may only be helping individuals exchange one idol for another. Further, if this new idol is just a Godless belief in self—one's own strength, self-sufficiency, bootstraps, or goodness—we may be contributing to an alarming condition where those we are trying to help are now further from God's grace than they were in their brokenness and humility.[224] These are sobering thoughts—especially for those who desire to serve fathers with distinctively Christian ministry.

Let's review some of what we've learned so far in part one:

1. The most powerful and fundamental evidence for the existence of a loving Creator is the beauty of human love seen especially within the context of a healthy family. (Chapter 1)

2. "The Trinity is at the center of the universe; perfect relationship is at the center of all reality."[225] And as St. Gregory of Nazianzus clarified, "Father designates neither the substance nor the activity, but *the relationship*, the manner of being, which holds good between the Father and the Son...the Only-Begotten Son who is in the bosom of the Father..."[226] (Chapter 2)

3. God, the Universal Father of all humanity, is seeking the lost so that he might be their Redemptive Father. (Chapter 3)

4. God is not male or female but has revealed himself as "Our Father." (Chapter 4)

5. The kingdom of God is the theme of the Bible and family is the foundational and oldest sovereign sphere of that kingdom. (Chapter 4)

6. Turning the hearts of children to their fathers is turning hearts toward God's ancient paths. (Chapter 5)

And this brings us to the core of what it means to recover God's heart for dads and why they're irreplaceable: Both moms and dads have

---

[223] Steve Corbett & Brian Fikkert, *When Helping Hurts* (Chicago, IL: Moody, 2009), 95.

[224] Psalm 34:18; Matthew 5:3; James 4:6.

[225] Brent Curtis and John Eldredge, *The Sacred Romance* (Nashville: Nelson, 1997), 73.

[226] St. Gregory of Nazianzus, *On God and Christ* (Crestwood, NY: St. Vladimir's Seminary Press, 2002), 84.

exceptional value to God in that they partner with Him in turning the hearts of their children toward His ancient paths. As sociologist Christian Smith concluded in analyzing the data on who is really leaving the faith and why, "Without question, the most important pastor a child will ever have in their life is a parent."[227] Moreover, given that He has revealed himself as "Our Father," dads are arguably in the most strategic position on the planet to pass on the possibility of friendship with God to their children. Could there be any greater privilege? Any more sobering responsibility? Make no mistake, friend, if you're a parent– and especially if you're a dad who loves God—you are the primary conduit for passing on His heart to your kids.

But being a good dad is hard, and not only have there been massive shifts in culture since biblical times, we now face some unique challenges as well. It's to these shifts and challenges that we now turn.

---

[227] https://www.thegospelcoalition.org/article/who-is-really-leaving-the-faith-and-why/

PART TWO: CULTURE SHIFTS AND CHALLENGES

"We didn't start the fire
It was always burning, since the world's been turning
We didn't start the fire
No, we didn't light it, but we tried to fight it."

—Billy Joel

CHAPTER SIX: IRREPLACEABLE MOMS AND MARRIAGE

I ain't the kind to hang around
With any new love that I've found
Since movin is my stock 'n trade,
I'm moving on I won't think of you when I'm gone...
I've got a hundred more like you, so don't be blue
I'll have a thousand 'fore I'm through[228]

The cold, detached attitude reflected in these lyrics may have been part of what made Gordon Lightfoot famous; however, his actions—not much different than these lyrics—took a devastating toll on his family.

For those who don't know, Lightfoot was one of the brightest stars of the folk music genre, famous especially for his strong use of emotion and the consistently high-quality of his compositions. His music, especially this song, was at the center of the culture shift that took place in attitudes toward marriage during the 1960s. David Brooks helps us put that shift in historical perspective:

A study of women's magazines by the sociologists Francesca Cancian and Steven L. Gordon found that from 1900 to 1979, themes of putting family before self dominated in the 1950s: "Love means self-sacrifice and compromise." In the 1960s and

70s, putting self before family was prominent: "Love means self-expression and individuality." Men absorbed these cultural themes, too. The master trend in Baby Boomer culture generally was liberation—"Free Bird," "Born to Run," "Ramblin' Man"...[229]

Now a rugged, 84-year-old man, Lightfoot's life provides an honest and long-term case study for our purposes. "If You Could Read My Mind," his first song to go number one, and arguably one of his finest, is about the collapse of his first marriage in the 60s.[230] In the 70s, he was in a brief relationship with singer Cathy Smith, who was with John Belushi on the night of his fatal overdose.[231] Lightfoot is on his third marriage now and he has six children. Regret has always been a common theme in his music. For instance, in his song "Second Cup of Coffee," written in 1972, he confesses, "my sleep was filled with dreaming of the wrongs that I have done / And the gentle sweet reminder of a daughter and a son."

The daughter referenced is Ingrid, his oldest from his first marriage. She finally asked him to stop singing the lyrics our chapter began with:

I didn't want him to sing it, because it made me angry... I knew it was about my mom. It's pretty self-explanatory. "I'm not the kind to hang around" and "the new love that I've found." My dad was going through a lot of women. My mom didn't need to be reminded of that.[232]

We'll talk more about Lightfoot's regret, repentance, and view on atonement in the final chapter of this book. But for now, he'll serve as a great example of how *not* to treat our wives or the mother of our

[229] https://www.theatlantic.com/magazine/archive/2020/03/the-nuclear-family-was-a-mistake/605536/

[230] https://www.rollingstone.com/music/music-features/gordon-lightfoot-interview-80-years-strong-tour-844868/ from June 11, 2019.

[231] https://www.rollingstone.com/music/music-features/gordon-lightfoot-interview-80-years-strong-tour-844868/ from June 11, 2019.

[232] Nicholas Jennings, *Lightfoot.*(Viking, 2017), 232.

children. And, as we see in Ingrid's comments above, how we treat our spouse or our child's mother deeply affects our kids. In the real world, unlike the character Reese Bobby, Ricky's Bobby's father in *Talladega Nights*, cheating spouses and dead-beat dads don't make us laugh: They bring pain, hurt, and unhappiness of the worst kind.

Happy Together: Moms, Dads, & Healthy Marriage

An integral part of recovering God's heart for dads is recovering His heart for healthy marriage and moms, too. In God's ideal and design, they are a package deal: There is no motherhood or fatherhood without marriage.

Mothers are essential, full partners in raising healthy kids and marriage is intimately tied to fatherhood. Moreover, it's been said that the best way for a man to love his children is to love their mother. After thirty-five years of marriage, I whole-heartedly agree and many social scientists, including David Blankenhorn, also concur:

> Scholars who study this issue know full well that . . . the institution of marriage is the essential precondition for, and therefore the most accurate predictor of . . . effective, hands-on, nurturing fatherhood.... ignoring marriage is like wanting the crops without plowing the ground, or wanting the ocean without the roar of its waters.[233]

Further, "American men see marriage and parenting as a package deal; when the marriage breaks up, parenting deteriorates as well."[234] A simple way to summarize the research on marriage is that it shows that marriage tends to function as the glue that holds the father to his children. My friend and the former President of National Fatherhood Initiative, Roland Warren, likens this aspect of marriage to the three rules of real estate: location, location, location. In other words, marriage provides proximity to children—a prime location of closeness. It is easiest to be involved, responsible, and committed

---

[233] March 16, 2009 letter to President Obama.
[234] *The Cambridge Companion to Christian Ethics, Second Edition* (Cambridge: Cambridge UP, 2012), 259.

when you live in the same house as your kids and their mother. "Nearly every negative outcome for children increases statistically without the presence of a committed man in the home."[235] Put simply, it's much harder to be involved, responsible, and committed to your children when you don't live in the same house.

What Marriage Was and What It Became

Although the primary culture shift that took dads out of the home dates back to 1760 and the Industrial Revolution (more on that in the next chapter), changes in *attitudes* toward marriage are more recent, dating back to the 1960s. Earlier we saw how the Bond franchise, launched in 1962, mirrored this culture shift that was aggressively delinking sex from marriage and parenting. The sacred ties between marriage and parenting began to fray as children became optional and, worse, expendable. Although there are positive changes[236] associated with this shift, some of the negative changes related to the weakening of marriage as an institution can be illustrated as follows:

Marriage *was*:	Marriage *became*:
Primarily focused on raising the next generation of healthy children	Primarily focused on creating and maintaining adult happiness
An institution	A personal relationship only
Used to accomplish a collective purpose	More individualistic—used to satisfy two people
Determined by what's good for society	Determined by what's good for me
Seen as normal, with divorce and unwed childbearing seen as abnormal and disastrous	Seen as optional, with divorce and unwed childbearing seen as normal

---

[235] Bruce Wydick, "Married with Benefits," *Christianity Today*, 60, no. 6 (July/August 2016), 74.

[236] As a friend pointed out in reviewing a draft of this project, positive changes would include "increased penalties and lower tolerance for domestic violence; increased equality in father involvement within married parenting brought on by increased gender equality; growing recognition of divorce as the result of chronically broken marriage vows (rather than the initial breaking of those vows); more holistic, godly views of healthy sexuality within marriage, etc."

Five Current Views on Marriage

Fast forward to the 21rst century: According to a 2018 Census Bureau survey, only 35 percent of 25- to 34-year-old men were married, a rapid plunge from 50 percent in 2005.[237] Let's look at several perspectives on marriage that we've inherited or remain since the sixties, the first two less common among those who identify as Christians.

View #1: Marriage as a problem, not a solution

Toni Bentley, author of *The Surrender: An Erotic Memoir,* said monogamy is, "a charade we insist on, thus institutionalizing dishonesty."[238] For Bentley, the societal pressure to be with one sexual partner at a time is "an unnatural act for homosapiens" and one of the "remaining vestiges of patriarchy."[239] In this view, since marriage represents one of the most institutionalized forms of monogamy, it's a form of oppression in that it denies humans—especially women—their independence and sexuality.

But Bentley misses the fact that as humans we crave something beyond our primal sexual urges—we crave intimacy. And marriage—far from being a dishonest, "unnatural act"—is actually the context that best satisfies and protects that craving. Andy Stanley, pastor and author of *The New Rules for Love, Sex, and Dating,* makes this case brilliantly:

Cassettes are obsolete. Monogamy is more like an endangered species. Rare. Valuable. Something to be protected.

Women and children do not fare well in societies that embrace polygamy and promiscuity. Sexual freedom undermines financial and emotional freedom. If we are only biology, monogamy was probably a flawed concept from the start. But

---

[237] https://www.christianitytoday.com/ct/2020/july-august/marriage-save-church-declining-christians-global.html

[238] Toni Bentley, "Monogamy Is a Charade," *Time Magazine*, September 11, 2015, accessed November 14, 2016, http://time.com/4028153/toni-bentley-is-monogamy-over/.

[239] Ibid.

very few of us live as if we were only biology. I've officiated my share of weddings and done my share of premarital counseling. I always ask couples why they are getting married. Survival of the species never makes the list.

We desire intimacy—to know and be fully known without fear. Intimacy is fragile. Intimacy is powerful. And intimacy is fueled by exclusivity.[240]

View #2: Marriage as less desired than unrestrained casual sex

In this take, marriage is less nefarious, but still an unwelcome straitjacket for those in their prime. Again, we already touched on this view in chapter two, but here's just one example from the Bond movie franchise's *The World Is Not Enough*:

Elektra King: "What do you do to survive?"

Bond: "I take pleasure in great beauty." (Defined in this context, as I take pleasure in lots of casual sex with beautiful women.)

View #3: Marriage as less desired than cohabitation

In my work at Care Net, I've found it interesting that 86% of women who have abortions are unmarried and, of those unmarried, 31% are cohabiting with their partner.[241] The ministry, Axis, notes:

[I]n theory, cohabitation could be considered a way of trying out marriage before committing to it. But as Barry Schwartz points out in *The Paradox of Choice*, "What we don't realize is that the very option of being allowed to change our minds seems to increase the chances that we *will* change our minds. When we can change our minds about decisions, we are less satisfied with them... Knowing that you've made a choice that you will not reverse allows you to pour your energy into improving the relationship that you have rather than constantly second-guessing it."[242]

---

[240] Nancy Gibbs, "Is Monogamy Over?" *Time*, September 21, 2015, accessed November 14, 2016.
[241] Guttmacher Institute.
[242] Axis Culture Translator Vol. 8, Issue 6, February 11, 2022

Consider also the following research on cohabitation vs. marriage:

- People who get married earlier report slightly higher levels of sexual satisfaction and conflict resolution in their relationships.[243]
- Women who waited until marriage to live with a partner and also married between 22 and 30 had some of the lowest divorce rates in the country.[244] On this and the stat above, Axis again notes, "We don't want to put undue pressure on teens that they need to rush to find 'the one,' but it's helpful to point out that some of the happiest couples have made romantic choices that are not the cultural norm."[245]
- Mark Regnerus, Professor of Sociology at the University of Texas at Austin and co-founder of the Austin Institute for the Study of Family and Culture observed that "meeting a mate seemed more likely to occur—or be on its way soon—when our interviewees focused on holiness before loneliness."[246]

View #4: Marriage as capstone, not foundation

This is a view formulated and best articulated by Regnerus, who we just cited above. He describes it as follows:

Marriage, even in the minds of most Christians, is now perceived as a capstone that marks a successful young adult life, not the foundational hallmark of entry into adulthood. The nomenclature attests to this. A capstone is the finishing touch of a structure. It's a moment in time. A foundation, however, is what a building rests upon. It is necessarily hard-wearing. In the foundational vision, being newly married and poor was common, expected, and difficult, but often temporary. In the capstone standard, being poor is a sign that you're just not marriage material yet.

---

[243] http://nationalmarriageproject.org/reports/
[244] https://www.wsj.com/articles/too-risky-to-wed-in-your-20s-not-if-you-avoid-cohabiting-first-11644037261
[245] Axis Culture Translator Vol. 8, Issue 6, February 11, 2022
[246] https://www.christianitytoday.com/ct/2020/july-august/marriage-save-church-declining-christians-global.html

Regnerus illustrates the capstone mentality in an interview with Chloe, a 27-year-old from Michigan. She says, "You have your 20s to focus on you… and then [after that] you try to help others." Regnerus then makes this amazingly important observation for our times: "This approach, common among [Chloe's] peers, is poor preparation for marriage. Self-sacrifice is learned behavior, not a gift for your 30th birthday."[247]

View #5: Marriage as foundation and as God designed

From a biblical perspective, marriage is the foundational institution of the human race.[248] God designed it to be a creation thing (for society as a whole), not just a Christian thing (for those who identify themselves as Christians). It is a multifaceted gift from the Creator of love and life. And although marriage is a celebration filled with joy, it is also a serious decision involving a lifetime commitment. Marriage, as God designed it, has seven primary purposes:

- To help overcome individual aloneness.[249]
- To provide a man and woman with the gift of "togetherness," and a committed context to learn to be "soul mates."[250]
- To provide a safe place for enjoying sexual expression.[251]
- To grow the human race.[252]
- To provide the best environment for raising healthy children.[253]
- To curb the hurt in society caused by pre-marital sex and extra-marital affairs.[254]
- To be a picture of the intimacy God desires with us through Christ.[255]

---

[247] Ibid.
[248] Genesis 2:22–25.
[249] Genesis 2:18.
[250] Ecclesiastes 4:9–12; Matthew19:4–6; Ephesians 5:28–29.
[251] Proverbs 5:15–20; Ecclesiastes 9:9a.
[252] Genesis 1:28.
[253] Psalm 127:1, 3–5.
[254] 1 Corinthians 7:1–2; 1 Thessalonians 4:3–5.
[255] Ephesians 5:25–32.

Related to this last benefit, Regnerus reminds us that "marriage is… a vehicle for spiritual progress that provides daily (if not hourly) opportunities to exhibit sacrificial, incarnational love."[256]

Last year, Pam and I celebrated our 35th wedding anniversary. Despite facing struggles, we still look each other in the eyes and thank God that we're still standing, still in love, and that He is rich in mercy and mighty to save. This definition of marriage we learned and embraced even before we took our vows has been one of the most helpful tools throughout our relationship: "Marriage is the joining together of two needy sinners into a relationship in which the two of them together is better than either one of them would ever have been separately."[257]

That's Pam and me: sinners, better together, and, gratefully, "still the one" for each other. "Sinners" isn't a word that stirs up warm fuzzies, nor will it ever be included in the title of a Hallmark channel movie. Still, it's a foundational concept for a good marriage because it sets realistic expectations. As sinners, we're not always loveable. That's why a good marriage requires a lot of longsuffering and selflessness. It's not a 50/50 arrangement. It's 100/100. Don't get me wrong—I'm all for fire and romance, and I've enjoyed plenty with Pam, but in real life that's not all that a healthy marriage consists of.

What I Learned from Kay Hymowitz

Although many Christians are clear on what the Bible teaches about marriage, most have never thought deeply about what it does for society. For me, my horizons were expanded when a black urban pastor first introduced me to *Marriage and Caste in America* by Kay S. Hymowitz. Hymowitz is an incisive American author and senior fellow at the Manhattan Institute. She is also a contributing editor for City Journal, and her writing has appeared in the Wall Street Journal.

---

[256] https://www.christianitytoday.com/ct/2020/july-august/marriage-save-church-declining-christians-global.html.
[257] Adapted from a definition in Sinclair Ferguson, *Discovering God's Will* (Edinburgh: Banner of Truth, 1982), 92.

Her analysis, although not faith-based, is data-driven and shows family breakdown at the heart of our nation's most obstinate social problems, especially poverty and inequality.

Hymowitz believes that in the healthiest societies, fatherhood and marriage go together. "[N]o culture has ever designed a model of fatherhood without matrimony,"[258] she notes. When severed, she argues, the result is entrenched multi-generational poverty. "Thirty-six percent of female-headed households live below the poverty line. Compare that with 6 percent of married couple families in poverty.... Dads in the hood have children by several different women who themselves may have sons and daughters with different men. The end result is a maelstrom of confusion, jealousy, rage, abandonment and violence."[259]

A Life Script and a Marriage Orientation

Hymowitz says every society needs a life script. For example, for many it is childhood first, then adolescence or school or some other preparation for self-sufficiency. Marriage often comes next and then children. In this orientation, marriage provides a healthy and committed structure for raising the next generation.

One of Hymowitz's greatest insights is that society needs people with a marriage orientation, not just marriage itself:

Educated women still believe in marriage as an institution for raising children. Marriage orders life in ways we only dimly understand. Further, marriage makes it more likely that children will grow up with a dad in the house. Women with a marriage orientation organize their lives around a meaningful and beneficial

---

[258] Kay S. Hymowitz, *Marriage and Caste in Society* (Chicago: Ivan. R. Dee, 2006), 9, 22.

[259] Ibid., 9. Although Hymowitz's data is outdated, the trend and impact she identifies still exists: "Single mothers are much more likely to be poor than married couples. The poverty rate for single-mother families in 2020 was 23.4%, nearly five times more than the rate (4.7%) for married-couple families. Among children living with mother only, 38.1% lived in poverty. In contrast, only 7.5% of children in two parent families were counted as poor." For more see https://singlemotherguide.com/single-mother-statistics/

life script. A marriage orientation demands that a woman keep her eye toward the future. She must go through life with deliberation. She must use self-discipline, especially when it comes to sex...[260]

To summarize, a marriage orientation provides a helpful map that encourages you to live with care and purpose in a way that prioritizes the well-being of children.

Married Parents and "The Mission"

This life script and marriage orientation, Hymowitz continues, leads to the proliferation of nuclear families.[261] Why does this context work so well for children? For one thing, Hymowitz points out, there is the "strength in numbers" theory, meaning that two parents are more likely to have two incomes. More money means more stability, less stress, better daycare and health care, more books, more travel, and a home in a better school district. It leads to educational and workplace success. Married couples can support each other if one is laid off or would like to pursue more education. Married couples can take turns caring for children. The bottom line is that a husband and a wife, together for the long haul, can provide better opportunities for their children.[262]

In Hymowitz's view, when mom and dad work together in marriage, parenting becomes a strategic "mission." Hymowitz defines this mission as a parental team effort to help their children thrive:

[It is] the careful nurturing of a child's cognitive, emotional, and social development, which, if all goes according to plan, will lead to the honor roll and a spot on the high school debate team, which in turn will lead to a good college, then perhaps a graduate or professional degree, which will all lead eventually to a fulfilling career... house... and a sense of meaningful accomplishment.[263]

---

[260] Ibid.
[261] A nuclear family is technically a father, a mother, and their children living in the same home, and we'll talk more about this topic in chapter eight.
[262] Ibid., 26–27.
[263] Ibid., 25.

Over the years, I've found Pam's coaching and perspective invaluable in connecting with my kids heart-to-heart. For example, during my son Matthew's high school years, I had difficulty communicating and connecting with him. On one occasion, I was frustrated because he wanted to visit his girlfriend and her family on our weekly family night, and I wanted him home. I thought Matthew should have more respect for this "sacred space" I was trying to guard to keep our family connected. Matthew, however, was getting older, had scheduling desires of his own, and wanted to make more decisions independently. Pam could see this clearly, but I could not. It was through her coaching that I came to see my issues of control. She helped me see that by getting in Matthew's face and pulling him closer, I was actually driving him farther away. He was growing up, making wise choices, and I needed to modify my expectations and give him freedom. Had I been a single parent, without the benefit of Pam's insights, I would have not only lacked self-awareness, but also further frustrated Matthew and damaged our relationship.

Giving Moms the Honor They Deserve

As I [Paul] remember your [Timothy's] tears, I long to see you, that I may be filled with joy. I am reminded of your sincere faith, a faith that dwelt first in your grandmother, Lois, and your mother Eunice and now, I am sure, dwells in you as well (2 Timothy 1:5, ESV).

I've spent a good part of my career championing fathers and sharing research that shows dad's primary spiritual influence even over moms. The verse above along with a recent major study by Pew Research Center, however, are important reminders to not undervalue mom's fundamental spiritual influence.

One of the most compelling studies I've encountered is a 1994 study from Sweden that found, "if a father does not go to church, no matter how faithful his wife's devotions, only one child in 50 will become a regular worshiper."[264] In analyzing this study, Vicar Robbie

---

[264] https://www.thegospelcoalition.org/blogs/justin-taylor/a-fathers-role-in-his-children-going-to-church-when-they-are-adults/

Low noted in 2003, "mothers' choices have dramatically less effect upon children than their fathers', and without him she has little effect on the primary lifestyle choices her offspring make in their religious observances."[265]

Fast forward twenty years to a Pew study from the US, and we see a very different scenario:

Most Americans who were raised by a biological or adoptive mother and father say their parents played an equal role in their religious upbringing. But among the roughly four-in-ten adults who say one of their parents (either biological or adoptive) was "more" responsible for their religious upbringing, far more name their mother than their father.[266]

Christianity Today, in analyzing this data, notes:

The higher level of religious commitment among women than men has been well documented; in Pew's study, 83 percent of those with affiliated/unaffiliated parents reported that their mother was the religious one. And both men (30%) and women (33%) told Pew that the wife was more religious than her husband. (About 60% said the spouses were equally religious.) Mothers mostly take the lead in their children's religious upbringing. Among Protestant couples, 66 percent took equal responsibility for their children's religious education. Another 28 percent said their mother was more responsible, and only 5 percent said their father was more responsible. The same held true for Catholic and unaffiliated couples: most said their parents shared responsibility (64% Catholic, 58% unaffiliated); where one took on more responsibility, it was overwhelmingly the mother (29% Catholic, 12% unaffiliated).[267]

---

[265] http://www.touchstonemag.com/archives/article.php?id=16-05-024-v
[266] http://www.pewforum.org/2016/10/26/one-in-five-u-s-adults-were-raised-in-interfaith-homes/
[267] https://www.christianitytoday.com/news/2016/october/protestant-parents-kids-keep-faith-catholics-nones-pew.html

Why do the findings from the 1994 study and the 2016 study tell different stories? Is it some cultural difference between Sweden and the US? Global cultural changes in the last two decades? Comparing apples and oranges? Did one (or both) have a faulty methodology? Might it be that dad has the primary influence on church attendance specifically, while mom has the primary spiritual influence overall? While resolving these questions is beyond our capacity here, truth be told, 2 Timothy 1:5 that we referenced above and the recent Pew study reflect the experience of millions: When it comes to passing on the faith, more often than not, moms have had greater influence than dads.

We see this even in the earliest centuries of the church. Monica, the mother of one of the most significant Christian writers and pastors in the history of the Church, St. Augustine, is a perfect example: For over thirty years, she prayed for Augustine. In his *Confessions* (c. AD 400), Augustine famously quotes a North African pastor, who, when Monica came to him weeping over her son's need for salvation, promised her, "The son of these tears shall not perish."[268]

My son, Timothy, who holds a master's degree in theology from an Augustinian university, notes:

Augustine implies a double meaning here: on the one hand, here is a pastor who's trying to get a woman to quit crying. It's as if he's saying, "Lady, your kid is probably going to be fine if you're getting *this* worked up about him." On the other hand, Augustine is implying that his mother's tears and prayers were both a means and sign of God's grace. By fretting over his salvation and praying for him, she became an instrument of God's salvation. Augustine wrote the following about his mother:

[S]he did not relax her weeping and mourning. She did not cease to pray at every hour and bewail me to You, and her prayers found entry into Your sight. But for all that You allowed me still to toss helplessly in that darkness.[269]

---

268 III.12.21.
269 III.12.11.

That's an episode from when Augustine was seventeen or eighteen. He didn't decide to be baptized until he was thirty-two. Even though his dad didn't become Christian until much later in his life, Augustine's mom was a Christian, and he was brought up "in a Christian home," as it were. Moreover, Roman North Africa during Augustine's upbringing was, in a lot of ways, like the Arkansas of the Bible Belt of the Roman Empire. So the problem wasn't that he didn't know the Gospel. The problem was that he was deliberately running from it. But Monica wept and prayed for him all the while.

I think about the ripple effect of my mom's sacrificial love, prayers, and tears in my own life, and how these are now impacting new generations with my kids and grandchildren. Not only is she associated with my earliest spiritual memory[270] but she is also now my only remaining parental spiritual influence (since my dad rejected faith). What we share in Christ is precious, and I honor her positive impact and ongoing presence in my life and family! To this day, she prioritizes both regular private time with God and involvement in a healthy church community. Despite her own devastations that have included divorce and cancer (twice a survivor now), she has chosen to carry her suffering with dignity and view life primarily through a lens of grace. She is an example to us all, both in choosing courage over comfort, and being a quiet, steady presence that celebrates the beauty of creation, literacy, and honest conversation.

In wrapping up our discussion of moms and marriage, I hope your perspective has been challenged, strengthened, or fortified. I pray it has not only given you a greater respect for the moms in your life, but also a greater love and appreciation for God's ideal and design for marriage. As irreplaceable as fathers are, mothers too are essential and often the primary spiritual influence in children's lives. And the best way for fathers and mothers to raise healthy children is through the shared mission of married parenthood. As Bruce Wydick, professor of economics at the University of San Francisco poignantly observed:

---

[270] I write about this in chapter one of *How I Became a Christian Despite the Church.*

[You will find] the marriage institution all over the world because, despite all its challenges, it is hard to find another form of organizing the sexes that does as good a job at promoting human flourishing.[271]

🔥 Takeaways:

- Remember, one of the best ways to love your kids is to love their mother. And on a related note, one of the best ways to pass on fiery passion for healthy marriage to your kids and others is reflected in this golden insight from Regnerus' research:

> One Russian interviewee remarked, bad examples serve as "a sort of vaccine against marriage." By contrast, good examples inspire the next generation… "How parents live their marriage will make a strong impression," he said. "And I imagine that if the relationship is sweet, if there is really love, I think that generates enthusiasm in a young person to say, 'I want something like my parents have.'"[272]

- Notice that tears are not only part of Monica and Augustine's story but Paul and Timothy's as well (again, see 2 Tim. 1:5 above). This reflects a deep love and heart-to-heart connection. If you have shed tears for your children or your parents, be encouraged. Your experience is shared by the greatest of saints.
- Pray regularly for your kids and grandkids. Love them and never give up. Only God knows the key to someone's heart.
- Make sure you thank your parent(s) and/or grandparent(s) often for their sacrifice and influence in your life or in the life of your kids. Your loving reminders are especially important in

---

[271] Bruce Wydick, "Married with Benefits," *Christianity Today*, 60, no. 6 (July/August 2016), 74.
[272] https://www.christianitytoday.com/ct/2020/july-august/marriage-save-church-declining-christians-global.html

their later years when they might feel increasingly invisible, powerless, and unimportant.

CHAPTER SEVEN: A BRIEF HISTORY OF DADS' CHANGING ROLES

One of the many things I'm grateful to my mom for is passing on some of her dad's books and correspondence to me. My grandfather, Ralph Whitson Seaman, was a Lutheran minister with excellent diction, a gift for learning languages, and a fascination for words. He also had a good sense of humor.

At that time, his denomination and others were making changes in response to the feminist movement[273] that ranged from updating documents—including the Bible—with more gender-inclusive language to the total eradication of patriarchy; that is "father-rule." These later changes stretched from perspectives that no longer wanted to call God "Father," but "Father" and/or "Mother," to simply eliminating any hint of gender and sex altogether by calling God something generic like "Source of All."

On April 13, 1979, my grandfather wrote the following to his denomination as a humorous but gentle critique (he was not a harsh

---

[273] The goals of the feminist movement or women's rights movement of my grandfather's day were wide-ranging and not always unilateral: "They want equal pay for equal work, and a chance at jobs traditionally reserved for men only. They seek nationwide abortion reform – ideally, free abortions on demand. They desire round-the-clock, state-supported child-care centers in order to cut the apron strings that confine mothers to unpaid domestic servitude at home. The most radical feminists want far more. Their eschatological aim is to topple the patriarchal system in which men by birthright control all of society's levers of power – in government, industry, education, science, the arts." (Time magazine's "Who's Come a Long Way, Baby?" from August 31, 1970)

man) of those he felt were going too far in trying to diminish the role of men and fathers:

Dear Sir:

Now that, thanks to the actions taken at our last synodical convention, the constitution of the synod has been thoroughly and mercilessly demasculinized, I feel that the next logical step should be taken...

My suggestion is this: that we go through the clerical role of Synod and the name of every pastor whose present name ends with the hateful suffix, -MAN, substituting the apparently more acceptable term, -PERSON.

Take the name VOGELMAN, for example. Is it not illogical—perhaps even irreverent—for such a name to appear on the clerical roll of the thoroughly emasculated North Carolina Synod? Surely henceforth this fine young pastor should be known as Jon VOGELPERSON!

Then there is the name PERRYMAN, another of our fine young pastors. For shame! Surely, following the 1979 Convention of the Synod, the name PERRYPERSON should appear on our roster. And, if he becomes head of a committee (as well he might), let us be sure to refer to him as CHAIRPERSON PERRYPERSON!

Further, there are names on our roll that end in -SON, a masculine term if ever there was one! Should not a less sex-oriented suffix be substituted? -CHILD, for example, or -OFFSPRING, or -PRODIGY. Dale PEDERPRODIGY sounds a bit cumbersome, though, and PEDERCHILD smacks of being somewhat non-ministerial. Let him henceforth be called Pastor PEDEROFFSPRING!

In this connection, is it not unthinkable that the presidents of our two institutions of higher learning are named AnderSON?

Perhaps the lawyers in our midst can help us repent of our past negligence and enable us to compel these noble gentlemen scholars to change their names to Drs. ANDEROFFSPRING.

In the spirit of consistency and Christian love these humble suggestions are being made by the greatest sinner of all, who if the proper action is taken by the Synod at its forthcoming convention, shall henceforth be known as

Respectfully yours,

R. Whitoffspring Seaperson

P.S. Come to think of it, the hallowed term PERSON has as its second syllable the objectionable -SON. So I suppose we can't get away from it after all. Linguistically, at least, it is still a man's world. So let's forget the whole thing!

Although I don't agree that "it is still a man's world" and we should "forget the whole thing," I can relate to my grandfather's aversion to change in that many responses to cultural shifts are (or can seem) crazy or extreme.[274] Forgetting the whole thing is usually *not* the answer, but we do need some anchors to bring a shared script—that is, common ground—to the conversation. It used to be that the Bible and a Christian perspective could help with that, but increasingly, the Bible and Christianity are seen as part of the problem. Besides all the scandals and abuse, one of my observations about especially the conservative American church is that it is fiercely independent and often acts as if it has a stronger allegiance to Patrick Henry than Jesus.[275] Further, it has little interest in pausing and listening well when

---

[274] Since this was almost 44 years ago and lest anyone misunderstand, my grandfather was not here opposing gender-inclusive translations of the Bible that do not do violence to God as "Father" such as the NLT or NRSV. He was rather concerned with an agenda that threatened to erase history or a particular sex—agendas that often end up throwing out the baby with the bathwater.
[275] "Give me liberty or give me death" seems way more important to many than "Love your neighbor."

something like the #MeToo movement comes along. Instead of, again, listening well and learning from the stories, many reflexively denounce and circle their wagons. The "man's world" must be protected.

In the next chapter, we'll look at some of the more "hot topic" cultural challenges like the eradication of patriarchy ("father rule"), the denigration of the nuclear family, and the LQBTQ+ movement. Challenges we're right in the midst of. Challenges we need to acknowledge, be in conversation with, and provide guidance on.

In this chapter, however, we'll take a very brief and broad historical overview, starting with the ancient Near East during biblical times, looking at some of the major cultural shifts that have affected dads and especially their ability to father well and pass on a spiritual heritage to their children. We'll also address one of the rarely called-out lies the conservative church has promoted and protected—a lie that has sucked life and joy out of many moms and dads working together day-to-day to survive and provide for their families.

The Ancient Near East and Biblical Times

The biblical ideal for fatherhood in the Ancient Near East (ANE) is one of *influence* (Prov. 31:23) and *involvement* in the daily routine of his children's lives (Deut. 6:4–9). In the first century, the father—like God the Father—takes the role of protector and provider seriously. He models himself after God, who cares about the needs of his children (Phil. 4:19) and gives them good gifts (Matt. 7:9–11; James 1:17).

The Post-Biblical Early Church

The *Didascalia* is a Christian treatise that presents itself as having been written by the Twelve Apostles at the time of the Council of Jerusalem; scholars, however, agree that it was actually a composition of the third century, perhaps around 230 AD.[276]

The *Didascalia* encourages the church in general and elders in particular to include those without fathers in the life of the congregation:

---

[276] Gregory W. Woolfenden, *Daily Liturgical Prayer: Origins and Theology* (Farnham, United Kingdom: Ashgate, 2004), 26.

If any child among the Christians is an orphan, it is well that if any brother has no children, he should adopt the orphan in place of children . . . And you who are overseers: Watch carefully over the orphan's upbringing that they lack nothing! When a virgin girl is of age, give her in marriage to a brother [in Christ]. As a boy is brought up, let him learn a craft so that, when he becomes a man, he will earn a worthy wage.[277]

Despite the patriarchal perspective, note the practical focus on child well-being and connecting fatherless children with the childless in the church. Further, note the real-world emphasis on providing well for their needs by marriage or by helping young men learn a skill that would bring them a family-supporting wage. There is a lot of wisdom here for, as we learned from Kay Hymowitz in the last chapter, both marriage and vocation involve "an orientation to the future." Again, here's Hymowitz on how this close connection plays out in our times:

Men do not get married because they have a steady job; they get married because they are *the kind of person* who can get and keep a steady job.... The very task of looking for "the right woman" means projecting yourself into the future and taking a mindful approach to life... Both marriage and vocation are part of the script—trying to master life and shape it into a coherent narrative.[278]

The Medieval Church

Hailing from the 1200s, the Roman Catholic scholar Thomas Aquinas is recognized today even by Protestants as the greatest systematic theologian of the Middle Ages. According to the late professor Don Browning from the University of Chicago's Divinity School, Aquinas believed that "family, because of biological tendencies of parents to give preferential care to their own children, has a *prima*

---

[277] Didascalia Apostolorum, 17, quoted in Timothy Paul Jones, *Perspectives on Family Ministry* (Nashville, TN: Broadman & Holman, 2009) 21.
[278] Kay S. Hymowitz, *Marriage and Caste in Society* (Chicago: Ivan. R. Dee, 2006), 107.

125

facie [plain or clear] competence and right to care for its offspring. The tendency of families . . . is based on the intentions of God in Creation and stamped into the structure of Nature."[279]

Aquinas further believed, according to Browning, that "children are the semblance or partial image of their parents,"[280] but they are also gifts of God and made in His image. Based on this, he drew an important conclusion: "Since God's goodness spills over into all children, Christian adults should cherish all children whether they are directly their own or not."[281]

Again, as in the early church, we see a focus on cherishing children. We also see a theological justification for the rights of the nuclear family (something we'll discuss more in the next chapter) based on biological relationship—a relationship that for Aquinas is directly connected with the intentions of God.

The Reformation Era

Martin Luther, the father of the Protestant Reformation, was known for his humor, earthiness, and candor. He echoes this same theme of loving and caring for children seen above: "The purpose of marriage is not pleasure and ease but the procreation and education of children and the support of a family. People who do not like children are swine, dunces, and blockheads, not worthy to be called men and women, because they despise the blessing of God, the Creator and Author of marriage."[282]

Note how Luther adds the "education of children" to the historical sketch given above, yet still retains the simple focus on the blessing of children closely connected to a mom and dad in marriage.

---

[279] *The Cambridge Companion to Christian Ethics, Second Edition* (Cambridge: Cambridge UP, 2012), 262.

[280] Ibid., 265.

[281] Ibid.

[282] Martin Luther, "Martin Luther: The Later Years," *Christian History*, 39, accessed November 14, 2016, https://www.christianhistoryinstitute.org/uploaded/50cf7fdbd09b24.47881377.pdf.

The Puritan Era

It is in the Puritan Era that the "education of children" seems to have morphed into a passionate fixation on the transmission of structured content through the practices of family worship and family catechesis.[283] Unfortunately, in many cases, this focus tended to eclipse earlier simple priorities like enjoying relationships, having a healthy marriage, or learning a trade with a family-supporting wage. Due to a similar fixation and focus in the Reformed communities I've had the most experience in in recent years, I will provide some specific examples from one prominent Puritan voice, Richard Baxter.

Richard Baxter and the Case for Catechizing Families

I am humbled by how Richard Baxter's devotional classic written over four hundred years ago, *The Reformed Pastor*, still helps my heart. Many have experienced the Puritans' unique ability to expose and attack sin, but also give wise and tender counsel that heals. I also appreciate Baxter because he too saw the home as the primary conduit for passing on the Christian faith, saying "You are not likely to see any general reformation, till you procure family reformation. Some little religion there may be, here and there; but while it is confined to single persons, and is not promoted in families, it will not prosper, nor promise much future increase."[284] How did Baxter go about promoting reformation in households? He pioneered the practice of catechizing families.[285] "We must have a special eye upon families, to see that they are *well-ordered*, and the *duties* of each relation *performed*," he wrote. The goal was to work against "*careless, prayerless, worldly*" families; to "*labour*" to "*get a promise* from them" to "*learn to do better*," and to "*tell them*" of their "*sin and shame*."[286] (emphasis mine)

To stay connected and prioritize our marital relationship, Pam and

---

[283] Catechesis is simply teaching from a catechism. And a catechism is simply a collection of questions and answers designed for memorization and recitation. We will talk more about these in chapter nine.

[284] Richard Baxter, *The Reformed Pastor* (Carlisle, PA: Banner of Truth Trust, 2007), 102.

[285] John R. W. Stott, *Between Two Worlds: The Challenge of Preaching Today* (Grand Rapids, MI: Eerdmans, 1982), 29.

[286] Baxter, *The Reformed Pastor*, 87–111.

I tried to go on a date every Sunday night when our children were in their later teens and beginning to get more independent. Before that, our practice was to have a fun family night on Sunday nights. Often this included a brief devotional or prayer, but not always. How would Baxter say our Sunday evenings should have been spent? *"Persuade* the master of every family *to cause* his children and servants to *repeat the Catechism* to him, every Sabbath evening, and to *give him some account* of what they have heard at church during the day."[287] (emphasis mine)

Notice the words I italicized in the two quotes above. Taken as a whole, they can give the feeling of a gray existence—a colorless Christianity where living is all work and duty. Further, a dedication to this dutiful well-orderedness often manifests itself in individuals and families that can never relax, play, or take joy in simple gifts like food and drink or spending time with those they love. There is a fixation on the fact that one is never good enough. In this model, passing on content, maintaining control, and conforming outwardly are the priorities, rather than developing relationships, enjoying life, and trusting in God to change desires over time. In this model, Christianity is taught more than caught. Duty trumps joy, and there is a morbid fixation on "the constant expectation of death," and the "uncertainty and the shortness of all men's lives."[288] Granted, life in the 1600s was far harsher and more fragile than twenty-first century American life. It has been my observation, however, that embracing Baxter's vision uncritically or without contextualization produces individuals and families with little emphasis on grace, play, and encouragement.

The Industrial Revolution

The central role of the father in the home was seriously altered due to the Industrial Revolution, which caused a massive shift that affected families much more than is commonly understood. In the 1970s and 80s, the conservative evangelical church circles I grew up in were largely ignorant of this history. Their shallow analysis of the struggle to provide financially decried working moms and double income families. Most in these circles believed that the *Leave it to Beaver*

---

[287] Ibid., 101.
[288] Ibid., 113–114.

or *Ozzie and Harriet* world of the 1950s was the biblical ideal. Serious Christians were those who unquestioningly made the stay-at-home mom model work. Those who struggled with this were deemed materialistic. Thus, rather than strengthening families, these churches passed on a fundamentalist guilt that has stolen much joy in the last fifty years from many husbands and wives working together to provide for their children.[289]

But before we get more into analysis and application, let me give a brief description of the Industrial Revolution. The Industrial Revolution was "the process of change from an agrarian, handicraft economy to one dominated by industry and machine manufacture."[290] This process began with Britain's economic development from 1760 to 1840, but spread to other countries and overlaps with what is often called the Second Industrial Revolution that lasted from 1870–1914, just before World War I.

According to the Encyclopedia Britannica, the Industrial Revolution involved technological, socioeconomic, *and* cultural developments. Just to get a glimpse of this, the technological changes included:

- Important developments in communication, including telegraph and radio
- A new organization of work known as the factory system, which entailed increased division of labor and specialization of function
- The use of new basic materials, chiefly iron and steel
- The use of new energy sources, including both fuels and motive power, such as coal, the steam engine, electricity, petroleum, and the internal-combustion engine, and this led to...

---

[289] For example, in the Bible, the ideal ancient Near Eastern woman or mom was intelligent, fully capable, respected, and worked to provide for her family financially: "Her husband has full confidence in her... She considers a field and buys it; out of her earnings she plants a vineyard... She makes linen garments and sells them, and supplies the merchants with sashes... let her works bring her praise at the city gate." (Proverbs 31:11a, 16, 24, 31b, NIV)

[290] "Industrial Revolution," Encyclopedia Britannica, accessed July 2, 2016, https://www.britannica.com/event/Industrial-Revolution.

- Important developments in transportation, including the steam locomotive, steamship, automobile, and airplane.[291] For the first time in human history, people were able to go faster than an animal could run!

To understand the challenge good dads and moms have to be physically and emotionally present, we need to understand the massive shift in how the Industrial Revolution affected work and a family-supporting wage. I am convinced that many couples miss out on much shared joy together because they miss the forest for the trees. Nancy Pearcey, in her book *Total Truth*, helps us see the forest in terms of the economic and structural changes that took place during the Industrial Revolution. She helps us understand what changed and why so many dads and moms now struggle to care for their families and make ends meet. It's not just about gas prices, the housing crisis of 2008–2009, the sin of materialism, regional cost of living, etc. Yes, these are or were real issues that impact or have impacted some, but they are not the full story.

Here is the fuller story, according to Pearcey:

> We... need to understand enough of modern thought to identify the ways it blocks us from living out the gospel the way God intends—both in terms of intellectual roadblocks and . . . in terms of economic and structural changes that make it harder to live by scriptural principles. It is enormously difficult for fathers in a modern industrialized society to function in the strong parental role Scripture calls them to—and as they did in earlier historical periods. It is likewise difficult for mothers to raise their children well, and still be faithful in honing their other gifts in a . . . calling.

> Historically speaking, the key turning point was the Industrial Revolution, which eventually divided the private realm of family and faith from the public realm of business and industry. To grasp these changes more clearly, let's start by painting a picture of life before the Industrial Revolution.

---

[291] Ibid.

In the colonial period, families lived much the way they have lived for millennia in traditional societies. The vast majority of people lived on farms or in peasant villages. Productive work was done in the home or in the outbuildings. Work was done not by lone individuals but by families and households. A family was a relatively autonomous unit, often including members of extended family, apprentices, servants, and hired hands. Stores, offices, and workshops were located in a front room, with living quarters either upstairs or in the rear.

It meant that the husband and wife worked side by side on a daily basis, sharing in the economic enterprise. For a colonial woman, one historian writes:

> [Marriage] meant to become a co-worker beside a husband . . . learning new skills in butchering, silversmith work, printing, or upholstering—whatever special skills the husband's work required.
>
> In their day-to-day life, fathers enjoyed the same integration of work and childrearing responsibilities that mothers did. With production centered on the family hearth, fathers were a "viable presence, year after year, day after day" as they trained their children to work alongside them. Being a father was not a separate activity to come home to after a day at work; rather it was an integral part of a man's daily routine. Historical records reveal that colonial literature on parenting—like sermons and child-rearing manuals— were not addressed to mothers, as the majority are today. Instead, they were typically addressed to fathers. Fathers were considered the primary parent, and were held to be particularly important in their children's religious and intellectual training.[292]

---

[292] Nancy Pearcey, *Total Truth: Liberating Christianity from Its Cultural Captivity* (Wheaton, IL: Crossways, 2005), 327–329.

Coming Into the Modern Era

Thus, until the Industrial Revolution, most husbands and wives worked "side by side," and fathers held a "primary" parenting role. These are critical points for churches and families to grasp. It's sad when newly married Christian couples can find more encouragement in a classic *Carpenters' song* than in their church:

> We've only just begun to live
> White lace and promises
> A kiss for luck and we're on our way...
> Sharing horizons that are new to us
> Watching the signs along the way
> Talkin' it over, just the two of us
> Workin' together day to day
> Together[293]

The cultural stereotypes of dad as breadwinner or provider and mom as nurturer (again, think *Leave it to Beaver*) go back to the 1760s in North America and Europe, not ancient Palestine. Further, these are cultural roles related to changes that took dad out of the home. They are not biblical roles. As we pointed out in the beginning of this brief historical sketch, even in the ancient Near East, the Proverbs 31 woman participated in bread-winning and providing financially for her family (Prov. 31:11a, 16, 24, 31b) and dads were expected to be nurturers, involved daily in connecting heart to heart with their children (Deut. 6:4–9).

And this brings us to the lie I said I would address at the beginning of this chapter: I want to put to rest—once and for all—the cultural stereotype and false teaching that the bible says that men are supposed to be the primary financial providers for their families, and that women aren't or can't.

Yes, it's true that biologically, women on average are more nurturing than men, and men are on average 50 percent stronger physically than women. Physiology is and will continue to be a factor

---

[293] The Carpenters, "We've Only Just Begun" from the album *Close To You*, 1970.

in how parenting roles play out. Nonetheless, we no longer live in an agrarian society where physical strength is the most important quality for getting work. Now, technological proficiency and emotional intelligence are in greater demand, opening up more roles for both men and women.

Additionally, there are far fewer jobs with family-supporting wages and benefits. A standard of living that includes attention to family health and growth requires two incomes for most, or some creative juggling of several jobs.

Consider this data and analysis from just the last sixty years:

- In the 1950s-1970s: Kristen Du Mez, in her provocative book *Jesus and John Wayne* makes this astute observation about changes in employment opportunities for men and women:

> The postwar years had been marked by economic gains that made it possible for many men to serve as sole breadwinners for their families. The global economic restructuring beginning in the 1970s, however, resulted in a decline of American manufacturing jobs and stagnation of male wages. The breadwinner economy had always been as much myth as reality, but in the 1970s, this aspirational idea was becoming increasingly difficult to attain, even among members of the white middle class. In 1950, 37 percent of women worked for pay, but that number began to rise significantly in the 1970s. Linked in part to women's growing economic independence, rates of divorce began to increase dramatically in the 1970s as well. All of this amounted to a "crisis" of the family, and for evangelicals gender and authority, not global economic patterns, were at the heart of the crisis.[294]

And as David Brooks points out, "Starting in the mid-'70s, young men's wages declined, putting pressure on working-class

---

[294] Kristen Kobes Du Mez, *Jesus and John Wayne: How White Evangelicals Corrupted a Faith and Fractured a Nation* (New York: Liveright, 2020), 82.

families in particular."[295]

- In 2009: Pew research found that 59 percent of women work or are actively seeking employment. An even higher percentage of women with children ages 17 or younger (66%) work either full or part-time. Among those working mothers, most (74%) work full time while 26% work part-time.[296]

- In 2014: Married fathers were responsible for about 65 percent of their households' hours in the paid labor force (39 hours a week), while wives performed 35 percent (21 hours a week), according to the Pew Research Center. In fact, more than three quarters of married mothers do not wish to work full-time: 53 percent prefer part-time work and 23 percent prefer to be stay-at-home mothers. (This stands in marked contrast to married fathers: 75 percent of them think working full-time is ideal and an additional 13 percent prefer part-time work...) Sociologist Brad Wilcox weighed in on this contrast saying, "Here, I suspect that ordinary married mothers' desire to invest time, affection, and supervision in their children's lives outweighs their desire to lean in at work, at least while their children are young."[297]

A Few Concluding Thoughts & Parenting Together in 21st Century

I said at the beginning of this chapter that the role of the ANE father was one of influence and involvement. We have also traced a steady line through the early, medieval, and reformation era church that demonstrated that children were cherished and cared for in Christian homes. We highlighted three main priorities in raising children: to prepare them for a healthy marriage, to teach them a trade with a family-supporting wage, and to provide them with an

---

[295] https://www.theatlantic.com/magazine/archive/2020/03/the-nuclear-family-was-a-mistake/605536/
[296] Pew Research Center, http://pewsocialtrends.org/2009/10/01/the-harried-life-of-the-working-mother/ Oct. 1, 2009.
[297] "Surprisingly, Most Married Families Today Tilt Neo-Traditional" by W. Bradford Wilcox February 26, 2014.

education—especially a religious education through catechesis. The father's role was central in all of this; he was a protector, a provider, a nurturer who fostered heart-to-heart connection, and a guide.

Ecclesiastes 9:7-10a offers a fitting corrective and conclusion to this chapter:

> Go, eat your bread with joy, and drink your wine with a merry heart, for God has already approved what you do. Let your garments be always white. Let not oil be lacking on your head. Enjoy life with the wife whom you love, all the days of your vain [fleeting] life that he has given you under the sun, because that is your portion in life and in your toil at which you toil under the sun. Whatever your hand finds to do, do it with your might… (ESV)

🔥 Takeaways:

- Although it takes two to tango and you can't control another person's heart (e.g. make someone "enjoy" you), make no mistake, from God's point of view, your spouse should be your greatest treasure and a joyful, healthy marriage is one of the greatest gifts you can pass on to your kids.
- Be careful of over-emphasizing head above heart, duty above desire, and things like regimented family worship and catechesis above relationships, rest, grace, play, and encouragement.
- Make it a priority to help your sons and daughters discover what is in their hands. Help them cultivate their passions, gifts, and talents in such a way that, when they're older, they'll not only provide a family-supporting wage, but also be something that they use with pleasure and strength to the glory of God. And here's the best advice I've heard to date on helping older teens and young adults discern their calling.[298] Tell them to:
  - Mark out the possibilities. Yeah, professional gambling or prostitution may be off-limits, but God really has

---

[298] I got this outline and a few of these thoughts from a chapter called "Consider Your Calling" in Sinclair Ferguson's excellent little book *Discovering God's Will*.

given us a lot of freedom.

- o Consider their gifts. As John Murray has well said, our gifts are "the divine index to the call." At this point it can be helpful for a son or daughter to ask a parent, pastor, elder, etc. to write down what they think their strengths and weaknesses are. "In the multitude of counselors, there is safety."
- o Consider the needs of the world. Love requires that we think about and care about the world and believe that God likely put us here "for such a time as this."
- o Consider their settled interests and desires. We learn by trying new things and experiencing what we like and are good at as well as what we don't like and may not be good at.

- In view of all that we've discussed related to what really took men especially out of the home to work, many moms and dads need to climb out of the repressive swamp of fundamentalism with renewed and more accurate biblical and historical perspective. Further, they need to stop longing for the past, feeling guilty if mom works, and instead enjoy once again working together to the glory of God. If raising children on only one income works for you then that's great. My heart's cry in this section, however, is to bring clarity and freedom to many moms and dads who carry false guilt or have allowed themselves to be affected by the judgment of others.

- Once we've unshackled ourselves from these narratives, we can then help ourselves and fresh generations wrestle with the challenges that come with a two-income family in today's culture. Working together for the glory of God in our day means sharing many duties we didn't see our parents or grandparents share. It means supporting spouses as they grapple with the work habits and cultures of our competitive job market. It means getting creative about childcare and school options. And amidst these challenges, it often requires extra effort to find a healthy support system. Here are a few questions to discuss with your friends or spouse:

o   How did this chapter give you peace?
o   What challenges come from this change of perspective?
o   How can these refreshed biblical and historical insights fuel better conversations to overcome these challenges?
o   What kind of support system do you have currently and are you willing to ask for help?[299]

[299] I'm indebted to my friend and colleague Alex Hettinga for his insights and questions here.

CHAPTER EIGHT: PATRIARCHY, THE NUCLEAR FAMILY, AND THE LGBTQ MOVEMENT

As we come to understand God's heart better and see our irreplaceable role in passing that heart on to our kids, it's imperative that we—like the men of Issachar—are equipped to understand our times.[300] In this chapter, we will touch on some of the unique cultural challenges related to being a dad like the eradication of patriarchy ("father rule"), the denigration of the nuclear family, and the aggressive promotion of the LQBTQ movement. Again, these are challenges we're right in the midst of. Challenges we need to acknowledge, be in conversation with, and give our children guidance on. But first...

Defining Terms

As some of the topics and terms in this chapter may be unfamiliar or unclear, we need some simple and shared definitions of sex, gender, LGBTQ, the nuclear family, and patriarchy.

Sex and Gender

In our culture of extreme gender confusion, Carolyn Custis James helpfully delineates our first two terms, sex and gender, and reminds us that "theologians and social scientists generally agree that sex and gender are *not* the same.

- *Sex* refers to biology—to *physical differences* in anatomy that distinguish males from females.

---

[300] 1 Chronicles 12:32.

- *Gender* refers to how a particular culture defines what it means to be a male (manhood/masculinity) or what it means to be a female (womanhood/femininity)."[301]

LGBTQ

This "is an acronym for lesbian, gay, bisexual, transgender and queer or questioning. These terms are used to describe a person's sexual orientation or gender identity."[302]

Nuclear Family

Our fourth term, the *nuclear family*, designates a father, a mother, and their children living in the same home. It's a high ideal that, sadly, many feel is now irrelevant or was never even important until 200 years ago when biological family units were elevated to a place they never were previously.

Patriarchy

Our fifth term, *patriarchy*, can be defined as "father rule." Although it's related to both sex and gender, the cultural challenges surrounding patriarchy are related more to gender. Again, Carolyn Custis James provides valuable insight:

All forms of patriarchy are not equally bad—patriarchy is a continuum. It ranges from radicalized violent fundamentalists, such as the Taliban or ISIS (but that exist in every religion, including Christianity), to kinder, gentler versions embraced and promoted by cultural traditionalists and some western evangelicals. Despite the vast variety of expressions, the root issues... run deeper than gender; they are about what Jesus warned us—of the original sin of self-interest, privilege, dominance, and power over others[303]

---

[301] Carolyn Custis James, *Malestrom* (Grand Rapids: Zondervan, 2015), 22.
[302] gaycenter.org/about/lgbtq/ Note: the LGBTQ acronym is at times lengthened to LGBTQIA+ to include Intersex and Asexual, but this is beyond the scope of our discussion here.
[303] Op. Cit., 30.

Listening Well to Tough Questions

For many, calling God "Father" is associated with the worst examples of patriarchy throughout Scripture: like Lot and his daughters; Jepthah's vow; or Abraham and Hagar. How do we interpret the male orientation of the Bible, especially as it is related to the Fatherhood of God? Further, is patriarchy a biblical construct or just the cultural backdrop in which the Bible was written?

Let's unpack just one of the afore mentioned examples to make sure we appropriately feel the challenge of these questions: Lot, the "righteous" nephew that Abraham pleads with God for in the Genesis 19, seems to value hospitality so highly he's fine offering his virgin daughters to a mob set on sexual assault, ("do to them as you please") if the townspeople will just not harm the strangers Lot welcomed as guests. The Oxford Study Bible calls his behavior here "a foolish and cruel, unfatherly act" and that, it seems to me, is putting it mildly.[304] Even the more conservative ESV Study Bible notes that what Lot did here was "a shocking, cowardly, and inexcusable act (even if he intended this only as a bluff, or expected the offer to be rejected)."[305]

We will discuss the LGBTQ movement later but for our purposes now, in discussing how Lot stewarded his "father rule," I want to challenge the way many Christians so readily use the Sodom and Gomorrah passage to condemn homosexuality but say nothing about a man who offered his daughters up for sexual assault. What's worse in this story: homosexual rape or a father being OK with offering his daughters up to be raped?

My purpose in asking this particular question is not here to promote my particular take on LGBTQ issues or patriarchy. Rather, it's to help us pause and listen better to some real cultural challenges to our faith. I'm convinced that if we listen better, it's more likely that our answers will be better. Further, to not pause and listen well or—worse—"to answer *before* listening" is a "folly and shame."[306]

---

304 *The New Oxford Study Annotated Bible*, Fifth Edition, 37.
305 *The ESV Study Bible*, 83.
306 Proverbs 18:12, NIV.

Challenges to the Nuclear Family

In the thirteen years I worked for National Fatherhood Initiative (NFI), I was keenly aware of individuals and movements that wished to dismiss the traditional family and downplay the unique and irreplaceable role of fathers. It came as a surprise, however, to see this message promoted and sponsored by a prominent para-church organization.

In 2006, I was invited to speak at a two-day training for youth and community workers in the Bronx on the topic of fragile families and related issues. The training was sponsored by one of the largest Christian relief organizations in the world.

My goal in participating was to further cultivate the relationship, introduce attendees to NFI and our resources, and to learn more about working with fragile urban families. The event had been presented as an honest forum to discuss "the good, the bad, and the ugly" of fragile family situations.

When I got there, although I had been invited to be part of a forum, I was surprised to learn I would only have ten minutes to speak. Realizing I did not have time to present what I had prepared, I tried to keep my primary message clear: "It is critical for youth workers who want to improve the lives of fragile families to engage, rather than ignore fathers. If we want to bring about positive change, the research shows we can't just focus on mom and extended kin. NFI is a non-profit that specializes in engaging fathers and we are here to serve you."

After I finished, the rest of the presentation time—over two hours—was given to one guest. His sessions centered on subjective and "novel" interpretations of Scripture at the expense of research, objective truth, and ancient wisdom. His joy seemed to be tearing down time-tested paradigms held by participants and replacing them with his own pet interpretations. Although he was entertaining, he made several statements that did not sit well with me. The one that bothered me the most was, "There was no idea of the nuclear family until the 1800s." Although he said nothing further to back up or unpack this statement, his comment had the effect of de-emphasizing the contribution and involvement of my organization as "a partner" to these young practitioners. Worse yet, his rhetoric had the effect of making efforts to engage fathers and strengthen nuclear families seem unnecessary or misguided in building up fragile families. And yet, as experienced social workers know well, the truth is this: In addressing fragile families, the goal is always to reunite a child with their nuclear family; extended family only come in when the biological family is too broken, dysfunctional, or nonexistent.

Unlike the above, there are other more credible challenges to the nuclear family– or at least, certain kinds of nuclear families. A case in point is the one Jamie Smith makes in his excellent book *Desiring the Kingdom*. In arguing for the importance of ancient liturgy, he says that the vows taken by the congregation when a child is baptized involve a "relativizing of 'blood lines.'"[307] By "relativizing" he means that our ancestry or biological family ties are now relative, dependent, or secondary to what we now share in Christ. In other words, from Smith's perspective, the church becomes our "first family." He then calls out the "privacy of the family" for being just "another sphere of rabid autonomy in late modernity."[308] Smith is concerned with "the idolization of family," where the family functions as a "closed, self-sufficient, autonomous unit."[309]

Some critiques of the nuclear family are related to its exclusion of the extended family. And there is certainly much to say on the value of grandparents, aunts, uncles and the role of shared parenting. Or even the value of a larger community (the village) including a healthy church family for that matter. *The New Dictionary of Christian Ethics and Pastoral Theology* attempts to give some clarity on this while also weighing in on whether or not the nuclear family is rooted in Scripture:

> Many biblical references to parenthood relate to the concepts of protection and inheritance, often strictly codified. Yet parenting itself was clearly shared within the extended family or household, possibly with servants. **There is no description of the nuclear family**, considered so desirable recently in the West. Perhaps Christians adopted the model as it seemed a

---

[307] Smith, *Desiring the Kingdom,* 185.
[308] Ibid., 186.
[309] Ibid.

143

practical outworking of the NT teaching on sexual continence within marriage, as well as honoring the teaching codes of conduct and respect between parents and children (1 Cor 7 and Eph 6:1–4)...

The family of Jesus himself is the only clear NT model [of the nuclear family]: the son of Joseph and Mary, he is known to have brothers and sisters (Matt 13:55–56). The only extended family member referred to is Elizabeth, Mary's cousin (Luke 1:36), and she was not local. Christians, therefore, may well also have tended to adopt this pattern as supporting the idea that the nuclear family is the norm in present times. They have generally paid less attention to the extended family, though worldwide there are, of course, cultural variations.[310]

Despite intentions, the authors above leave the waters muddy regarding whether or not the nuclear family is biblically supported and should be championed and protected. Notice the statements I've placed below and bolded above:

- "there is no description of the nuclear family"
- "the family of Jesus himself is the only clear NT model"

It's an all-too-common example of the unwarranted hesitancy—again, even in the Christian community—to acknowledge the nuclear family's prominence since the beginning (think Adam, Eve, Cain, and Abel) and extol its virtues. Yes, the extended family (grandparents, aunts, uncles, etc.) is also important in raising children and should be valued and affirmed. This is no reason, however, to downplay the significance of the nuclear family or give serious attention to the model in which Jesus himself was born into and raised.

How the Holy Family Helps Us

In my current vocational role as Executive Director of Church Outreach and Engagement at Care Net, the Christmas story and the

---

[310] *New Dictionary of Christian Ethics & Pastoral Theology* (Downers Grove, IL: IVP, 1995), 651-652.

family Jesus was born into is especially significant, as it deals with the most famous "unplanned" pregnancy in history.[311] I have a great visual on my bookshelf to remind me of this as I write. It's a white figurine of Joseph standing with a lamp in his left hand and his right arm wrapping his cloak around Mary. She is kneeling with baby Jesus in her arms. The statuette is a beautiful and uncommon representation of the nuclear family with Joseph as a significant presence, protector, and guide. Joseph and Mary are united in love and marriage and their child is safe. The figurine was originally my grandparents and several years ago, given that my life's work has primarily focused on strengthening fathers and families, my mom gave it to me. Now a cherished fixture in my office, it is a daily reminder of eternal priorities and perspective. It gives laser focus to my efforts to equip churches and pregnancy centers in offering compassion, hope, help, and discipleship to men and women facing unplanned pregnancies. And it applies equally here to your mission as an irreplaceable dad.

Here's how:

- **The Holy Family is an *icon* that invites unity.** All three branches of the Christian church—Orthodox, Roman Catholic, and Protestant—use and love the nativity story. It's a celebration of the incarnation and birth of Christ. Further, the Christmas traditions of most Christian families include setting up a manger scene. Children grow up playing with and being fascinated by it. Baby Jesus gets carried around and many of us have even seen baby Jesus' cows, donkeys, etc. with broken arms or legs because they've been played with so much!

  For many of our children, the holy family is their first introductory glimpse into the gospel described in John 1:14: "The Word became human and made his home among us. He was full of unfailing love and faithfulness. And we have seen his glory, the glory of the Father's one and only Son."[312] Again, whatever our Christian expression, the biblical Christmas story has played and continues to play a significant role in our

---

[311] This is, of course, from Mary and Joseph's perspective. From God's, it was the most *planned* pregnancy in the history of the world!
[312] NLT.

spiritual formation. As we mature in our faith and come to better understand the cross, we identify with these lyrics from Julie Miller's, *Manger Throne*: "That dirty manger was my heart, too. I'll make it a royal throne for you."

- **The Holy Family is an *image* that presents and preserves the ideal of the nuclear family.** What of Jamie Smith's earlier critique that many nuclear families are "closed, self-sufficient, autonomous" units comprised of moms, dads, and their children who have little interest in their church or spiritual family? He's absolutely right. Many families (traditional or non-traditional) are fairly closed to the outside world. It's all about building their white picket fence and there's little interest in getting to know neighbors, meeting needs in their community, or changing the world. The problem to address here, however, is self-focus and a lack of care and inclusion on the part of some nuclear families, not the nuclear family structure unit itself.

And, yes, the extended family (grandparents, aunts, uncles, cousins, etc.) is also important in raising children and should be valued and affirmed. Even in Mary's case, we see that relationships– especially extended family– can be critical in a crisis.[313] Again, this is no reason, however, to diminish the critical role of nuclear families or denigrate the model in which Jesus himself was born into and raised. Indeed, as we noted above in talking about fragile families, many individuals and social workers have no choice but to focus on extended kin because the nuclear family is weak, fragmented, or non-existent.

- **The Holy Family is a *picture* that focuses us on gospel potential.** Helen Keller famously said, "The saddest thing in the world is a person who can see but has no vision." Let me share how I apply this particular point in talking to pregnancy centers workers: I ask them, "When a client comes into a

---

[313] In facing her "unplanned pregnancy" (again, from a human perspective at least!), she went to stay with her cousin Elizabeth for three months (See Luke 1:39-44, 56).

center seeking help or considering abortion, what or whom should we see? Certainly, we should see the vulnerable life of the unborn infant. Life-affirming work, however, isn't just about saving a baby; it's about raising a child." Research shows that baby's outcomes, on average, are not very promising without a dad in the picture. The most effective pregnancy centers, then, are those who see dads as potential Josephs who have unique, important roles.

Further, if we're in sync with Jesus' vision for the world, we'll recognize idols of the heart, too: convenience, a woman's body elevated over that of a baby, adult plans and potential held as more important than a child's, etc.

We'll also see and share hope—the message of the cross and the forgiveness of sins. Bottom line, we'll have an eternal vision for all as those that need to become disciples of Jesus Christ— the pregnant mom, her baby, and her boyfriend/father/ partner.

Finally, in making our case for the critical importance of strong, loving, and outwardly-focused nuclear families we need to make one final point: Denigrating the traditional nuclear family ignores basic biology and the findings of evolutionary psychology. These show that "individuals are not only concerned with their own specific genes; they are also concerned with the survival of those who carry their genes— offspring."[314] In other words, we are most likely to care for what is part of us.

Special Considerations for Churches

To those of us who champion the nuclear family as part of God's design– who believe the manger family is still a model for the modern family, *New York Times* commentator David Brooks offers the following critique:

---

[314] *The Cambridge Companion to Christian Ethics, Second Edition* (Cambridge: Cambridge UP, 2012), 264.

Conservatives have nothing to say to the kid whose dad has split, whose mom has had three other kids with different dads; "go live in a nuclear family" is really not relevant advice. If only a minority of households are traditional nuclear families, that means the majority are single parents, never-married parents, blended families, grandparent-headed families, serial partnerships, and so on. Conservative ideas have not caught up with this reality.[315]

I believe Brooks' words are a helpful mirror for the church in this cultural moment, helping us ask some important questions:

- Are we providing realistic help to those whose situation looks different than ours, or different from the "ideal"?
- Do our words and actions communicate love and hope to those who've been hurt, abandoned, or abused? To rebels? To those who are powerless or have fallen off the cart of life? To those whose families are a maelstrom of confusion?
- Is the language we use sensitive to the growing number of broken or alternative (including LGBTQ) family structures?

As Christians, we have to live with the fact that our religion is one with exclusive truth claims: Sometimes there is just one way that leads to life and many ways that seem right but lead to death.[316] We believe God, the Creator, has the right to call the shots on what is or isn't His design and how humans approach Him. We can't change, for instance, the fact that "God resists the proud but gives grace to the humble."[317] Nor can we remove the requirement of repentance in making God's ways accessible: "This is what the Sovereign LORD, the Holy One of Israel, says: 'In repentance and rest is your salvation, in quietness and trust is your strength, but you would have none of it.'"[318]

In thinking about the last bulleted question above, we need to be

---

[315] https://www.theatlantic.com/magazine/archive/2020/03/the-nuclear-family-was-a-mistake/605536/
[316] John 14:6; Judges 21:25; Prov. 14:12.
[317] James 4:6.
[318] Isaiah 30:15, NIV.

sensitive when using the term "natural" to refer to the traditional nuclear family. With the widespread breakdown of the traditional nuclear family, many individuals may view their family situations as subpar, that is, broken or unnatural. Yes, sometimes becoming aware and honestly acknowledging that our current situation is less than ideal can bring hope and be a step toward healing. The point I'm trying to make, however, is related to sensitivity and compassion. To say it another way: we want to be conduits of God's goodness that leads to repentance, not purveyors of shame.[319]

We need to love all, pointing each (including ourselves!) to the One whose "mercies are new every morning."[320] Our challenge in doing this is to stay strong in holding up God's ideal or design. The Apostle Paul provides us with a great example. He strategically reached households.[321] In first-century culture, this included the nuclear and extended family, as well as servants—all who lived under the same roof. The heads of household in these examples were forces for good, bringing blessing to all through their decision to embrace the gospel.

We are blessed to live in a culture that— on the whole– cares about the well-being of children (at least, those that have been born) and has mostly abandoned authoritarian and ugly forms of patriarchy. It is to the detriment of many children, however, that the nuclear family is increasingly deemphasized or disparaged in favor of alternative family structures.

As we continue to wrestle with the realities and challenges of alternative families, we have some choices to make. We can sit smugly inside our own walls, thanking God that we are not like those out there. A fortress mentality like that, however, is a far cry from the one Jesus, "the friend of sinners," had. It's also opposite the prayer for mercy at the heart of true Christianity. Other choices we might make include panic or preparation. My heart is that we would reject panic and choose preparation, courageously tearing down walls like Joshua.[322] I pray that we will do this, however, with the love and grace of the later Joshua

---

319 Romans 2:4.
320 Lamentations 3:23.
321 Acts 10-Cornelius,16- Lydia and the Philippian jailor.
322 2 Timothy 1:7; Joshua 1:9.

(Joshua means "Savior"), who died to justify the ungodly.[323]

Lest we forget, *we* are among the ungodly who Jesus died to justify, as are our growing number of human brothers and sisters forming alternative identities and households—some choosing to be part of– and raise children in– the LGBTQ community. It is to this difficult challenge that we now turn.

Gay Fathers and the LGBTQ Revolution

During my time with NFI from 2004–2015, I also did "Engaging Fathers for Successful Reentry" trainings for the pre-release, probation, and parole staff of State Departments of Corrections (DOCs). Over time, the topic of gay parenting came up more and more. For example, in 2014 in conducting a training for twenty-six Kentucky DOC's Probation and Parole officers, one female officer mentioned she often observed that lesbian moms have a strong bias against men and don't want their child to have anything to do with dad. In being asked to weigh in on this kind of scenario, I could not answer from a religious perspective, so I would say something like this:

> One's rights or sexual orientation is not one of NFI's issues. We help fathers wherever they are. If they want to be involved, responsible, and committed to their children, we want to encourage them in this. The only thing that NFI would want to avoid in helping children is a perspective that denigrates mom or dad as unnecessary to children's well-being.

> When you frame the issue of parenting around what is best for a child—instead of what one has a right to do individually— the research strongly shows kids are served best by both a mom and a dad.[324]

---

[323] Romans 4:5.

[324] At the time, I found this response not only avoided the political landmine of gay marriage and related issues, but also silenced any aggressive pro-gay agenda and gave everyone something to think about. For example, most gay men who wanted the right to parent or adopt did not want to be perceived as trashing mom or her role.

While much research exists about parenting in general, there is much less data available on gay parenting. Further, "studies of children raised by same-sex parents have almost exclusively focused on families headed by lesbian mothers."[325] Still, it is estimated that "between 1% and 12% of children are being raised by a gay or lesbian parent."[326] Michael Lamb, a Cambridge scholar widely considered to be the definitive authority on the role of fathers in child development, notes that most positive claims on gay fathers are based on self-reporting— that is, gay fathers describing themselves—rather than hard research. For example, gay men report themselves as being "more emotionally available than most heterosexual fathers" or "more child centered than most heterosexual fathers could through their greater openness and tolerance of their child's choices."[327]

Lamb also notes that many of these "reconceptualized" family relationships boast of being "based on love rather than biology"[328] This last phrase may sound progressive to many, but it falsely pits biology against love and ignores research where biology is clearly related to increased commitment toward and decreased vulnerability for the child. For example, "the most powerful taboo in human society" is "the incest taboo."[329] In discussing this in his book, *Fatherless America*, researcher David Blankenhorn notes that while "most stepfathers do not molest their children," numerous studies confirm that stepfathers are far more likely to do so than biological fathers.[330] Another study revealed that in many cases, the absence of a biological father contributes to increased risk of child maltreatment. The results suggest that Child Protective Services (CPS) agencies have some justification in viewing the presence of a social (rather than biological) father as increasing children's risk of abuse and neglect. It is believed that in families with a non-biological (social) father figure, there is a higher

---

[325] *The Role of the Father in Child Development*, ed. Michael E. Lamb, 5th ed. (Hoboken, NJ: John Wiley & Sons, 2010), 322–327. The 2021 HBO documentary *Nuclear Family* is also a recent example of this.
[326] *The Role of the Father in Child Development*, 320.
[327] Ibid, 326.
[328] Ibid.
[329] Blankenhorn, *Fatherless America*, 40.
[330] Ibid.

risk of abuse and neglect to children, despite the social father living in the household or only dating the mother.[331] The point here is not to feed into the false and extremely harmful stereotype that gay men are more likely to be pedophiles than straight men. Nor is it to disparage stepfathers—many are great dads—but only to show clear research on how biology is more often a protector of children than a barrier to love.

Although some of the studies Lamb discusses, "did not show a higher incidence of psychological disorder" or "gender identity confusion" among children with gay parents, the following may be the most troubling consequence associated with gay parenting: "More young people from lesbian-mother families than from heterosexual families had *experimented* in same-sex relationships."[332] For those who consider the Bible trustworthy when it comes to sexual ethics, this should be especially concerning, because it is a recipe for seriously wounded children. When children and teens are encouraged to experiment with rather than protected from sexual encounters that God forbids,[333] wounds and conditioning occur. As humans, we remember our first sexual experiences, and these shape us in mysterious and profound ways.[334] This can be a good thing if our first experience is positively associated with the person we have decided to marry, and with whom we made serious vows. The power, beauty, and intense pleasure of sexual experience is then associated with committed love, trust, and God's design. But outside of biblical marriage, early experimentation can bend or solidify the desires and preferences of children, teens, and young adults in certain directions. Chosen identities become confirmed, leading to painful distortions and entanglements later in life.[335]

---

[331] "CPS Involvement in Families with Social Fathers." *Fragile Families Research Brief* No.46. Princeton, NJ and New York, NY: Bendheim-Thomas Center for Research on Child Wellbeing and Social Indicators Survey Center, 2010.

[332] *The Role of the Father in Child Development*, ed. Michael E. Lamb, 5th ed. (Hoboken, NJ: John Wiley & Sons, 2010), 327.

[333] Here is where the Bible mentions homosexual behavior: Genesis 19:1-28, Leviticus 18:22, Deuteronomy 23:17-18, Romans 1:26-27, 1 Corinthians 6:9-10, and 1 Timothy 1:10.

[334] 1 Corinthians 6:18.

[335] In using the term "chosen identities," I am in no way implying that same-sex attraction is always chosen. Many have experienced a gay orientation long before

Indeed, even the latest research strongly suggests that recent increases in LGBTQ orientation are more the result of nurture than nature; that is, more the result of conditioning than being "born this way." These are the cultural waters we are all swimming—sometimes marinating—in; none are unaffected. Gallup's annual poll showed that the LGBTQ population grew to over 7 percent in 2022, doubling data from ten years ago.[336] And "the number of transgender people in the U.S. has grown to 1.6 million, with the sharpest rise among young adults and teenagers."[337] Even comedian and social commentator Bill Maher recently used this data to draw attention to the clear "trendiness" of being LGBTQ among Gen Z, joking "If we follow this trajectory, we will all be gay in 2054!"[338]

In conclusion, Christian psychologist and Wheaton College Provost Stanton Jones observes:

> Our biology, including our genes, likely does influence our sexual orientation, but this is only one among a set of factors. There is also research, ignored by many, suggesting that family and experience are powerful influences on the development of same-sex attraction (Jones & Kwee, 2005).[339]

Jones then weighs in on the ethics of all of this, bringing further clarity: "We all inherit inclinations that reflect our brokenness and sinfulness. The core ethical question is not, 'Why do I want to do the things that I want to do?' The core ethical question is 'Should I do the things I want to do?'"[340] As William Willimon has well said, "The gospel is not simply about meeting people's needs. The gospel is also

---

their first sexual encounter. For more on this, see Wesley Hill's excellent book *Washed and Waiting*.

[336] https://www.nbcnews.com/nbc-out/out-news/percentage-lgbtq-adults-us-doubled-decade-gallup-finds-rcna16556

[337] https://www.nytimes.com/2022/06/10/science/transgender-teenagers-national-survey.html

[338] https://www.youtube.com/watch?app=desktop&v=mMBzfUj5zsg&feature=youtu.be

[339] *Psychology and Christianity: Five Views* (Downers Grove, IL: IVP, 2010), 123.

[340] Ibid., 125.

a critique of our needs, an attempt to give us needs worth having."[341]

🔥Insight: In light of these challenges, here are four practical takeaways for irreplaceable dads:

- Focus and work on your own issues and sins, rather than everyone else's. This means tending to our own business—our own sexual impurity and weak marriages. Even in thinking about LGBTQ issues, as Christopher Yuan aptly reminds us, "Homosexuality is not the worst sin. Our sin is just as odious to God."[342] In wrestling with my own disordered desires, I've found Professor Wesley Hill's guidance convicting and helpful:

> While those in the grip of Christ's love will never experience ultimate defeat, there is a profound sense in which we must face our struggles now knowing there may be no relief this side of God's new creation. We may wrestle with a particular weakness all our lives. But the call remains: *go to battle.* "There is much virtue in bearing up under a long, hard struggle," a friend of mine once told me, even if there is no apparent "victory" in the short run… Significantly, this kind of long-suffering endurance is not a special assignment the gospel gives only to gay and lesbian persons. Many believers of all stripes and backgrounds struggle with desires of various sorts that they must deny in order to remain faithful to the gospel's demands.[343]

- Because the gospel is good news, be known in your family and community for what you're for more than what you're against.
- Especially with younger children, make lavish use of manger scenes to pass on the Christian faith. As a mom, dad, or

[341] William Willimon, *Pastor: The Theology and Practice of Ordained Ministry* (Nashville: Abingdon, 2002), 95–96.
[342] https://www.christianitytoday.com/ct/2014/june-web-only/why-matthew-vines-is-wrong-about-bible-same-sex-relationshi.html?paging=off
[343] Wesley Hill, *Washed and Waiting* (Grand Rapids: Zondervan, 2016), 88.

member of the extended family, you are a storyteller of a nativity narrative. What's more, in dependence on God, you can become an intentional conduit to see that story played out in the lives of all those who receive him (John 1:12).

- Especially in working with older teens and adults, lay aside your bias and agenda to love others intentionally and authentically in the space and chapter they're in. I pray you'll have the loving patience and sensitivity to the Holy Spirit's work that one of my co-workers recently exhibited in one of her comments about a client she is mentoring who is in a polyamorous[344] relationship: "There are so many things I want to share with her, so many things I want to say, but she doesn't want to hear those things. For now, I will continue to care about her and walk with her, and we will get there sometime."

---

[344] Polyamorous relationships are those "characterized by or involved in the practice of engaging in multiple romantic (and typically sexual) relationships, with the consent of all the people involved" (Oxford Dictionaries @ Oxford University Press).

PART THREE: YOUR IRREPLACEABLE LEGACY

"Each of us is born with a box of matches inside us but we can't strike them all by ourselves."

—Laura Esquivel

"The most powerful weapon on earth is the human soul on fire."
—Ferdinand Foch

CHAPTER NINE: ALL "I"S ON HERO-DADS
PART 1

It happened suddenly and unexpectedly one cool August morning in 2005 at Montana's Glacier Mountain National Park. Johan Otter, 44, and his daughter Jenna, 18, were only 90 minutes into their hike when a huge female grizzly bear, apparently in an effort to protect her cubs, suddenly appeared on the trail running straight toward them. Jenna was knocked aside, suffering only minor injuries. Johan, however, was a different story. Hoping the bear would stay focused on him rather than his daughter, he bore the brunt of the bear's attack and "Johan was left with 20 wounds, including broken ribs and a fractured eye socket." He was also nearly scalped and miraculously survived a horrific, nearly fatal neck fracture. "Doctors said that if the bear had applied just a bit more pressure on his head, the bear's fangs would have penetrated his brain." Johan said later, "[Death] was not going to be an option that day. I had to protect my daughter."[345]

This story gives a dramatic glimpse into the life of a hero-dad and what it means to love our children well. Any good dad would give his life for his kids, if necessary. And many good men do give their lives for their children—every day—in small, seemingly insignificant ways.

Earlier, in the beginning of the book and in chapter seven, we defined the roles of a good dad as protector, provider, nurturer, and guide. In this chapter and the next, I'd like to expand on that simple description with this second, more robust, and biblically-informed

---

[345] "Father Bears Brunt of Grizzly Attack to Protect Daughter," *ABC News,* September 14, 2005, accessed November 14, 2016, http://abcnews.go.com/GMA/OnlyinAmerica/story?id=1124199.

definition:

The ideal father is *interconnected* with his kid's heart(s) and always in prayer for them (Job 1:5). He chooses *involvement* (Deut. 6:4–9), *intentionality*, and *influence* (Prov 31:23) over *isolation* (Prov. 18:1). Although he is deeply aware of his *inadequacy* to provide all that his kid(s) need in and of himself (Matt. 5:3; John 15:5), he *imitates* the wisdom and love of the Triune God: the Father, who cares about his children's needs (Phil. 4:19) and gives them good gifts (Matt. 7:9–11; Jas. 1:17); the Son who served out of a profound self-awareness (John 13:3-4), and the Holy Spirit who becomes the long-term, always-accessible Comforter, Counselor, and Helper (John 14:16).

In the next two chapters, I want to more deeply explore each of these "I" concepts in this order:

- Hero-dads are *interconnected* with their kid's heart(s) and are always in prayer for them.
- Hero-dads are *involved* in the daily routine of their kid's lives.
- Hero-dads are *intentional* about passing on their faith.
- Hero-dads are aware of their *inadequacy* to provide all that their kid(s) need.
- Hero-dads avoid *isolation.*
- Hero-dads care about and grow in competence to *influence.*
- Hero-dads seek to *imitate* the wisdom and love of the Triune God.

All seven of these "I's" describe the "hero" dad of the Bible. They also embody the biblical concepts that helped me the most in raising my kids.

Hero-dads are *interconnected* with their children's hearts and are always in prayer for them.

The Old Testament saint Job as the quintessential example of this. The book begins by describing Job as "a man... totally devoted to God" who "hated evil with a passion."[346] And here's the example given to illustrate this devotion:

---

[346] Job 1:1, The Message.

His sons used to go and hold feasts in one another's houses in turn; and they would send and invite their three sisters to eat and drink with them. And when the feast days had run their course, Job would send and sanctify them, and he would rise early in the morning and offer burnt offerings according to the number of them all; for Job said, "It may be that my children have sinned, and cursed God in their *hearts*." This is what Job *always* did.[347]

Note the two words I've italicized above: Job was concerned about his kid's *hearts*, and it was something he *always* did. And although it doesn't say the state of his kid's hearts kept him up at night, it certainly got him up early. "As the priest of a patriarchal household, Job is responsible for the welfare of his family."[348] We might be tempted to view Job's actions here as obsessive or excessive. But his habit is a reminder that involved, responsible, and committed dads are intensely focused on, and at times, distracted by, the health of their kid's hearts. Related to this is an observation made by Tim Keller that "once you become a parent you will never be happier than your unhappiest child. Your heart is tied up with them."[349]

Moreover, it turns out that research suggests that this heart-to-heart connection is *the* most important characteristic of a hero-dad:

- "Having an emotionally close relationship with fathers may provide a broad, secure foundation that is more important than specific interactions around religious topics."[350]
- "Emerging adults tend to match the level of religiosity of their fathers particularly if they are attached to their fathers."[351]

What the Job passage adds to the importance of heart-to-heart connection, however, in passing on faith is 1) prayer and 2) a deep

---

[347] Job 1:4-5, NRSV.
[348] Norman C. Habel, *The Book of Job* (Philadelphia, Westminster, 1985), 88.
[349] Tweet from May 11, 2014.
[350] Greg Priebbenow, "Dad Matters! . . . The Spiritual Influence of Fathers," Formingfaith, accessed November 14, 2016. https://formingfaith.wordpress.com/2015/06/18/dad-matters-the-spiritual-influence-of-fathers/. Used by permission.
[351] Ibid.

awareness of our kid's need for the atonement of sins. Of course, on this side of the cross, we know that the sacrifices and "burnt offerings" that Job and other Old Testament saints offered pointed ultimately to Christ. The Message translation of Hebrews explains this clearly and beautifully:

> Every priest goes to work at the altar each day, offers the same old sacrifices year in, year out, and never makes a dent in the sin problem. As a priest, Christ made a single sacrifice for sins, and that was it!... It was a perfect sacrifice by a perfect person to perfect some very imperfect people. By that single offering, he did everything that needed to be done for everyone who takes part in the purifying process... Once sins are taken care of for good, there's no longer any need to offer sacrifices for them.[352]

Again, the author Hebrews continues, getting even more practical:

> So, friends, we can now—without hesitation—walk right up to God, into "the Holy Place." Jesus has cleared the way by the blood of his sacrifice, acting as our priest before God. The 'curtain' into God's presence is his body.

> So let's do it—full of belief, confident that we're presentable inside and out. Let's keep a firm grip on the promises that keep us going. He always keeps his word. Let's see how inventive we can be in encouraging love and helping out, not avoiding worshiping together as some do but spurring each other on, especially as we see the big Day approaching.[353]

On this side of Jesus clearing the way "by the blood of his sacrifice," prayers for our kid's hearts should be done with full confidence in God's loving acceptance and faithfulness to us. What's more, those prayers should be packaged together with tons of creative

---

[352] 10:11-18, *The Message.*
[353] 10:19-25, *The Message.*

encouragement, emotional connection, and regular participation in a healthy church.

Hero-dads are *involved* in the daily routine of their kid's lives.

These commandments that I give you today are to be on your hearts. Impress them on your children. Talk about them when you sit at home and when you walk along the road, when you lie down and when you get up. Tie them as symbols on your hands and bind them on your foreheads. Write them on the doorframes of your houses and on your gates (Deut. 6:6-9, NIV).

As we learned in chapter seven, the Industrial Revolution took many fathers out of the home, disrupting the pattern from most of history, where most moms and dads worked together on the family farm or business with their kids. Note the variety of "involvement" postures taken from the celebrated passage above:[354]

- Sitting
- Walking
- Lying down
- Getting up

All of these bodily positions highlight the sacredness of the ordinary; that is, the huge significance God places on the habitual, seemingly mundane, parts of our daily routine. These descriptors also remind us of the importance of our presence—remember the old saying, "kids spell love T.I.M.E.," both quality and quantity. Indeed, many of our parenting joys and "wins" happen unexpectedly "along the road."

As an example, in June 1994, Pam's pop-pop had just died, and I needed to take her and our infant son Timothy to the airport so she

---

[354] This passage is part of the Jewish "Shema," a word that literally means to listen, heed, hear, and do. In the Hebrew mind, hearing is an effectual hearing that leads to obedience. And so, fast-forwarding to the NT, when Rabbi Jesus said, "He who has ears to hear let him hear," he also was implying an effectual healing; that is, a hearing that effected or showed up in how one lived.

could fly to the funeral. At the time, I was attending seminary in Louisville, KY and working part-time as a youth pastor. That day there was a huge Christian Music festival going on in Louisville. I had taken the youth group earlier in the day, but missed seeing some of my favorite artists because I had to leave to get Pam to the airport in time. Later that night, however, Michael W. Smith was doing a special acoustic set with his early band members. And because of this I planned to go back, bringing my two-and-a-half-year-old son Matthew along. I knew he liked Smith's music as he would often pick out Smith's album, *Go West Young Man,* and ask us to play it for him so he could hear "Michael."

Matthew and I arrived back at the stadium about 9 pm, before "Michael" came on. Matthew was definitely a little overwhelmed by the crowd, so I bought him a bucket of popcorn to keep him busy. The youth group kids loved that my son was there, so he and his popcorn got passed from lap to lap. I put cotton in his ears, and Michael W. Smith came out with his band at full volume! Matthew was a little afraid of all the lights, noise, and excitement, but I kept saying, "It's OK, it's Michael!" After two to three songs, Matthew started smiling and clapping like everyone else. When Michael played the piano intro to "Place in This World," Matthew's favorite song at home, something clicked and he looked up at me with a big smile and said, "That's Michael!" As we were walking to the house from the car that night, Matthew looked up at me and said, "We had a good time with Michael."

Although that's one of hundreds of parenting memories I'll treasure forever—let's be honest—some recollections are downright terrifying! The scariest moment I remember took place one winter when we were sledding with friends in Morgantown, PA. The sledding was great because the sun was shining, causing a thin layer of melting ice on the packed snow. You could barely walk without falling. My son, Tim, no more than two at the time, was heavily bundled up in his snowsuit and sledding with older kids who held him and steered. I was watching from nearby when suddenly, he climbed on one of the sleds by himself in the direction of the parked cars and started down the hill. He was lying on his belly with his head stretched up and a big smile on his face, heading straight toward the front of a car with a steel bumper! As his momentum increased, I saw no way he would not snap his neck once his face hit the bumper. I felt horror as I realized that there was no way I could get to him in time. My heart sank, and everything went into slow motion. Somehow, he missed and was fine. I have no idea how, but guardian angels may well have been involved.

Thankfully, although some involved parents face incredibly difficult challenges, it's not all fighting grizzlies! In the end, whether scary or fun, exhausting or exhilarating, sad or joyful, there's nothing like being an involved, responsible, and committed dad and watching your kids grow.

Hero-dads are *intentional* about passing on their faith.

Let's look at the Deuteronomy 6 passage again, this time through a different lens, noting the "intentional" images that I've italicized:

> These commandments that I give you today are to be on your hearts. *Impress* them on your children. *Talk about* them when you sit at home and when you walk along the road, when you lie down and when you get up. *Tie* them as symbols on your hands and *bind* them on your foreheads. *Write* them on the doorframes of your houses and on your gates (Deut. 6:6-9, NIV).

The Case for Catechesis

These verbs—*impress, talk about, tie, bind,* and *write*—reflect an intentionality that flows out of a heart for God. Many families put this intentionality into action through the use of catechesis—a word that, for a variety of reasons, is unknown or has fallen out of favor with many. My friend, Jay, recalled his first experience with the word: He went to play ball with his neighborhood buddy but found, unfortunately, his buddy wasn't available. Why? He had to go to something called "catechism" first. And so Jay followed his buddy to the Catholic church and waited for him on the steps. Then, after "catechism" was finally out of the way, they got to play ball.

Like my friend as a young boy, many view catechesis as a foreign

165

and unwelcome experience—a boring interruption in an otherwise fun day. Others see the practice as antiquated, irrelevant, or even potentially brainwashing. We'll deal with some of the most common objections below, but first let's define catechesis and look at some positives.

Despite the bad press,[355] catechesis is a biblical practice related to one of the marks of the earliest Christians: devotion to the apostles' teaching (Acts 2:42). The word comes from the Greek *katechein* and means to teach orally or to instruct by word of mouth. For example, here is how the apostle Paul used the term in Galatians 6:6: "The one who is *catechized* must share all good things with the one who *catechizes*."

Broadly defined, catechesis is the practice of "grounding and growing God's people in the Gospel and its implications for doctrine, devotion, duty, delight."[356] Catechisms, then, are simply collections of questions and answers designed for memorization and recitation. Tim Keller in his introduction to the *New City Catechism Devotional* gives four reasons why catechisms are still relevant and important:[357]

- Classic catechisms "take students through the Apostle's Creed, the Ten Commandments, and the Lord's Prayer—a perfect balance of biblical theology, practical ethics, and spiritual experience."

- "The catechetical discipline of memorization drives concepts deeper into the heart and naturally holds students more accountable to master the material than do discipleship courses."

- "The practice of question-answer recitations brings instructors and students into a naturally interactive, dialogical process of learning."

- Catechetical instruction helps us be less individualistic and

---

[355] Admittedly, much of this bad press is deserved. As my son, Tim, pointed out in reading this section: Some branches of Christianity are "pretty mediocre at linking catechesis with any kind of internal development, spiritual discernment, personal commitment, or emotional journey. Basically, catechesis has been unmoored from... a lifelong journey and struggle to be present with God day-to-day."

[356] J.I. Packer and Gary Parrett, *Grounded in the Gospel: Building Believers the Old – Fashioned Way* (Grand Rapids, MI: Baker, 2010), 182.

[357] *The New City Catechism Devotional* (Wheaton, IL: Crossways, 2017), 8.

more communal. It reminds us that Jesus taught us to pray, "Our Father," rather than "My Father."

Catechizing also gives a framework so that Christian words and phrases are understood in theologically accurate and historically-informed ways. To use an image from carpentry, think of a classic catechism as a solid "mental foundation on which... spiritual life will be built."[358]

What happens when we don't have a theologically robust and time-tested framework for healthy spirituality? In construction, when you don't have a sound framework that's to code, it affects everything: insulation, drywall, plumbing, electrical, HVAC, etc. Building codes specify "minimum standards" and their main purpose is "to protect public health, safety and general welfare as they relate to the construction and occupancy of buildings and structures."[359] In a similar way, classic catechisms were painstakingly crafted to promote spiritual "health, safety, and general welfare."

Without a strong framework or a knowledge of minimum standards—spiritual building codes if you will, we settle for chicken-houses, shanties, and cardboard boxes. To say it another way, without a solid foundation rooted in historic Christian teaching, it's easy to become homeless spiritually or settle for an "abandominium." Abandominium—that's a word my ex-offender friend, who now works with other ex-offenders in Camden, taught me. It's basically an old condominium that's now abandoned. Many of the residents of his halfway house jokingly say, "I got me an abandominium."

One emotionally unhealthy gentleman I knew—I'll call him Jack—had a brilliant mind. With no strong catechetical framework, however, he was susceptible to spiritual leaders who played on his emotions and claimed supernatural experience (e.g. "God spoke to me..." or "God told me in a dream..."). Without a strong understanding of historic Christianity, Jack gravitated to teachers who tended to yell loud, have little training, and always interpret the Bible

---

[358] *The New City Catechism: 52 Questions for Our Hearts and Minds* (Wheaton, IL: Crossways, 2017), 8.
[359] https://guides.libraries.psu.edu/c.php?g=3

literally (when a great deal is manifestly poetry, and so on).[360]

Today, he's tormented by inaccurate beliefs about hell, the unpardonable sin, suffering, and the silence of God. Fear and shame are his masters, not Christ. He clings to his spiritual abandominium and it's difficult to get him to consider living anywhere else. In some ways, it would be better if he knew nothing about the Bible and Christianity. I've often wished there was some way to bulldoze his shack-like thinking so he could get a fresh start with a proper foundation and framework. Yet, we all know—even from experience with ourselves: it's hard to teach old dogs new tricks. And as we get older, it becomes easier and easier to paint ourselves into a corner we can't get out of.

That's why catechesis is largely preventative work. We catechize our children so they don't go through life vulnerable to "every wind of doctrine" like Jack.[361] Yet, even as adults with bad habits and various forms of "stinkin thinkin," there's hope: we can unlearn things. Scripture memory (more on this below) and catechesis help. As noted above, memorization drives messages deeper into the heart. It also drives out lies, replacing them with truth.

Concerns with Catechesis

Not everyone is a fan of catechesis—or even intentional Scripture memorization—and in what follows, I'd like to address seven common concerns, concluding with a personal confession and some practical guidance:

- **"Catechesis is brainwashing"**— British philosopher and author A. C. Grayling said that "Religions survive mainly because they brainwash the young."[362] Is he right in saying this?

---

[360] Always taking the Bible literally, especially when one simultaneously devalues theological education; mainstream science; a thorough knowledge of the Old Testament, ancient Near Eastern and first-century culture is a recipe for spiritual abuse and malpractice. As the late Bruce Metzger, one of the foremost NT Scholars of the last century, said: "The Bible doesn't always mean what it literally says but it always means what it literally means."

[361] Ephesians 4:14.

[362] A more nuanced and helpful statement that takes Grayling's challenge seriously is this one by Soren Keierkegaard: "There are two ways to be fooled. One is to believe what isn't true. The other is to refuse to accept what is true."

Even many thoughtful Christians wonder, "Isn't catechizing children a form of brainwashing?" It's a great question, and in answering it let's first define terms. Brainwashing is:

- A method for systematically changing attitudes or altering beliefs, originated in totalitarian countries, especially through the use of torture, drugs, or psychological-stress techniques. Or...
- Any method of controlled systematic indoctrination, especially one based on repetition or confusion: brainwashing by TV commercials.[363]

This second meaning applies the most to our question and helps to ask it even more pointedly: "Is catechizing a method of 'controlled systematic indoctrination' based on 'repetition'?" The answer is, yes. But then, by this definition, so is spending hours on a smartphone, or consuming hours of Disney or PBS KIDS. Which brings us to this question: "Is using a catechism to pass on the essentials of the Christian faith a good and helpful form of "controlled systematic indoctrination," akin to memorizing multiplication tables or even a verse like John 3:16? How you answer this question will largely be determined by whether you think a particular catechism (or certain portions of it) teaches truth and is good for kids. If you believe it does, you'll likely use it. If you believe it doesn't or you're A.C. Grayling, you'll likely have a different take. Yes, it's true that, in catechizing children, they don't fully understand the full implications of what they're learning at the time that they're memorizing select questions and answers. But there are plenty of things we teach our children before they fully understand, for their own good. Remember, as a parent, you have the ability to determine how in-depth you want to go in presenting concepts to your child(ren).

- **"I'm not a fan of liturgy and meaningless repetition"**– Some are averse to any kind of formulaic worship, responsive readings, prayers that are written out ahead of time and read vs. those that are spontaneous and informal, etc. Often

---

[363] Dictionary.com

Matthew 6:7 is pointed to where Jesus said, "And when you are praying, do not use meaningless repetition as the Gentiles do, for they suppose that they will be heard for their many words."[364] But Jesus' issue here is not repetition[365] as much as it is "showy" repetition or repetition that is disconnected from a heart for God. In other words, Jesus' command is more a reflection of God's words in Isaiah: "These people say they are mine. They honor me with their lips, but their hearts are far from me…"[366] Catechesis and memorized prayers like The Lord's Prayer or memorized creeds like The Apostle's Creed are not "meaningless repetition" if the heart is engaged. And let's be honest, whether we prefer formal worship, informal worship, or some mix of the two, we'll constantly have to deal with our wandering hearts. Whether worshiping publicly or privately, we'll never outgrow the need to have our hearts called back to God's ancient paths.

- **"Memorization makes me sweaty"**—A friend's wife had a young grade-schooler who had a hard time helping out or doing his work. When asked why, in his characteristic whiney lisp, he'd say, "I can't, Mrs. Irwin, it makes me sweaty." Yes, he was serious and that's what made his response so hilarious. It's a classic line that's been a joke around our house for years. I often tell my daughter when she asks me to move her car or do the dishes that I can't because it makes me sweaty. This certainly applies to memorizing something like a catechism or learning Spanish. If we find memorization valuable, however, we'll push through the sweatiness and do hard things![367]

---

[364] NASB.
[365] The Psalms are full of repetition. See especially Psalm 136.
[366] 29:13a, NLT.
[367] In reading this section, one friend noted that "ADHD can make memorization extremely difficult for some children. In these instances, if parents want to make memorization a positive experience, they will likely need to get creative with incentivizing or the physical way memorization is done. For example, a lot of kids with ADHD do much better studying when in motion, that is, while doing something."

- **"Change happens at the level of desire, not knowledge"**— Individuals like Jamie Smith in his book *Desiring the Kingdom* have made the case that true, transformative change happens primarily at the level of desire, not knowledge. In other words, you don't start the fire of faith by memorizing facts or verses. Many (myself included), however, although agreeing strongly with Smith, see catechesis as laying "kindling and logs in the fireplace, so that when the Holy Spirit ignites your child's heart, there will be a steady, mature blaze."[368]

- **"I'd rather focus on heart than head, the practical rather than the intellectual"**—Sometimes, especially in reformed circles, there is a tendency to elevate head knowledge— including catechesis—over topics like relationships, healthy marriage, vocation, emotional health, or a heart for God. That's why for some "attention to doctrine is sometimes actually avoided, lest it induce contention and cold-heartedness and thereby diminish devotional ardor."[369] But as J.I. Packer pointed out, "rote memorization of catechisms without a lively, interactive relationship of didactic exchange between catechist and catechumens was not... the Reformers' intent..."[370] Their aim was to change the heart through habit and repetition, but if catechesis doesn't happen through "lively, interactive" exchanges in the context of loving relationships, familiarity breeds contempt. In these instances, what is memorized will be like an empty train that no longer delivers. It just clatters along but no one pays attention to it anymore. Undeniably, much harm has been done to the reputation of good catechisms by their association with rigid, curmudgeonly proponents.

- **"I'm concerned about heart, not brand"**—Related to the above, some push back on catechesis because their thought is,

---

[368] *The New City Catechism: 52 Questions for Our Hearts and Minds* (Wheaton, IL: Crossways, 2017), 8.
[369] J.I. Packer and Gary Parrett, *Grounded in the Gospel: Building Believers the Old – Fashioned Way* (Grand Rapids, MI: Baker, 2010), 17.
[370] Ibid., 65.

"My goal is to pass on a heart for God, not indoctrinate my kids into a particular sect of Christianity (i.e. Catholic, Reformed, non-Reformed, etc.)." Given that our journeys are all different (for example, we may have had a bad experience with a certain church or denomination), I sympathize with this view. If this is your position, my only advice is to make sure you're intentional about whatever you do. For example, if you're not comfortable with formal catechesis, follow the example of Job who regularly prayed for his kid's hearts or Jesus who successfully resisted the temptations of the devil through skilled use of memorized Scripture.[371]

- **"Scripture is better"**—The idea here is that if you're going to take the time to memorize something, why not just memorize Scripture? As Deuteronomy 11:18 says, "You shall put these words of mine in your heart and soul..."[372] Or as Psalm 119:11 teaches, "I have stored up your word in my heart that I might not sin against you."[373] Again, how did Jesus himself resist temptation and defeat Satan? It was through his clearly internalized use of memorized Scripture.

I grew up from the fourth grade on in a Christian school environment. During most of that time, my classmates and I were required to learn three verses a week and one chapter per month. Honestly, it wasn't too hard because we repeated the three verses out loud several times a day. We did the same with the chapter of Scripture once a day as a group (e.g. Psalm 1, 23, the Beatitudes, etc.). All the memorization was in the King James Version (KJV). Over the course of my life, I'm amazed at how many times scripture stored in my heart has benefited me, and how much I still recall. Isaiah 55:11 says that God's word will not return void—that is, empty or with no effect. In other words, it will accomplish what God wants it to. But this positive affirmation about the power of God's word should

---

[371] See Matthew 4:1-11.
[372] NRSV.
[373] ESV.

172

not be used to disparage the value of classic catechisms as valuable tools that supplement Scripture in passing on the essentials of the Christian faith.

A Personal Confession and Some Guidance

As a pastor and intentional father, I certainly passed a lot of Christian content on to my children, but, especially during certain seasons, I struggled to do this as part of a daily routine. What I did do, however—together with Pam—was prioritize making a heart-to-heart connection, sharing stories of God's faithfulness, and passing on a heart for God. As we discussed earlier, research shows that *the* most important thing in passing on faith is to prioritize warm, accepting, safe, and enjoyable relationships.[374] Much of my kids' learning came through simple informal conversations "along the way," more than formal catechesis or devotional time. Looking back, I think this was the right call. As I've previously shared, significant things often happen at insignificant moments. The trick then (besides just making it through some days!) is to prioritize plenty of quality time with your children; the kind that includes lots of hugs and fun—making as much space as possible for both spontaneous and intentional conversations.

How do we do even more of this in our already busy lives? The ministry Axis gives this sage advice:

> When you have downtime, talk; when you're on the go, talk. Whatever else you're doing, build conversation into it. It almost sounds too simple, but Deuteronomy 6 says that this is how we pass on the legacy of faith to the next generation.

And here are a few resources that can help strengthen both your formal and informal spiritual conversations with your kids:

- The Ten Commandments, The Beatitudes, or The Lord's Prayer

---

[374] Prioritizing "warm, accepting, safe, and enjoyable relationships" is also in sync with one of Malachi's characteristics of the "good life" from chapter five: "to be secure in the love of God—so secure and healed internally that we live with a carefree playfulness…"

- The Apostles Creed, The Heidelberg Catechism, The Westminster Shorter Catechism (WSC), or the New City Catechism.[375] Check out at least what is often referred to as Heidelberg #1, the first question in the Heidelberg Catechism, and the first question of the WSC.
- *Creeds, Confessions, and Catechisms: A Reader's Edition* compiled by Chad Van Dixhoorn– this is a great "one-stop-shop" and a way to introduce yourself to some of the greatest statements of Christian faith.
- *The Jesus Story Bible: Every Story Whispers His Name* by Sally Lloyd-Jones (ages 2-6)
- *Children of God Storybook Bible* by Archbishop Desmond Tutu (ages 4-7)
- *Leading Little Ones* to God by Marian Schoolland (ages 4-10)
- *The Biggest Bible Story Book*– written by Kevin DeYoung and illustrated by Don Clark (ages 6-11)
- *The Adventure Bible* from Zondervan (ages 7-11)
- *Training Hearts, Teaching Minds: Family Devotions Based on the Shorter Catechism* by Star Meade (11- adult)
- *Comforting Hearts, Teaching Minds: Family Devotions Based on the Heidelberg Catechism* (11-adult)
- *The Apostle's Creed for All God's Children*- text by Ben Myers and Art by Natasha Kennedy (has a coloring book that can be ordered too)
- *Be Thou My Vision: A Liturgy for Daily Worship* compiled by Johnathan Gibson

---

[375] The *New City Catechism* is informed by six of the classics, especially the Heidelberg, and has a free app with some great features.

CHAPTER TEN: ALL "I"S ON HERO-DADS PART 2

Hero-dads are aware of their *inadequacy* to provide all that their kid(s) need.

It was the morning after my oldest son's wedding and I was lost in thought. Just the night before, at the glorious end of a full day of celebration, Pam and I had watched as he, his beautiful bride, and many friends danced with all their hearts to Coldplay's "Sky Full of Stars." Standing there watching their joy and knowing what marriage signifies was one of the best moments of our lives. Now we were riding in the car, returning serving equipment to the caterers, and I was suddenly overcome with tears of painful emotion. Pam asked me what was wrong. As I searched my soul for the answer, I finally said, "I just hope we gave him our best. I know I failed him at times, but I hope we gave him what he needed."

Few questions loom larger for good parents than, "How do I give my kid(s) my best and what they will need to succeed?" And we defined success earlier in the book as raising kids who are wise, self-aware, empathetic, culturally literate, pure, and God-fearing; who have their vocational direction and self-worth rooted in the cross; who enjoy relationships and are prepared for healthy marriage (whether they'll marry or not); who care about beauty, justice, and—to the extent they have the capacity—are able to make a positive impact on their world.

The first part of our two-part question above, "How do *I*," reminds us that we can only give what we have. There are no perfect parents, and even the best parents fail, wound, and pass on baggage to their kids. This thought grips us at times and can cause us to be hesitant, but understanding our profound need for grace helps us come to terms with our deficiencies. The answer to the second part of the question, "*What* they will need to succeed,"—must be supplied by God in a variety of ways—not just through us. Although our hearts are to give our best, hero-dads are profoundly aware that we don't have everything they need.

I've had times of financial hardship and unemployment where I lacked money for tuition, class trips, transportation, and other things my kids required for high school and college. In one instance, God prompted two single friends to pay for my children's transition to a private Christian school (providentially, that school also turned out to be where all three met their spouses!). During my kids' college years, an aunt and uncle unexpectedly gave $20,000 and a car to two of our kids when I was going through a bumpy job change. God using others to fill in for our lack in these times was both severely humbling and faith-building. Parenting will regularly put us in situations where what we have to give is not enough. But here's the comfort: "The heart of man plans his way, but the Lord establishes his steps."[376] Giving our kids all that they need is definitely a bigger task than we can handle, but gratefully, God has our backs!

Hero-dads avoid *isolation.*

"I knew he loved me… but he would lock himself away."

I've heard many versions of this over the years from adult children who've had dads that were physically present but emotionally absent, and it's a real problem. Batman may do some of his best work in a cave, but hero-dads need to think through the healthy and unhealthy parts of isolation—including our legitimate need for solitude, quietness, and rest—so we don't hurt our families. This can be tough, as we all have different personalities and have been influenced more than we know by the example of our parents and others, including our favorite musicians, sports figures, actors, authors, and other cultural celebrities.

My journey toward manhood was full of loner-types like Robert

---

[376] Proverbs 16:9.

Redford in *Jeremiah Johnson*, Sylvester Stallone as Rambo, or Chuck Norris as *Lonewolf McQuade*. Even as a child, I remember reading a biography about Daniel Boone and resonating with his mother's observation about why he could spend days alone in the woods: "I think thee loves the quiet…" At fifteen, given my love for solitude and the outdoors, I wanted to be a forest ranger but eventually was dissuaded from this vocational direction, partly through a sermon my pastor preached on how God's will always involves people. My thinking at the time was that since I didn't enjoy lengthy interactions with people, I might be misguided in my vocational interest. In other words, if God's will always involved people, maybe I needed to lean into professions where people were more front and center. Although I now disagree with these youthful conclusions,[377] I'm still grateful for the role this sermon played in steering me toward all God has planned for me.[378]

Over time, I learned I was an introvert—someone who was energized by time alone and quiet. After learning this, one of my favorite books became *Quiet: The Power of Introverts in a World that Can't Stop Talking* by Susan Cain. Cain helped me understand that "there is a place in God's kingdom for sensitive, reflective types. It's not easy to claim but it's there."[379] She has also helped me understand that just as "it can be hard for extroverts to understand how badly introverts need to recharge at the end of the day…, it is also hard for introverts to understand how hurtful their silence can be."[380] Sadly, I haven't always gotten that right.

I love music and have pretty eclectic tastes. I especially love introspective melodies[381] that are perfectly matched with honest lyrics that express the good, the bad, and the ugly of the human condition. I agree with Bernie Taupin and Elton John that sometimes "sad songs

---

[377] I heard little in church those days about a more expansive view of what it means to seek God's kingdom here and now, or from passages like Rom. 8:19-23 that clearly teach creation-care and how God's will also involves nature. For more on this, see *Simply Christian* or *Surprised by Hope* by N.T. Wright.

[378] See Psalm 37:23 and Ephesians 2:10.

[379] Susan Cain, *Quiet: The Power of Introverts in a World that Can't Stop Talking* (New York: Broadway Paperbacks, 2013),67.

[380] Ibid., 228.

[381] Regina Spektor, Jon Foreman, and Gordon Lightfoot are a few examples.

177

say so much." But in certain past melancholy or dark moods, although certain "sad songs" soothed my soul, they weren't the remedy I needed. Sometimes they exacerbated my depression when I needed to choose joy. Or sometimes they kept me marinating in loneliness when I needed community. To be more specific, basking too long in certain music kept me from prayer, a much-needed conversation with Pam, or was a precursor to destructive habits like eating poorly and overeating, or viewing porn.

Interestingly, musician Gordon Lightfoot's journey toward addiction began with using alcohol to deal with the stress in his first marriage. His biographer notes, "when things got complicated with Brita, alcohol gave him an easy way to forget his problems—if only for a while. 'It made me feel better,' he says, 'and if I felt better, I could work better.'"[382]

Again, I can relate and in addressing my own unhealthy withdrawal and stress-avoidance, here's the verse that's helped me more than any other see that my proclivity to isolate is often a selfish and foolish choice: "Whoever isolates himself seeks his own desire; he breaks out against all sound judgment." (Prov. 18:1, ESV) As the German pastor, Dietrich Bonhoeffer, wrote, "Man's entire spirituality is interwoven with sociality."[383] Said differently, our spiritually and growth cannot take place apart from socializing with others; we need community to grow. In fact, if you think about it, even the fruit of our spirituality and growth can only be expressed in community. So how do we respond to stress, and get the solitude, quietness, and rest we need in ways that help rather than hurt our families?

Getting the Rest We Need Including Time Alone with God
Even extraverts need regular times of solitude to stay spiritually healthy. Ian Marcus Corbin, philosopher and research fellow at Harvard Medical School, reminds us:

Befriending oneself is a prerequisite for becoming a true friend

---

[382] Nicholas Jennings, *Lightfoot* (Viking, 2017), 91.
[383] Dietrich Bonhoeffer, *The Communion of Saints*, trans. Ronald G. Smith et al (New York: Harper & Row, 1962). 48.

to others. We do this by sitting quietly alone, coming to terms with who and what we are, forging some order out of the riot of thoughts, fears and desires that rages in our heads. [Unfortunately] ...now our various screens and speakers furnish ever-present mental and emotional stimulation, which displace the work of self-confrontation.[384]

In seeking God's heart regarding a healthy work-life balance, I've had to wrestle with the value of what some traditions call a "quiet time," or "devotions." Although I've left the legalism of the "have you done your *Quiet Time Diary* today?" of my youth,[385] this quote by George Mueller (1805-1898), the great man of prayer, has helped restore my faith in a regular time of Bible reading and prayer:[386]

> I saw more clearly than ever, that the first and primary business to which I ought to attend every day was, to have my soul happy in the Lord. The first thing to be concerned about was not, how much I might serve the Lord; how I might glorify the Lord; but how I might get my soul into a happy state, and how my inner man may be nourished... I saw that the most important thing I had to do was to give myself to the reading of the Word of God and to meditation on it.[387]

Mueller's perspective illustrates well the truth of Romans 15:4: "Such things were written in the Scriptures long ago to teach us. And the Scriptures give us hope and encouragement as we wait patiently for God's promises to be fulfilled." (NLT, emphasis mine)

Besides the spiritual refreshment that can come from personal

---

[384] https://www.washingtonpost.com/opinions/2021/01/22/technology-covid-pandemic-friendship/
[385] The *Quiet Time (QT) Diary* was a practical resource from Word of Life that was slavishly implemented in the "rules without relationship" religious culture of my childhood. In that context, if you had your daily QT, you got spiritual brownie points and were part of the spiritual elite.
[386] George Muller, Director of the Ashley Down orphanage in Bristol, England, spent his life caring for more than 10,000 orphans.
[387] Autobiography of George Mueller, comp. Fred Bergen (London: J. Nisbet, 1906), 152-154.

devotions and worship with friends at church,[388] here are nine other types of rest to consider:

- "Time away
- Permission to not be helpful
- Something 'unproductive'
- Connection to art and nature
- Solitude to recharge
- A break from responsibility
- Stillness to decompress
- Safe space
- Alone time at home"[389]

🔥 Pause here to reflect and identify one or two of the above that you need the most of right now. How might you build more of these into your life in the next week, month, or year? If these questions are not easily answered, consider asking a friend for their honest perspective and counsel. If you're married, consider asking your spouse what she might need and how you might help her.

Hero-dads care about and grow in competence to *influence*.

Dads who come out of their caves learn to care about their communities. They are like the dad connected to the virtuous woman in Prov. 31: "Her husband is known in the gates when he sits among the elders of the land" (23, ESV). To sit by the city gates was to sit among the civic leaders: listening, discussing problems, and making decisions that impacted the community. Good dads care about people and influencing the world—especially the world of their children, grandchildren, and great-grandchildren, and others in their sphere of influence. They listen, read, and learn not just for personal enrichment and enjoyment, but because they genuinely love others and show that love by their actions.

Although there are other ways to grow in competence to

---

[388] Hebrews 10:24-25.
[389] https://ninetypes.co/blog/nine-types-of-rest

influence, it has been my conviction over the years that cultivating a love for reading in ourselves and others will help us and them become the type of people others look to for leadership. This is why, in September 2009, I wrote this letter to my kids:

Dear Emily, Matthew, and Tim,

I know it may seem that I harp on you more often than you would like about not reading enough—watching too much TV or spending hours playing video games. I also know you sometimes roll your eyes (or are tempted to ☺) and seek to avoid that predictable question: "What have you been reading lately?" I have told you before that my heart is not to shame you or make you feel uncomfortable. It is also not to reinforce stereotypes I sometimes deserve of being too rigid, not able to relax, or sounding like a broken record. I am learning to "chill-lax" more—a word I learned from your friends—but there are important reasons why I want you to learn to love reading:

1. Reading quiets your heart and stills your soul. We live in a busy, crazy world. Much of the stress and demands on our time we have little control over. If you can get into a habit of daily or weekly non-homework reading, you will find your mind gets clearer and your soul re-centered. Find a quiet place. Stop texting for a bit—turn off your cell phone and read something you are interested in and enjoy. Read fun stuff like the *Harry Potter* series, *The Hardy Boys* or *Nancy Drew*, *Sherlock Holmes*, etc. These books (and other books like them) take you on fascinating journeys and help you relax. Again, set aside time each day or week. You know your schedule best.

2. Reading will help you be a strong person who others look to for leadership. Reading will help you be a better conversationalist, counselor, and writer. While it is true that not every reader is a leader, every leader is a reader. Reading keeps your mind sharp. It expands your world and thinking. It makes you feel smarter and grows your imagination. It makes you a person of breadth—someone who is balanced, well-rounded, curious, culturally-literate, intelligent, interesting, and wise—all qualities that make you a better person, friend, leader, and citizen of our great country.

3. Reading can help you be humbler. Pride, arrogance, and snobbery are some of the most unattractive qualities one can have. Few things are more sickening, however, than when pride is combined with ignorance and apathy. "I'm ignorant and proud of it!" Or, "I'm ignorant and don't give a rat's rip." These attitudes almost always go with a distaste for reading and a love of TV. Read fun stuff and fiction, but also read non-fiction. Reading great books—classics and those that have had staying power (e.g. have been around for more than thirty years)—will help you learn that the times you are living in are not the most important times. Anything older than you may seem lame, but the truth is that you are standing on the shoulders of thousands of great men and women who have gone before you. You get to know these folks primarily through books. Don't be guilty of what the great writer, C.S. Lewis, called "chronological snobbery"—that is, thinking that the times and culture you live in are the most important.

In closing, here is a quote I came across recently that speaks well to the points above: "Books enlarge us by giving direct access to experiences not our own. In order for this to work, however, we need a certain type of silence, an ability to filter out the noise. Such a state is increasingly elusive in our over-networked culture, in which every rumor and mundanity is blogged and tweeted. Today, it seems it is not contemplation we seek but an odd sort of distraction masquerading as being in the know. Why? Because of the illusion that illumination is based on speed, that it is more important to react than to think, that we live in a culture in which something is attached to every bit of time."[390]

I love you all very much and pray that you will be men, Tim

---

[390] *Los Angeles Times* book reviewer David L. Ulin [latimes.com, 8/9/09].

and Matt, and a woman, Emily, of great character, humility, and serenity who lead and serve—people whose lives are strong enough to enrich others, due in part because you learned to love reading. 　　　　　　　　　- Dad

Since that time, I've seen the need to add these two clarifications and corrections to what I wrote above:

- The ultimate goal is not reading itself but growing individuals who can explain what they've learned. Most of us take our ability to read for granted; however, "only 12% of the people in the world could read and write in 1820,"[391] and before that, literacy rates were even worse. That fact, combined with deeper reflection on Hebrews 5:11–14, has helped correct my thinking:

> We have much to say about this, but it is hard to make it clear to you because you no longer try to understand. In fact, though by this time you ought to be teachers, you need someone to teach you the elementary truths of God's word all over again. You need milk, not solid food! Anyone who lives on milk, being still an infant, is not acquainted with the teaching about righteousness. But solid food is for the mature, who by constant use have trained themselves to distinguish good from evil.[392]

The ability to explain what one has learned is implied in the phrase "by this time you ought to be teachers." In other words, it is *the ability to explain* that is key here, not the mastery of some study Bible or even the ability to read. This is really important as—if we don't understand it—we risk shaming some who, although they may desire to learn and grow, don't enjoy reading as their preferred way of learning.

- Audiobooks, video talks, and great podcasts are often better

---

[391] https://ourworldindata.org/literacy .
[392] Hebrews 5:11-14, NIV.

options for busy people or more auditory learners. In fact, given the rapidity of change in our world, some podcasts often offer a fresher, more timely perspective on certain topics. A book may effectively freeze a thought on a page but sometimes the conversation is too important to wait for the ice to form. This is part of living in the real world—outside our caves—where often we have to build the plane while flying it.

Hero-dads seek to *imitate* the wisdom and love of the Triune God.

On this last "I," I want to share a few powerful insights that we can learn about being an irreplaceable dad from each of the three persons of the Trinity.

First and foundationally, hero-dads imitate God, the ultimate father, who cares about the needs of his children; gives them good gifts; and will love them forever. Here's what the bible tells us about God the Father:

- "And this same God who takes care of me will supply all your needs from his glorious riches, which have been given to us in Christ Jesus" (Phil 4:19, NLT).

- "You parents—if your children ask for a loaf of bread, do you give them a stone instead? Or if they ask for a fish, do you give them a snake? Of course not! So if you sinful people know how to give good gifts to your children, how much more will your heavenly Father give good gifts to those who ask him (Matt 7:9–11, NLT).

- "Every good and perfect gift is from above, coming down from the Father of the heavenly lights, who does not change like shifting shadows" (James 1:17, NIV).

- "And I am convinced that nothing can ever separate us from God's love. Neither death nor life, neither angels nor demons, neither our fears for today nor our worries about tomorrow—not even the powers of hell can separate us from God's love. No power in the sky above or in the earth below—indeed, nothing in all creation will ever be able to separate us from the

184

love of God that is revealed in Christ Jesus our Lord" (Rom 8:38–39, NLT).

Turning our attention to the Father's relationship with the Son, we see the principle of affirmation before temptation.[393] This can be seen clearly in Mark 1:9–13:

> At that time Jesus came from Nazareth in Galilee and was baptized by John in the Jordan. Just as Jesus was coming up out of the water, he saw heaven being torn open and the Spirit descending on him like a dove. And a voice came from heaven: "You are my Son, whom I love; with you I am well pleased." At once the Spirit sent him out into the wilderness, and he was in the wilderness forty days, being tempted by Satan. He was with the wild animals, and angels attended him.[394]

God's example here demonstrates that as human fathers, we must lavish unconditional love, blessing, and affirmation on our kids often and early so when temptation comes, they will be fortified and resilient.

The popularity of DNA test kits, where individuals seek to discover more about their ancestors; find unknown relatives; and better discern those things that are unique and special about them give strong evidence of the hunger for affirmation and a better sense of identity in our culture.

As Sam Allberry observed:

> In earlier times… a lot of our evangelism began in Gen 3. We have to begin in Genesis 1. We don't live in a moralistic age where we need to prove people to be sinners. We live in an anxious age where we need to prove to people that they're worth something.[395]

This, I believe, is *the primary place* fathers can leave a unique and

---

[393] This insight is mentioned in the foreword and was shared with me several years ago by Roland Warren, former President of the National Fatherhood Initiative.
[394] NIV.
[395] https://www.youtube.com/watch?v=G-E4GS7dqJc

irreplaceable legacy because as Professor Carolyn Custis James says, "Most agree that a father's voice speaks… with unequaled significance. A father's affirmation can outweigh anyone else's criticism."[396] In the same way, the father's voice can inflict wounds that last a lifetime. We saw this in the example of my own father when at 82 his father's unloving and shaming "Boy, you sure know how to lose the good ones, don't you?!" still carried power. We also see this in how Julian Lennon still winces when he recalls what his father, the late John Lennon of *The Beatles,* said about him on one occasion:

> I've never really wanted to know the truth about how Dad was with me…There was some very negative stuff… like when he said I'd come out of a whiskey bottle on a Saturday night. Stuff like that. You think, where's the love in that? Paul [McCartney] and I used to hang about quite a bit … more than Dad and I did. We had a great friendship going, and there seems to be far more pictures of me and Paul playing together at that age than there are pictures of me and my dad.[397]

Second, hero-dads imitate Jesus, the Son of God, who served others out of a profound sense of self-awareness. We learn this in the preface to the most famous passage about Christian servanthood, where Jesus washes the disciples' feet:

> Jesus, knowing that the Father had given all things into his hands, and that he had come from God and was going back to God, rose from supper [to serve]…[398]

We learn from this classic text that Jesus' service flowed out of a deep knowing of himself (self-awareness). At this point in his ministry,

---

[396] Carolyn Custis James, *Malestrom* (Grand Rapids: Zondervan, 2015), 79.
[397] https://www.washingtonpost.com/news/morning-mix/wp/2015/04/02/how-cynthia-lennons-doomed-marriage-to-john-lennon-inspired-hey-jude/
[398] John 13:1 (ESV).

he did not need to "search for significance;"[399] his identity was intact. He knew:

- who he was ("the Father had given all things into his hands"),
- where he had come from ("he had come from God"), and
- where he was going (he was "going back to God").

Being a hero-dad is certainly Christian service of the highest caliber, and Jesus' example here reminds us that the best and healthiest service flows out of a deep spiritual awareness of who we are, where we've come from, and where we're going. Like Simba, mentioned in chapter five, we find our way back to "Pride Rock" by first remembering we have an identity rooted in the Father's love.

This brings us to our third and final insight about how hero-dads imitate the Holy Spirit. When Jesus—the ultimate servant—finished his mission on earth and ascended to heaven, he left us with a mission and the presence of the Holy Spirit: "And I will ask the Father, and He will give you another Helper (Comforter, Advocate, Intercessor—Counselor, Strengthener), to be with you forever."[400]

The Holy Spirit's role is especially meaningful to me these days. Although I'm still a father, I'm now an empty-nester and grandparent, too. Like the Holy Spirit, my role is less visible, but I'm still an unseen influence in the larger life of my family. That is, I'm still very much a "helper." Together with Pam, I have my kids' backs. As a dedicated comforter and counselor, my prayer is that I can help my children and grandchildren "carry the fire," passing on the gift of friendship with God that can be with them forever.

Let's quickly review the "seven "I" statements:

- Hero-dads are *interconnected* with their kid's hearts and always in prayer for them.
- Hero-dads are *involved* in the daily routine of their kid's lives.
- Hero-dads are *intentional* about passing on their faith.
- Hero-dads are aware of their *inadequacy* to provide all that their kid(s) need.

---

[399] I am thinking here of the book and associated small group study called *The Search for Significance* by Robert S. McGee, which Billy Graham said "should be read by every Christian."
[400] John 14:16, Amplified.

- Hero-dads avoid *isolation.*
- Hero-dads care about and grow in competence to *influence.*
- Hero-dads seek to *imitate* the wisdom and love of the Triune God.

In conclusion, I want to add one final "I" statement:

Hero-dads stand against the *intimidation* of the evil one.

Although being a hero-dad is an exhilarating adventure, it's also a battle that involves spiritual warfare. We have an enemy, Satan, and there's nothing he hates more than God's image in us; what's more, he will oppose our efforts to polish that image in others—especially our kids. Yet, "Greater is he that is in you than he that is in the world."[401] This calls for courage and trust in the One who is greater as sometimes being a hero dad will bring us close to the gates of hell.

I experienced this in a chilling way one Saturday during a rebellious season that my then thirteen-year-old son Timothy was going through. We were dealing with deceit, an "I don't care" attitude, and half-hearted obedience; but what was even more concerning was the direction his heart seemed to be heading. After disciplining him that afternoon, I sent him up to his room. I was lying down in the living room, drained from our intense verbal interaction and dead tired from working a long week. I knew, however, that after several hours I needed to follow-up and check on him. "That's what good parents do," I reminded myself wearily.

We were alone in the house, and I went upstairs and found him asleep on the floor of his closet. I rustled him out of his slumber, and he suddenly spoke to me in a demonic-like voice. I felt terror but did not know how to process what was happening. It was surreal and I was afraid for my son; however, I was also physically and emotionally empty and exhausted. All I could think to do was pray, and so I got down with him on the floor and just cried out to God for his heart and soul. When I finished, he seemed to be OK and his spirit lighter, as if a weight had been lifted. I told him he needed to go take a walk in the

---

[401] 1 John 4:4b.

woods and do some business with God. He left, came back a couple hours later, and has never been the same since.[402]

We began the last chapter by thinking about a human father, Johan, doing his best to protect his daughter Jenna from a grizzly. And we conclude this one by returning once again to the all-powerful God who will not stand passively by while his kids are ravaged or exploited by evil. Rather, He is involved, responsible, and committed to His people—the spiritual "Israel."[403] He will not let His Eden be destroyed.

---

[402] In discussing this memory recently with My son, Tim, he does not remember speaking with a demonic-like voice, only feeling like his neck was constricted and seeming to be thrown down. He also remembers going into the woods, praying, and having a sense of hearing Christ say that he was not theirs to take.

[403] Again, we discussed this in depth in chapter five. See also Romans 9:6 and Galatians 6:16.

CHAPTER ELEVEN: BUILDING STRENGTH IN OUR FAMILIES

"I don't know if any of you have seen Ken Burns' film *Baseball*. In typical Burns' fashion, the documentary was well done and, along with a compelling play-by-play on the history of the game, it provides an excellent window into the lives and personalities of key players, such as Babe Ruth.

In Ruth's case, I really first became aware of him as a boy in the 1970s when Hank Aaron broke his record and I saw an old black and white movie about him. Oh, and that candy bar named after him is pretty tasty—it has always been one of my mom's and my favorites!

Ruth was born in Baltimore, and he had a very rough childhood. His father ran a local bar in town and had a difficult time parenting Ruth. Ruth was rambunctious and out of control and it's reported that his dad beat him mercilessly. When the beatings didn't work, his dad declared him to be 'incorrigible' and shipped 7-year-old Ruth off to reform school.

This was a very difficult time for Ruth because his family almost never visited him. In fact, it's reported that he told a fellow schoolmate that he was 'too big and too ugly' for anyone to visit him. The only bright spot for him at reform school was that he discovered that he could really play baseball and, at 19-years-old, the Baltimore Orioles signed him. Longing for a family that he never really had, he married shortly after this and had a daughter.

However, after he was traded to the Yankees and his fame began to grow dramatically, he moved his wife and young daughter to a farm in Massachusetts and began living in an expensive apartment in one of

New York City's finest hotels. He also began living a life of self-indulgence, drinking heavily, partying constantly, and frequenting prostitutes. He even took a long-time mistress. He was rarely home due to the long baseball season. Eventually, his behavior contributed to his wife's nervous breakdown. When this happened, Ruth took a bit of a '7th inning stretch' to reflect, but he soon returned to 'playing' his life as usual.

It's a bit ironic that a man who exhibited so much discipline at the plate chose to 'strike out' so consistently at home.

In 1923, the Yankees moved from the Polo Grounds to the newly built Yankee Stadium. In the first game at the new park, Ruth hit a well-timed home run and this caused the stadium to be forever dubbed 'The House that Ruth Built.' I suppose that this is very accurate given the success of the Yankees franchise. But I must admit that for me Ruth's legacy is more of a foul ball than a homerun given what I learned about *the home that he failed to build* for his wife and young child."[404]

Whether your family legacy is strong or laced with failure, Ruth's story raises some important questions:

- What kind of house are you building?
- What priorities does it reflect?
- What or whom are you dependent on as you build it?

Whether you're a seasoned parent, grandparent, or just getting started, Psalm 127, which we'll unpack in this chapter, is just what you need to answer these questions well.

> Unless the Lord builds the house,
> those who build it labor in vain.
> Unless the Lord guards the city,
> the guard keeps watch in vain.
> It is in vain that you rise up early
> and go late to rest,

---

[404] This opening illustration has been significantly edited for my purposes and is used with permission from the author. It was originally from Roland C. Warren's "The House that Ruth Didn't Build" published in National Fatherhood Initiative's Father Factor Blog, October 1, 2010.

eating the bread of anxious toil,
for he gives sleep to his beloved.

Sons are indeed a heritage from the Lord,
the fruit of the womb a reward.
Like arrows in the hand of a warrior
are the sons of one's youth.
Happy is the man who has
his quiver full of them.
He shall not be put to shame
when he speaks with his enemies in the gate.[405]

Psalm 127 is the first in a trilogy of wisdom poems; Psalms 127, 128, and 133. This trilogy is part of a larger collection of "pilgrimage psalms" or "Songs of Ascent" (120–134) that were written for the nation of Israel's "going up" (*ascending* a hill or mountain) to Jerusalem for festivals. For example, 133 is about the joyful arrival at one of their celebration events.

In what follows, I want to take a look at the three main sections of this epic family psalm, in a way that fortifies you with insight and encouragement for building a strong legacy.

Our Best Efforts are Useless Without God's Blessing

Unless the Lord builds the house,
those who build it labor in vain.
Unless the Lord guards the city,
the guard keeps watch in vain. (Psalm 127:1, NRSV)

The verse is striking and, given the events of even the last few years, we all know well that you never know what you are going to wake up to, do you?

For a builder or a sentinel of an ancient city, there was always the threat of hostile invasion. There could be attacks, drought, pestilence, disease, a raging fire, or a thousand other incidents. And to help blow

---

405 Psalm 127, NRSV.

the dust off this ancient Near Eastern psalm, let's look at a few examples of how our world is more similar to the ancient Near Eastern world than we might realize.

On the other side of a global pandemic, we've become painfully aware of our frailty and susceptibility to disease. My wife and I lost several friends to early versions of the COVID-19 virus and we almost lost my father.

Post 9-11, we all have a heightened sense of vulnerability to attack. In recent years, we've witnessed Russia's invasion of Ukraine. In the US, a violent insurrection at the Capital, mass shootings, and racial tension that literally burst into flames following George Floyd's murder.

Droughts of all kinds still threaten us, too. On a global scale as part of our changing climate, and personally or metaphorically as well: Many face extended periods of unemployment where our funds dry up and we are left asking things like, "If my child does excel in their studies, will I have enough to cultivate his or her gifts? Will I have enough to help get them into a good school and get a good start on life? Will I have enough for retirement? Will I be able to pay my monthly bills? Will I have enough for nursing care?"

The human condition is one of extreme vulnerability and Psalm 127:1 reminds us that somewhere between human effort and human achievement or success is the mystery of God's sovereignty. Indeed, there's a huge unknown gap that no amount of human vigilance or watchfulness can control:

- Consider the work of God: who can make straight what he has made crooked?[406]

- Many are the plans in the mind of a man, but it is the purpose of the Lord that will stand.[407]

Psalm 127:1 is a warning against the sin of presumption and trusting in our own strength. Or to put it differently, it's a wise reminder to put our ultimate trust in God alone.

Several years ago, when our family was moving from Pennsylvania to New Jersey, I had my kids memorize Isaiah 55:8-9:

---

[406] Ecclesiastes 7:13, ESV.
[407] Proverbs 19:21-ESV.

194

For my thoughts are not your thoughts, neither are your ways my ways," declares the Lord. "As the heavens are higher than the earth, so are my ways higher than your ways and my thoughts than your thoughts.[408]

I did this because I didn't want them to get discouraged if God closed a door he at first seemed to be opening. At that time, I shared with a friend what we were memorizing and he suggested I add Jeremiah 29:11:

"For I know the plans I have for you," declares the Lord, "plans to prosper you and not to harm you, plans to give you hope and a future."[409]

Why did he suggest this? Because my friend didn't want my family or me to forget the character, love, and passion of the one who is also holy, wholly other, and totally beyond us. That is, he wanted to remind us that the God who is mysterious and sovereign is also good... that God is *for* us.

And I don't want you to forget that either. Are you going through some great difficulty right now? Don't forget his character as you go through your time of struggle. We may not know why certain things—even unspeakably, horrible things—happen,[410] but we do know that Jesus himself was "a man of sorrows, acquainted with deepest grief."[411] Further, he does not want us to live in a constant state of anxiety. That's why this next part of Psalm 127 is so encouraging.

God Gives Rest to Anxious Hearts

It is in vain that you rise up early
and go late to rest,
eating the bread of anxious toil,

---

[408] NIV.
[409] NIV.
[410] Ecclesiastes 8:17.
[411] Isaiah 53:3, NLT.

for he gives sleep to his beloved. (Psalm 127:2, NRSV)

I can so relate to this verse, as I've often struggled with insomnia. It might be because I don't know how to solve a particular problem or heal a painful relationship. Or, it might just be that my mind is so full of detailed ideas or problems that I can't sleep. In other words, an exciting project might keep me up just as much as a difficult problem might.

Men especially can wonder, "Do I have what it takes to lead my family, to maintain our household, or to take us to the next level? What if I fail?" And as we get older, have less energy, or have made some mistakes, we can become risk averse. It can seem easier to stop trying rather than risk failing. Yet the only real failure in our lives is the one we learn nothing from.

Fear of failure mixed with worry about things like we mentioned in verse one—disease, attack, or drought—is a particularly nasty cocktail. As one singer-songwriter put it, "It's dust to dust, until we learn how to trust."[412] Whether we're building a house, defending a city, or earning a living, without God we're just wasting our energy. If he's not involved—if he's not the wind behind our backs—there will be no eternal value to our actions.

So, the point of Psalm 127:1-2, when taken together, is that work done independently of God is futile. It's not that people shouldn't be diligent. In fact, Psa. 128, part of the family trilogy, encourages hard work: "You shall eat the fruit of the labor of your hands; you shall be blessed, and it shall be well with you."[413] There *should* be intentionality, effort, and perseverance.

Even the book of Proverbs has a lot to say about hard work and its connection to competence. Here are just two examples:

- "Work hard and become a leader; be lazy and become a slave."[414]

---

412 This is a lyric from "Dust to Dust" by Keith Green from the album *Jesus Commands Us to Go, The Ministry Years Vol. I 1977–1979* and *Make My Life a Prayer to You: Songs of Devotion.*
413 128:2, ESV.
414 12:24, NLT.

- "Do you see a man skillful in his work? He will stand before kings; he will not stand before obscure men."[415]

Again, it's not that we shouldn't be diligent; rather, Psalm 127:2 stresses that working long days without dependence on God will ultimately be unsuccessful. Prov. 3:5–6 captures the essence of this kind of dependence well: "Trust in the Lord with all your heart and lean not on your own understanding; in all your ways acknowledge him, and he will make your paths straight."[416]

If you're having trouble sleeping (and it's not because of a crying baby or having too much caffeine the night before), I encourage you to look at anything that may be troubling you and ask: What does belief in a sovereign God look like for your situation right now? If God really is sovereign, then he's in charge and running the universe *even while you sleep*:

- "I will lie down and sleep in peace, for you alone, O Lord, make me dwell in safety."[417]
- "He tends his flock like a shepherd: He gathers the lambs in his arms and carries them close to his heart; he gently leads those that have young."[418]

What all this means for the Christian, for those of us with the cross at the center of our faith, is that we must lay down our self-sufficiency. Moreover, we must come to God, as Jesus describes in the Beatitudes, as those who are "poor in spirit;" that is, spiritually bankrupt.

Dependence (trust) and repentance really are the primary marks of following Jesus. As the old hymn says, "Nothing in my hand I bring; simply to your cross I cling."

Holocaust survivor Corrie Ten Boom once recalled a powerful insight that helped put her anxious heart in perspective:

Somebody said to me, "When I worry I go to the mirror and say to myself, 'This tremendous thing which is worrying me is

---

[415] 22:29, ESV.
[416] NIV.
[417] Psalm 4:8, NIV.
[418] Isaiah 40:11, NIV.

197

beyond a solution. It is especially too hard for Jesus Christ to handle.' After I have said that, I smile and I am ashamed."[419]

Friend, know this beyond a shadow of a doubt: Your worry and striving will not empty tomorrow of its troubles—only tonight of its rest and tomorrow of its strength.

And now for the final section of Psalm 127:

Children are God's Treasures to Change the World

Sons are indeed a heritage from the Lord,
the fruit of the womb a reward.
Like arrows in the hand of a warrior
are the sons of one's youth.
Happy is the man who has
his quiver full of them.
He shall not be put to shame
when he speaks with his enemies in the gate (Psalm 127:3-5, NRSV).

Verses 3–5 focus on another meaning of building; that is, to raise a family. Although this passage focuses more on sons as we will see, "fruit of the womb" includes both sons and daughters. The main thought is that children are not our achievement but God's gift, just like a completed house and a guarded city.[420]

In discussing the historical context of Psalm 127, Old Testament scholar Leslie Allen notes:

> The psalm concentrates upon the particular value of sons born to a man not too late in life: they would be old enough to protect their father in his declining years. If he were wrongly accused in the law court just inside the city gate, they would rally around, ensuring that he was treated justly and defending

[419] Corrie Ten Boom, "Each New Day," Christianity Today, Vol. 31, no. 13.
[420] Carson, D. A. (1994). *New Bible Commentary: 21st century edition.* Rev. ed. of: The new Bible commentary. 3rd ed. / edited by D. Guthrie, J.A. Motyer. 1970. (4th ed.) (Ps 127:1). Leicester, England; Downers Grove, Ill., USA: Inter-Varsity Press.

his interests in a way denied loners in society, such as widows and orphans. They were God's arrows against injustice within the local community.[421]

The ancient Near East scenario was akin to the classic TV western *Bonanza* or John Wayne's *The Sons of Katie Elder*. Although the world has changed much since the days of America's westward expansion, our nation's sense of masculinity still bears the imprint of towering figures like John Wayne. As one of the great Hollywood icons of the twentieth century, he was "emblematic of strong, silent manhood, of courage and honor in a world of timidity and moral indifference."[422] Gratefully, despite pervasive gender confusion in our day, our culture's shared sense of masculinity is evolving to include nurture and emotional health as part of what it means to be a healthy man and father.

Child Psychologist Michael Thompson, in his 2006 PBS documentary *Raising Cain*, took the pulse of the emotional development of boys growing up in America. He observed that boys desperately needed fathers and father-figures in their lives to show them a better model of manhood. He found that so many of our nation's boys were filled with sadness, pain, and loss. And many were trying to raise themselves in a vacuum. In a world with so many conflicting messages, they needed men to teach them life skills and how to be a man.

Thompson's research[423] showed that when these boys reached puberty, they experienced a "culture of cruelty" from their peers. Many of us know well—through personal experience or as a result of raising boys—that sixth, seventh and eighth graders can be so cruel. Thomson found that during these middle years one in four boys is bullied. Many then enter the "the culture of the streets," which is the gang version of manhood and a very distorted version at what it means to be a man. Thompson further observed that this distorted view was actually a

---

[421] Leslie Allen, *Word Biblical Commentary*, Psalm 101-150 (Waco: Word) 1983, 181.
[422] Kristen Kobes Du Mez, *Jesus and John Wayne: How White Evangelicals Corrupted a Faith and Fractured a Nation* (New York: Liveright, 2020), 105.
[423] *Raising Cain*, 2006.

"mask of masculinity," where boys "posture" themselves and get together and beat their chests. And often this includes a life full of addictions to mask deep emotional pain. And for too many of our nation's children, this leads to incarceration.

Thompson concludes his documentary by saying we need "a better understanding of the psychology of boys" and then makes these outstanding observations:

- Boys as much as girls have an emotional life.
- Boys have their own way of learning which must be accommodated in "the classroom" (whether in-person or virtual). Space will not allow going into detail here, but, on average, what Thomson was recommending was a more physical, active, and hands-on education experience. [Even today, young men are "falling behind" when it comes to higher education. The *Wall Street Journal* reports that two women will now earn a college degree for every man that completes theirs.[424] And the *New York Times* points out that the gender imbalance has existed on college campuses since the 1970s.[425]]
- Boys need to have a father or father-figure—an adult male who can model manhood and teach boys that there are many ways to be a man and that being a man means being responsible, caring and emotionally available.

Again, the last part of Psalm 127 concentrates on sons, who had the power to protect their older parents or defend the family's honor, but "fruit of the womb" includes all children, male and female alike. And "in a world where parents are called 'breeders' and people openly attack others for having multiple children as 'climate-destroyers,' it is more important than ever that we communicate that our children, at any age and at any ability level, are a blessing from the Lord."[426]

Moreover, the message of the psalm as a whole is that strong families are blessings to the places that they live. Our children—

[424] https://www.wsj.com/articles/college-university-fall-higher-education-men-women-enrollment-admissions-back-to-school
[425] https://www.nytimes.com/2021/09/09/upshot/college-admissions-men
[426] Axis' *The Culture Translator Premium* Vol. 7, Issue 20, May 14, 2022.

whether boys or girls and whether part of our biological or church family—are God's arrows. Although often a passage like this where children are arrows has been misused in militant ways, a friend recently sent me some insights she had gleaned from a pastor who reframed the issue for her. "A good archer," she said, summarizing her pastor's words, "handles their arrows with tender care, being cautious not to apply too much pressure to avoid warping, making sure the arrows have all the individual pieces necessary for a successful flight, etc. Children, like arrows, are very powerful but also delicate and prone to injuries that can result in 'missing the mark.' What characterizes a good archer then isn't just how accurate they are in shooting but how well they are caring for their arrows long before it's time to shoot."[427]

These insights about the tender care needed on the part of the archer are consistent with the vivid New Testament images of mothering and fathering that Paul uses to describe his team's pastoral ministry among the Thessalonians.[428] After noting how "we were gentle among you, like a nursing mother taking care of her own children," Paul describes the members of his team as fathers:

> You are our witnesses, and so is God, that our conduct towards you who believe was pure, right, and without fault. You know that we treated each one of you just as a father treats his own children. We *encouraged* you, we *comforted* you, and we *kept urging* you to live the kind of life that pleases God.[429]

The first two italicized verbs, *encouraged* and *comforted*, are "practically synonymous."[430] The third, "*kept urging*," has a "more authoritative nuance than the two preceding verbs."[431] "Urging" calls to mind the intentional "push to achieve" fathers often bring to the table. As someone said, "No one ever rose to low expectations." The first two verbs, however, can help us "raise the bar without lowering

---

[427] This quote was used with permission.
[428] Paul also references spiritual fathering in 1 Corinthians 4:14–15.
[429] 1 Thessalonians 2:7–12, GNT- italicized words, mine.
[430] F.F. Bruce, *Word Biblical Commentary: 1 & 2 Thessalonians* (Waco: Word Books, 1982), 36.
[431] Ibid.

the boom."[432] In other words, they remind us that our kids need that same foundation (encouragement and comfort) that we do as we lovingly push them to achieve.

Returning to Psalm 127, our children are God's arrows, cared for and raised in our "quiver," and then sent out to make a difference in the world. But that world can be a wild and scary place, and some of our neighborhoods need a lot of help. Here's a passage that's meant a lot to me over the years, reminding me that God has my back—and he's there for you too:

> The Lord will guide you continually, watering your life when you are dry and keeping you healthy, too. You will be like a well-watered garden, like an ever-flowing spring. Your children will rebuild the deserted ruins of your cities. Then you will be known as the people who rebuild their walls and cities.[433]

Remember, it's not so much about what we're building... It's what God is building through us.

♦ Prayer: Lord, thank you for this epic wisdom psalm and now please help us apply it to the definition of success we highlighted in the last chapter.

By your grace, we recommit ourselves:

- To unite our efforts to grow kids who are wise, self-aware, empathetic, culturally literate, pure, and God-fearing; who also have vocational direction and their self-worth rooted in the cross; who enjoy relationships and are prepared for healthy marriage (whether they'll marry or not); who care about beauty, justice, and—to the extent that they have the capacity—are able to make a positive impact on their world.

---

[432] I got this phrase from Frederick Buechner, although I cannot find the source. "Lower the boom" means "to harshly reprimand someone or punish him severely... The phrase was first used to mean to deliver a knockout punch in a boxing bout; however, it is an allusion to the boom on a ship, which is a spar on a mast that may be raised and lowered." (grammarist.com)
[433] Isaiah 58:11-12, NLT.

- We ask you for strength to do all this with humility, realizing that our best efforts are useless without Your blessing.
- Finally, we ask that you help us pursue quiet and untroubled hearts, knowing that you are running the universe even while we sleep.

CHAPTER TWELVE: DADS AND DAUGHTERS

On November 19, 2017, one of the most notorious murderers of the 20th century died: Charles Manson.

After the second set of murders associated with his name on August 10, 1969, one of the Manson cult-killers wrote "Helter Skelter" on the refrigerator of the house in which the murders took place. The phrase was from the Beatles' *White* album and innocently referred to a British amusement park ride. In his deranged state, Manson somehow turned a phrase about a theme park ride into a vision of a race war and murder.

Almost 20 years later, the band U2 tried to address Manson's distorted translation. In the opening track of their 1988 album *Rattle & Hum*, Bono shouts, "This is a song Charles Manson stole from the Beatles, and we're stealing it back!"

Similarly, there is an ancient wisdom poem from the Bible about an "ideal" great and godly woman that uneducated, silly, and surface interpretations have stolen from many, and we're going to steal it back!

After we reclaim this precious passage, we'll look at another lesser-known wisdom passage that showcases a great dad's attitude toward his daughters. I'll then share some reflections related to my daughter, Emily, as well as some research on why dads are so important in daughters' lives. We'll then close out the chapter by rethinking some harmful stereotypes that have relegated women to the status of sidekicks in the male adventure of life.

The Proverbs 31 Woman: An Important Corrective for Our Times

If we took a quick survey of the average person who has some familiarity with this passage, responses might include:

- "Oh no, not her again!"
- "The description of what she does makes me feel exhausted!"
- "Overwhelming..."
- "Mary Poppins"—practically perfect in every way!
- "Where are the guys? It seems that the women are working harder than the men..."

Bottomline, this passage has often been used to set unrealistic expectations which can depress women and reinforce all sorts of ugly patriarchal expectations for both men and women. Again, God's intent for this lofty picture has been stolen and we need to steal it back!

In order to do that, we need first to take a broad overview of the passage to understand three things:

1. Proverbs 31:10-31 is an elegant poem following a strict structure. In fact, it's an acrostic: each verse begins with a successive letter of the Hebrew alphabet and the author likely chose this structure for two reasons:
   - To make it easy to memorize and internalize.
   - To demonstrate that this woman's character runs the whole range of excellence. It's no accident the poem begins and ends with the woman's "excellence" (vv.10, 29-31). It's best to think of these uses of excellence as bookends, or two slices of bread that sandwich together important information.

2. The description looks a little old-school or weird because it was written 3000 years ago in an agricultural society. As such, we would expect many women to be married and have servants. Moreover, as we discussed in chapter seven, up until about 200 years ago with the Industrial Revolutions, much of the world lived this way.

3. "The Proverbs 31 woman" serves as "an ideal" for all humans to emulate, not just women. For example, Proverbs 7 gives us

the anti-"ideal" in the adulterous or bad-news woman. In a similar, but more mic drop kind-of-way, Proverbs 31 gives us the "ideal" of the virtuous or good-news-woman. Indeed, in this second case, we need to see her as the embodiment of "the full character of wisdom commended throughout the book."[434] Up until this point, the majority of concrete situations Proverbs has envisioned have involved a cast of males. Placing her at the end—as a kind of grand finale illustrating many of the major themes of the book, shows she's intended to be an example for all God's people; albeit, in a way that also promotes the "ideal" great and godly woman. Further evidence that she serves as an example for all can be seen in the use of *inclusio*. This is another literary sandwiching device where "fear of the LORD" is used in the key verse at the beginning of Proverbs (1:7). And then "fear of the LORD" is used at the end of the book (31:30) in a way where the Proverbs 31 woman is used as the quintessential illustration of that quality.

With this background, we can now get into the details of Proverbs 31's relevance to how dads view and treat their daughters. Like the Bond movies I mentioned in chapter two, I also love strong, capable female characters in books and movies, especially spy thrillers.[435] As a pastor, however, I fully acknowledge that degrading and oppressive attitudes and actions toward women have been rampant throughout history– both in entertainment and in real life. Sadly, many of these attitudes and actions have been vehemently defended by various religions and religious institutions, including Christian ones. Our irreligious "brave new world" promotes plenty of harmful views toward women, as well. Although some religious figures have twisted Proverbs 31 to create harmful, degrading standards for "godly women," the chapter understood rightly corrects these views.

Here are just a few of the vivid portraits this ancient poem paints:

- **She's intelligent and makes decisions independently.**

"She considers a field and buys it; with the fruit of her hands

---

434 *ESV Study Bible*, 1190.
435 Diana Rigg in *The Avengers* from the 60s, Angelina Jolie in *Salt*, and Jessica Chastain in *Ava* are a few examples.

she plants a vineyard." (16, ESV) "She considers a field," indicating wise judgment, and "buys it," indicating control of a substantial amount of money.

When my daughter Emily was in high school, to give her a great example of an influential, intelligent woman, I asked her to do a research paper on Dorothy Sayers. Born June 13, 1893, the only child of Reverend Henry and Helen Mary Sayers, Dorothy excelled in languages, learning French and Latin at a young age.[436] Later Sayers received a scholarship to Somerville College in Oxford. In 1915, she graduated with highest honors in modern language and was one of the first women to receive a degree from Oxford.[437] A contemporary of C.S. Lewis, she was one of the greatest minds of the 20th century. Remembered today for her mystery novels and plays, she was also a lay theologian who had a passion to excavate church doctrine layered beneath "stuffy clergy jargon," and prove Christianity to be an exciting adventure. Her example reminded my daughter, as it reminds us, that God celebrates women who work with head as well as hands; that is, with mental acuity, not just mad-baking skills.

- **She works hard and is an excellent manager.**
"She rises while it is yet night and provides food for her household and portions for her maidens… She perceives that her merchandise is profitable… and does not eat the bread of idleness." (15,18b, 27b, ESV)

At first glance, it might seem like this woman never sleeps! But this isn't the picture that's intended. Rather, she's an "unbelievably energetic and competent woman… the epitome of the hard worker."[438] She is diligent to complete her work both in the morning and in the evening, and her rejection of

---

[436] Galli and Olsen, 130.
[437] Siepmann and Baker, 870.
[438] Tremper Longman III, *Proverbs: Baker Commentary on the Old Testament* (Grand Rapids, MI: Baker, 2006), 540.

idleness embodies one of the chief virtues of Proverbs. In other words, she does not lie in bed and wait for servants to attend to her. Additionally, her planning enables everyone in the household to be productive throughout the day.

- **She engages in business outside of the home.**
"She considers a field and buys it; with the fruit of her hands she plants a vineyard... She makes linen garments and sells them; she delivers sashes to the merchant." (16, 24, ESV)

Again, the Proverbs 31 woman shows a remarkable amount of financial independence and is "engaged in real estate and agricultural ventures."[439] As I mentioned in chapter seven, Pam's and my experience as newlyweds in the church was plagued by a narrative that went something like this: "A woman shouldn't work outside the home as it's not her job to financially provide for her family. Men are the financial providers and women the nurturers. Godly women stay home with the kids." But this ancient Near eastern passage blows this false, disempowering, and guilt-inducing paradigm out of the water.

- **Her heart is for her family first, but extends to the community.**
"She opens her hand to the poor and reaches out her hands to the needy... Her husband is known in the gates... She looks well to the ways of her household...." (20. 23a, 27a, ESV)

Longman notes, "the implication is that her husband can achieve such a significant status only with the support of his wife. She takes care of the household while he works in the community. Her reputation also enhances his."[440] Her care, however, extends beyond her home and family: "She opens her hand to the poor and reaches out her hands to the needy." Working not just with head and hands, she has a compassionate heart. She is "concerned about the plight of the

---

[439] Ibid., 544.
[440] Ibid., 546.

poor and afflicted," Longman observes, and "works for the betterment not only of her own household but also for those outside of it."[441]

- **Her focus is on character and inner beauty first.** "Charm is deceitful, and beauty is vain [fleeting], but a woman who fears the LORD is to be praised" (30, ESV).

Many discussions of beauty focus on modesty and the degrading sexualization of women at younger and younger ages. Indeed, as I watched the 2021 Grammys, I had a hard time understanding how Megan Thee Stallion or Cardi B's performance honored either black lives or women. Our culture may have come a long way in addressing pay disparities and calling out abuse, but it has devolved when it comes to the celebration of internal beauty and substance.

But what does character and internal beauty look like—especially for a Christian? In truth, it is the same for sons and daughters, moms and dads. Although we have already detailed some of the Proverbs 31 woman's character, there may be no better mirror of what internal beauty and godliness looks like than the Beatitudes. Here Jesus gives his disciples eight characteristics that evidence being in a state of blessing and approval by God:[442]

- o *The poor in spirit*—this is, again, viewing yourself as spiritually bankrupt before God.
- o *Those who mourn*—this is a reminder that being godly is not being happy all the time. It's also a reminder that God sees and will one day comfort all whose current situation is intolerable or incomprehensible.
- o *The meek*—meekness is not weakness and to be meek means to not be arrogant and oppressive; that is, meek

---

441 Ibid., 541.
442 These definitions are informed by New Testament scholar R.T. France's NICNT commentary on Matthew. D.A. Carson gives France "pride of place" as his first recommendation for the book of Matthew in his *New Testament Commentary Survey, Seventh Edition* (Grand Rapids: Baker Academic, 2013).

people don't throw their weight around.

o *Those who hunger and thirst for righteousness*—this means that, in God's eyes, beautiful people are those who are eager to live as God requires.

o *The merciful*—this is a generous attitude which is willing to see things from the other's point of view, forgives, and is not quick to take offense.

o *The pure in heart*—this has to do with truthfulness or integrity, as well as having a heart that actively seeks God.

o *The peacemakers*—this refers to those who actively try to make peace by seeking reconciliation with enemies, and also bringing together those who are estranged.

o *Those who are persecuted for righteousness's sake*—this reminds us that followers of Jesus are not isolated from culture but rather engaged. As such, there are times when their counter-cultural beauty will arouse opposition.

🔥 Insight: Let's make sure we're raising our daughters (and sons!) to see through our culture's idolization of sex, external beauty, and glamour. Let's make sure we point out how so many in our day spend thousands on an unforgettable wedding but invest little in building a strong marriage. Or, how we're overly enamored by unreal reality shows. Finally, let's make sure we make it clear that the Proverbs 31 woman was known for her reverence for God, not keeping up with the Kardashians.

Job's Daughters and My "Greater Blessing"

In thinking about daughters specifically, I've found Job 42:10–17—another section in the wisdom literature of the Bible—particularly fascinating, especially verses 13–15:

So the LORD blessed Job in the second half of his life even more than in the beginning. For now he had 14,000 sheep, 6,000 camels, 1,000 teams of oxen, and 1,000 female donkeys.

211

He also gave Job seven more sons and three more daughters. He named his first daughter Jemimah, the second Keziah, and the third Keren-happuch. In all the land no women were as lovely as the daughters of Job. And their father put them into his will along with their brothers.

Job lived 140 years after that, living to see four generations of his children and grandchildren. Then he died, an old man who had lived a long, full life. (NLT)

This is the post-apocalyptic period of Job's life where he enjoys even greater blessing. The beauty of his daughter is mentioned "as a public indication of special blessing."[443] Further, each of their names represents some form of beauty or beautification.[444] As we noted above in discussing Proverbs 31:30, outward beauty is not a bad thing in and of itself, but it is a fleeting gift. As Joan Collins said, "The problem with beauty is that it's like being born rich and then becoming poor."[445]

By giving his daughters an inheritance along with their brothers, Job demonstrates he continued a policy of justice and equity in his life that went beyond the practice of the ancient world. In Israel, for example, a daughter could only inherit the property of her father if there was no male heir.[446]

My daughter, Emily, has definitely been part of the "greater blessing" of my life. Over the years, we've cultivated our relationship in both simple and special ways like going on dates. Further, as far back as I can remember, she's had a special sensitivity to God. As a child and throughout her teens, her insights, or even quietly playing a song like "Before the Throne of God Above" on the piano, called my

---

[443] Norman C. Habel, *The Book of Job* (Philadelphia: Westminster, 1985), 585.
[444] Jemimah means "turtle dove." The dove was a symbol of beauty and love; Keziah means "cassia," an aromatic plant used in perfumes; Karen-happuch means "horn of eye shadow." (Habel, 585) By the way, if your spouse is asking for baby names, I've just given you several to impress her with and here are three more: Eugene Peterson gives Job's daughters these names in *The Message*: Dove, Cinnamon, and Darkeyes!
[445] David Gibson, *Living Life Backward* (Wheaton, IL: Crossway, 2017), 20.
[446] See also Num. 27:1-8.

wandering heart back many times.

Before the throne of God above
I have a strong and perfect plea,
A great High Priest whose name is Love,
Who ever lives and pleads for me.

My name is graven on his hands,
My name is written on his heart;
I know that while in heav'n he stands
No tongue can bid me thence depart.

When Satan tempts me to despair
And tells me of the guilt within,
Upward I look and see him there
Who made an end of all my sin.

Because the sinless Savior died,
My sinful soul is counted free;
For God the Just is satisfied
To look on him and pardon me,
To look on him and pardon me.[447]

While researching for this piece, I found this March 26, 2001 journal entry: "Emily recently blessed me by saying, "Daddy, I know why Jesus has to die." I said, 'Why honey?' She said, 'He got in trouble so we wouldn't have to.' Tears came to my eyes as I realized that God is working in her heart even at this young age."

On January 28, 2007—when she was 11 and unprompted by anyone else, she gave me a little American Girl booklet (it had come as a fill-in-the-blank template with one of her dolls) titled "I Love You, Dad." Opening the first page, she shared 4 Reasons I Love You:

- "being a great dad
- talking to me about God

---

[447] Original words for "Before the Throne of God" by Charitie Lees Bancroft (1841-1892).

- being a good example
- loving me"

She had then added some special memories between us: taking walks; a lunch date at a fun place called Oliver's Twist; eating donuts in bed from our favorite bakery; sleeping with our lab puppy; and snuggling on the couch while watching *Wonder Woman* and *I Dream of Jeannie*. It concluded with, "Here is one thing you taught me that I will never forget: How to be a great Christian and grow in the Lord."

As adults, "great Christian" might seem a bit overstated—something worthy of an eye-roll. If you know Emily, however, you'd also see it as consistent with her childlike dependence on God (even into adulthood) and eagerness to pray or share an encouraging verse or song. I can't tell you how proud I was when she graduated from her Christian high school on June 13, 2014, as valedictorian and received two of the four annual awards based on Luke 2:52: an academic one for "growing in wisdom," and a Christian character one for "growing in favor with God."

Why Dads are so Important in Daughters' Lives

In the terrific 2018 HBO documentary *Jane Fonda in Five Acts*, Director Susan Lacy examines Fonda's interesting, controversial life. One clear cohesive theme that emerges is her troubled relationship with her dad. Indeed, her life is another striking example of the power of the father wound. Pop Culture Critic John Powers notes:

It [*Jane Fonda in Five Acts*] starts with her father Henry Fonda, who behind his heroic image was a tense, judgmental, emotionally remote figure—whose love his beautiful daughter spent decades chasing. Her attempts to please him by being a good girl set her life's template—her pattern of adoring a man and then letting him create an identity that she would try to live up to... Lacy's film is surely correct that Fonda's shifting identities were tied to her men...[448]

---

[448] https://www.npr.org/2018/09/21/650460554/jane-fonda-in-five-acts-reveals-the-shifting-identities-of-an-icon

Undeniably, women with father issues will adopt riskier behaviors and may do some strange things when they're looking for love. In detailing studies from 2003-2018 on sexual activity and teen pregnancy as they relate to father absence, National Fatherhood Initiative summarizes:

[L]iving in a father absent home increases the likelihood of teen pregnancy. Father absence not only leads to earlier sexual debut and risky sexual behavior, but also increases the likelihood that young men and women will be vulnerable to sexual exploitation. Attitudes about childbearing and marriage also relate to father absence, as youth with absent fathers report a lower ideal age for childbearing than do their peers..."[449]

The flip side of this is that an involved, responsible, and committed father empowers and fortifies a girl, becoming her first love and teaching her how she should be treated. The research is clear:

- A daughter's self-esteem is best predicted by her father's physical affection. In fact, the Journal of the American Medical Association found that girls with doting fathers are more assertive.[450]

- Higher quality father-daughter relationships are a protective factor against engagement in risky sexual behaviors.[451]

Rethinking Harmful Stereotypes

As a dad, one of my life's priorities has always been being an involved, responsible father; however, I certainly haven't gotten it all right. I'm still learning and growing, and sometimes still finding harmful beliefs—ones I've even taught to others—that I need to eradicate or adjust. John Eldredge's teaching on the image of God, gender, and the soul is an important example to share in this context. Although there are others who do not share my experience, on the

---

[449] *Father Facts, Eighth Edition* (National Fatherhood Initiative, 2019), 28.

[450] Meg Meeker, *Strong Fathers, Strong Daughters* (Washington, DC: Regnery, 2006), 23.

[451] Bruce J. Ellis et al., "Impact of Fathers on Risky Sexual Behavior in Daughters: A Genetically and Environmentally Controlled Sibling Study," Developmental Psychopathology 24, no. 1(February 2012): 317–332.

whole, John Eldredge's *Wild at Heart* had a positive impact on my life. Among other things, his insights on Satan's strategy are probably the most helpful thing I've read on that subject.

Eldredge's influence was so profound in my ministry that his teaching on the differences between the masculine and feminine image of God in the soul showed up in my doctoral project. Here's an excerpt from my thesis that I'm now rethinking:

> God made us male and female… to teach us important things about Himself. That being so, here's an important truth: whatever virtues are associated with being male or female, God has them all! John Eldredge, in his popular book *Wild at Heart*, tries to root his work with men in what it means to be created in the image of God. Despite deficiencies in his teaching,[452] his contribution to men's ministry has yielded fresh and important insights:
>
>> So God created man in his own image, in the image of God he created him; male and female he created them" (Gen 1:27). Now, we know God doesn't have a body, so the uniqueness can't be physical. Gender simply must be at the level of the soul, in the deep and everlasting places within us. God doesn't make generic people; he makes something very distinct—a man or a woman. In other words, there is a masculine heart and a feminine heart, which in their own ways reflect or portray to the world God's heart.[453]
>
> He goes on to describe the masculine heart as having three distinct desires which consist of:
> - an adventure to live,
> - a battle to fight, and
> - a beauty to rescue.

---

[452] For example, see Christianity Today's article "A Jesus for Real Men" by Brian O'Brian, April 18, 2008.
[453] John Eldredge, *Wild at Heart* (Nashville, TN: Thomas Nelson, 2001), 8.

He suggests that we "think of the films men love, the things they do with their free time, and especially the aspirations of little boys and see if I am not right on this." For women, he also suggests three corresponding desires:

- "a yearning to be fought for, yearned for, and pursued;
- an adventure to share—to be caught up in something greater than herself; and
- a beauty to unveil."[454]

Although there's truth in Eldredge's provocative analysis above, I've come to see that the way he dissects and differentiates the masculine image of God from the feminine image of God is inaccurate, unbiblical, and damaging to both men and women.

Specifically, by teaching that the three bolded desires above are ONLY masculine, Eldredge diminishes the beauty, mutuality, and mystery of the sexes, and ultimately demeans women by denying the following truths:

- Women, as well as men, have an adventure to live; and men, as well as women, have an adventure to share. Separating these thoughts in any way is needlessly reductionistic. Women are not just passively waiting around to be unveiled, pursued, or yearned for. For example, many conservative Christians grew up being taught that "men are initiators and women responders." But is this nature or nurture? Is it part of God's design or someone's popularized opinion or experience? Is it biblical or just a reflection of a certain subculture? Women are so much more than objects of desire.[455] As Tremper Longman points out, in Song of Songs, "the woman is the main speaker and initiates the relationship."[456] We see this in the example of Ruth who boldly pursued and cared for her mother-in-law,

---

454 Ibid., 9.
455 One female friend observed that "Eldredge seems to assume men have adventures and women just want to come along as a sidekick. When really, we are all, men and women, called to share in God's adventure. We are all supposed to be the sidekicks in His plan."
456 Tremper Longman III, *Proverbs: Baker Commentary on the Old Testament* (Grand Rapids, MI: Baker, 2006), 540.

Naomi, on their shared, grief-stricken adventure into the unknown. Or think of the courage of Queen Esther whose timely initiative literally saved her people from extinction.

- Women are actively engaged in the battle of life. In looking at the Proverbs 31 woman, for example, in verse 11 it says, "Her husband can trust her, and she will greatly enrich his life." The Hebrew word behind "enrich his life" is plunder or the spoils of war. Longman notes, "the idea of the verse seems to suggest that the woman is a warrior in the battle of life. She goes out and fights on behalf of her family and comes back with the victor's spoils, which allow her family to thrive in the midst of the conflict."[457] This is a metaphorical example; however, another real-life exemplar from the Old Testament is Abigail. She mercifully went out to fight for her husband's life. Had she waited around to be pursued, things would have turned out very differently.[458]

- Women—not just men—care about rescuing beauty. Should "rescuing beauty" be confined to militaristically saving a damsel in distress? Is not a mom or dad's nurture and care for their children rescuing beauty? Might not it also be rightly applied to someone's passionate commitment to save unborn children or even an endangered coral reef? Preborn children and God's creation in nature are certainly beauties to rescue.[459]

Since writing my thesis, I have come to learn that a healthy view of male and female differences promotes mutuality, not one sex over, or at the expense of, the other. Yes, women can bear children and men can't. And, yes, on average men are physically 50 percent stronger than women. These are biological facts, and they play out differently based

---

[457] Tremper Longman III, *Proverbs: Baker Commentary on the Old Testament* (Grand Rapids, MI: Baker, 2006), 543.

[458] See 1 Samuel 25:2-42.

[459] Another prevalent evangelical teaching related to this is that "men care about significance and women security." But again, is this nature—part of God's design? Or just nurture—the way we were raised or thought it was supposed to be? In the adventure of life where there's beauty to rescue, why can't it be a human thing—something men and women do equally together—to care about both significance (Matt. 6:33) and security (Rom. 8:35–39)?

on the people involved, the voices they listen to, and the times they live in. But that doesn't mean strength is a masculine virtue and not a feminine one. Think of the great Old Testament military leader Deborah or her colleague– one of the first female assassins, Jael.[460] Again, note that strength is characteristic of the Proverbs 31 woman:

- "She girds herself with strength, and strengthens her arms." (31:17, KJV)
- And here's the same verse in the NLT: "She is energetic and strong…"

As Longman observes, in this verse, "the woman's strength is praised in a way that may surprise those who incorrectly believe that is reserved for men in the Bible"[461]

Finally, Eldredge's thought-provoking insights about how great literature and movies awaken or reveal core desires—although harmful when applied to men only[462] —are spot on when applied to both sexes: God, the reckless loving warrior who has placed eternity in our hearts (Eccl. 3:11), invites us into relationship and a spiritual battle. He's the God of Easter who gave us his only Son because we are part of his beauty to rescue.[463]

Learning from Eowyn

Much of what I've struggled to nuance and steal back in this chapter is captured in an intriguing scene in *The Lord of the Rings: The Two Towers*. Sauron's dark forces begin to overcome peaceful Middle Earth and its fate rests in the hands of two hobbits, a dwarf, an elf, and a man named Aragorn. Knowing that a militia of ruthless soldiers is heading for the country of Rohan, Aragorn comes to help its people. As he walks about the palace, he finds the King of Rohan's niece,

---

[460] See Judges 4.
[461] Tremper Longman III, *Proverbs: Baker Commentary on the Old Testament* (Grand Rapids, MI: Baker, 2006), 544.
[462] As real-world evidence of this, one female millennial who had read her father's copy of *Wild at Heart* as a young teen shared: "For what it's worth, the exclusive application of these qualities or desires to men is what made me think for a number of years in my early teens that I was transgender—although I didn't know the word for it at the time. So yes, these teachings as put forth by Eldredge are quite harmful."
[463] John Eldredge, *Wild at Heart* (Nashville, TN: Thomas Nelson, 2001), 16–17.

Eowyn, practicing with a large sword. She doesn't know Aragorn is watching. Though petite, she is formidable, wielding the large silver sword like an experienced soldier. As Aragorn suddenly steps out of the darkness, she reacts with agility, and their swords clash. Aragorn comments on her skill.

She replies, "The women of Rohan have had to learn that just because you do not carry a sword does not mean you cannot die upon one. I fear neither death nor pain."

Curious, Aragorn asks, "What do you fear?"

"A cage," she says. "To stay behind bars until use and old age accept them and all chance of valor has gone beyond recall or desire."

♦ Prayer: Lord, help us to love our daughters and granddaughters well. Please eradicate any disrespectful, inaccurate views that dismiss women as mere sidekicks on the male adventure. Please help us to "steal back" and champion God's heart for women, as well as a full-orbed view of internal beauty that sees the Beatitudes as essential qualities for *all* who claim to be Christians. Please forgive us for feminizing virtues like meekness, gentleness, a quiet spirit, purity, peacemaking, and mercy.

May we as men and women—equally and together— seek you, share in *Your* adventure, and work to see your beauty unveiled. May we raise sons and daughters like Eowyn who, with love as their weapon, effectively battle for truth in a way that 1) helps people leave their caged existences of fear, shame, anger, and resentment, choosing instead hope and possibility; and 2) strengthens others enough to not only carry their own load, but also bear the burdens of others.[464]

In doing this, please help us care for ourselves so that we can love our neighbors well. May you give us wisdom and discernment so that we might have proper boundaries, yet never forget what Annie Dillard said so poignantly:

> When the candle is burning, who looks at the wick? When the candle is out, who needs it? But the world without light is

---

[464] Galatians 6:1-5.

wasteland and chaos, and a life without sacrifice is an abomination.[465]

Amen.

---

[465] From *Holy the Firm*.

CHAPTER THIRTEEN: THE WOUND IS WHERE THE LIGHT SHINES THROUGH

Last year, my work on this book got seriously interrupted when the conditions my dad was living in forced me to stop and ask, "Does recovering God's heart for dads apply to my heart and actions toward my own father?"

By his own choice, my then eighty-one-year-old Dad had been living in an assisted living home for the last seven years. In early 2020, he got and survived COVID-19. Although the virus didn't take his life, it did take a lot out of him and, combined with the isolation and immobility from quarantine, left him dependent on a wheelchair 90 percent of the time.

Throughout 2020, I tried to see him weekly—first through a window, then outside, socially distanced with a mask. In the first half of 2021 we would visit inside, but still masked. Because of the quarantine, the facility hadn't sent anyone out for medical care unless it was an emergency. Under-resourced like many privately-run homes, his facility relied on an inexpensive transport service to get residents to medical appointments. Unbelievably, 75 percent of the time a vehicle either didn't show up or, if it did, it was one to two hours late. Bottomline, my dad was languishing and unable to get the medical care he needed, and I was the only family member in his life to do something about his situation.

In my last book, *How I Became a Christian Despite the Church*, I noted that the most important area of growth I'm still working on is "learning to love." And sometimes that growth is painful as love often costs and isn't easy—especially when it touches our wounds. Christians at times

223

fall into the trap of selectively pointing out certain sins in others they view as abominations, all the while tolerating their own sins—especially a lack of love. Yet as Annie Dillard noted at the end of the last chapter, "…a life without sacrifice is an abomination."

Looking inward, I began to ask, "What does sacrificial love for my dad look like?" and "What does honoring God look like in his situation?" I really wasn't sure, but I was losing sleep and knew I had to do something.

Windows of Grace for Wounded Healers

I mentioned at the beginning of this book that the painful parts of our story matter to God and can become windows of grace in our healing. I also said that I wanted to save the most thorough discussion of the father wound for this chapter. Again, this is because each of us—at our best—will always be "wounded healers." In other words, we don't have the luxury of understanding and eradicating everything wrong with us before we start "learning to love" and parenting.

This chapter's title is from Switchfoot's 2016 album *Where the Light Shines Through* and was inspired in part by Leonard Cohen's great lyric from his song "Anthem:"

> Ring the bells that still can ring
> Forget your perfect offering
> There is a crack, a crack in everything
> That's how the light gets in[466]

What determines whether one peeks through the cracks of one's wounds to find healing, or just works more frantically to patch them and build thicker walls? Further, where are the lines between God's sovereignty and power to lovingly overcome our facades, and our ability to resist Him?

I don't know all the answers to these questions. But what I do know—especially through journeying with my dad these last two years—is that light can shine through the father wound in at least six

---

[466] From the album *The Future* by Leonard Cohen (Columbia, 1992).

ways. And in what follows in this conclusion to our discussion, I'll share and unpack each.

1. The father wound presents an opportunity to practice our faith.

"Honor your father and your mother" is a command that's central to our faith, even if discerning exactly what that looks like is challenging in various seasons of life– whether we are the child or the parent. Many of us have personally experienced the emotional, physical, and psychological fatigue associated with caring for aging parents. As one friend recently shared, "It's an intense commitment with challenges dealing with the later stages of life, as well as working things out with siblings."

As I was researching this book, I came across this verse from Ephesians that I found particularly relevant: "For this reason, I bow my knees before the Father, from whom *every family* in heaven and on earth is named" (Eph 3:14).

The italicized words are more literally translated "every fatherhood" or "every paternity," as this is the meaning of the Greek word used here: *patria*. In this context, it's closely related to God the Father (pater). "Every fatherhood" also shows Paul's creative wordplay: "For this cause I bow my knees to the Father of our Lord Jesus Christ, of whom all paternity [every fatherhood] in heaven and earth is named…" (Eph. 3:14, DRB). Here's the Roman Catholic take on how this verse relates to honoring parents:

- "The divine fatherhood is the source of human fatherhood; this is the foundation of the honor owed to parents."[467]

In other words, our parents are our source and contributed to making and establishing us, regardless of the closeness we may or may not experience with them. For their role in our

---

[467] *Catechism of the Catholic Church* (Liguori, MO: Liguori Publications, 1994), 534. The Catholic Bibles, Catholic Public Domain Version (CPDV) and Douay-Rheims Challoner Revision 1752 (DRC 1752), both reinforce this foundation and insight by translating *patria* in 3:14 as "paternity." The point of this passage is to emphasize "the cosmic scope of God's reign and purposes . . . [all] as existing under the one God."

creation alone, they deserve our honor.[468]

- "As much as they can, they [the parents' children] must give them material and moral support in old age and in times of illness, loneliness, or distress."[469]

On one cool, breezy, Saturday morning in May—around the time I was experiencing insomnia over my dad's situation—Pam and I had the luxury of a three-to-four-hour uninterrupted conversation outside to talk. I shared with her that I was losing sleep over the care my dad wasn't receiving. Unexpectedly, we quickly came to a place of peace and complete agreement that we should ask him to come live with us. (We jokingly told our friends and kids later, "No, we weren't drunk!") We had to try, we thought, even if we might not know how it would end up. We called him that night to ask him, not knowing if he would accept, and the next day he called back to accept our offer.

Being in healthcare and managing the offices of three of the seven doctors my dad needed, Pam took point in getting a handle on and overseeing his healthcare. I went into construction management mode to get our master bedroom ready for him to move into in less than a month. Besides the cost and time it took to prepare our house to meet his needs, Pam and I also had to move upstairs to a room one-third the size of the master bedroom. This meant my clothes ended up in my home office and Pam's clothes were now spread across three floors.

2. The father wound provides a path to greater insight and healing.

As you might expect, it was an exhausting transition, even though my dad had a positive attitude and really tried to make it work. Besides caring for him, Pam and I both worked full-time in jobs with significant responsibilities. Plus, I was writing a lot and trying to plant a church. I thought things like assisting my dad with a shower would

---

[468] Note the parallels here to the universal and redemptive fatherhood of God discussed in chapter three: In the case of God and our parents, they are our source, maker, and establisher whether or not we have intimacy or *Abba* closeness with them.

[469] Ibid., 535.

be one of the hardest parts. It wasn't. It was the date nights, weekends away, and vacations Pam and I had to give up. It was keeping all his meds straight and making sure he got them. It was the plastic table in the middle of our main living space that affected the grandchildren's play area, making a once nicely decorated living room feel like an assisted living cafeteria. Of course, this wasn't his fault and I constantly reminded myself, "Do unto others as you would have them do unto you," as well as asked myself the rhetorical question, "What does sacrificial love look like?"

Honestly, the biggest challenge in caring for my dad was the emotional part, which I was not prepared for. I had experienced enough healing to forgive and see him for a half-hour a week. But now he was in my home 24/7. I wrestled with anger that became harder and harder to hide, especially from Pam. Eventually, the anger turned inward which led to depression. Being tired most of the time, I had a hard time understanding myself or communicating to Pam.

This forced me to face some dishonesty: I was good at pointing out my dad's lack of self-awareness to Pam and others. But what about my own? In caring for my dad, I saw I had not acknowledged the full hurt of my own father wound.

In late August, two months after my dad moved in, I finally got a chance to write out my feelings:

I'm angry and losing hope. Most of my life consists of pleasing other people, have-to's, trying to be a more loving person, and most of the time lately I don't have the energy for it all.

What do I want? More time for whimsy and to cultivate Pam and my relationship. More time to finish a book that's tied to my life's work and, for better or worse, also my relationship with my dad. When my dad was not living in our home, the feelings were in a manageable place. Having him here 24/7, however, has churned them all up. The anger that had dissipated or laid dormant has now resurrected and I don't know how to deal with these emotions.

In many ways, my dad is a pleasant fellow who fancies himself like his hero, Kermit the Frog—a "nice guy" who's always making lemonade out of lemons. So what was I angry about? That we weren't praying at meals anymore because he had been hurt by the church and was no longer a fan of organized religion. That he refused to acknowledge his own responsibility and gullibility in what happened at this cult-like church, and how he had hurt his family and put us at risk. That he had decided to isolate himself even further after my kids graduated, refusing to go to any of their weddings or even his own sisters' funerals. That he almost never asked about how Pam, I, or the kids were doing; or, if he did ask, it felt more like a polite nicety than a desire to really know. That he rarely listened and almost all of our "conversations" consisted in him airing his own opinions, listing his ailments or needs, or anything else *he* wanted to say. That the person I once viewed as thoughtful now no longer gives gifts or even acknowledges any of his family members' special days, including birthdays—ever. That he never made amends for any of his mistakes and instead continued blaming others.

It's as if his lack of healing, constant craving for affirmation, and years of isolation have collectively diminished his capacity to love. For my dad, relationships seem more about survival and manipulating resources than a healthy give and take. Even his expressions of appreciation—frequently mixed with over-the-top flattery—often feel more like a calculated investment in those he might need something from, rather than a genuine statement of gratitude. This last behavior especially has often made those closest to him feel unloved and used.

3. The father wound gives a greater awareness of our own sin.

In becoming more fully aware and acknowledging these wounds from my father, I also became painfully aware of some ugly things about myself. First, there were my judgmental attitudes. How could I know what my dad's deepest motives were? I'm not God: I don't have the ability to see the human heart or sort out its complexities. Then there was the unforgiveness that kept reappearing like an old picture of the Loch Ness monster, making me question what unforgiveness

228

still lurked deep in my heart. But besides the judgmentalism and unforgiveness, pride and a lack of empathy also surfaced.

For example, how did I know that his lack of self-awareness was primarily the result of pride or what I've often referred to as his, "being intoxicated with his own goodness?" What if his blindness has always been more the result of pain he's never fully healed from, including his own father wound? If this is even partially so, my dad deserves my compassion, not my judgment. Further, I stand on his shoulders; he learned the hard way so I wouldn't have to. In particular, much of what I've learned about toxic churches came at the expense of his experience.

The most difficult thing I've had to confront in myself is the way I despised the weakness and human frailty in my dad, while not acknowledging it in myself. This insight came one morning as I forced myself to look at a recent picture of my dad, my sister Vicki, and myself. I hated the picture. It was taken on a day I felt close to a breaking point due to caregiving responsibilities. My dad is seated in a wheelchair at the center of the picture—old, small, and frail—a shadow of the man I remember from when we both were younger. To the left is my 53-year-old-sister, whose brilliant writer's mind was irreparably damaged by a traumatic brain injury. She's holding her crippled arm tightly fisted—like a claw—against her chest, the other on my dad's back. On his right, I'm leaning forward, standing taller than both, with one hand on my sister's back and the other on my dad's shoulder. My facial expression is strained; my eyes betray anger and weariness. I look old and tired.

At first, I thought I didn't like the picture because of how I look in it, or because it reminds me of an unhappy memory. I later realized I hated the brokenness, weakness, aging, and frailty in the picture. I wanted to cut myself out of it. I wanted to be an exception to the human experience—strong, exciting, privileged, and forever young. Tears welled up as a hard truth flooded in, overwhelming my emotions: I'm not separate from this picture but part of it—as I too am part of the human condition; fallen, broken, weak, aging, and frail. In other words, this is my blood. My family. My sister. My father.

Rather than viewing them with contempt, they deserve honor as humans that—just like me—are fearfully and wonderfully made, loved by God, and created in His image. As part of fallen humanity, just like me, they are good, dear, sinful, deeply flawed, wounded, aging people who desperately need God... Just like me. The birth, death, burial, resurrection, and ascension of Christ is proof that they're loved by God. And if I know more about God than someone else, and share that knowledge with them, it's only as one beggar showing another beggar where to find bread.

Henri Nouwen has valuable insights that speak to my dad's spiritual condition:

> Over the years, I have come to realize that the greatest trap in our life is not success, popularity, or power, but self-rejection. Success, popularity, and power can indeed present a great temptation, but their seductive quality often comes from the way they are part of the much larger temptation to self-rejection. When we have come to believe in the voices that call us worthless and unlovable, then success, popularity, and power are easily perceived as attractive solutions. The real trap, however, is self-rejection. As soon as someone accuses me or criticizes me, as soon as I am rejected, left alone, or abandoned, I find myself thinking, "Well, that proves once again that I am a nobody." Self-rejection is the greatest enemy of the spiritual life because it contradicts the sacred voice that calls us the "Beloved." Being the Beloved constitutes the core truth of our existence. [470]

Although I don't see biblical support for self-rejection being *the* greatest enemy of the spiritual life,[471] I definitely agree with Nouwen that—in synch with Malachi's vision of the good life discussed in chapter five[472]—"being the Beloved constitutes the core truth of our

---

[470] Henri Nouwen, *Life of the Beloved: Spiritual Living in a Secular World*.

[471] It would seem that pride (James 4:6) and unbelief (Mark 3:22-30) are the greatest enemies.

[472] As a reminder, Malachi's picture of the "good life" was to be secure in the love of God—"so secure and healed internally that we live with a carefree playfulness, fearing nothing but God...."

existence."

4. Regret from how we've wounded others can lead to repentance and a heightened sense of our need for atonement.

In chapter six, we looked at Gordon Lightfoot's example of how *not* to treat mom or care for your marriage. I'd like to return to his example again—but this time fifty years later, to see what he's learned, albeit the hard way.

A lot has changed since Lightfoot's marriage ended in 1973. Reflecting back, he admits:

> "In my first family, I'm afraid, at that particular time I guess I wasn't around long enough to be of service to them, and I do regret that a great deal to this day," he said. "[I] keep the lines of communication open at all times and see them regularly and the two grandchildren as well… My new family is growing and needs more attention. Since I won't be following the route I did in my first marriage, I will be dealing with it practically. I hope I can handle it."[473]

Thankfully, "making amends for past mistakes… [has] become a priority. Responsibilities to… children…[are] now paramount." His biographer, Jennings notes: "If he's sinned in the past, Lightfoot's future was going to be all about redemption."[474] Indeed, the pain of regret, aging, a near-fatal brain aneurysm in 2004, and a third marriage to actress Kim Hasse have given him a softer heart and a wiser perspective than he had throughout his prime.

His children attest to this positive change: "He's definitely changed after the aneurysm," his daughter Ingrid said, "paying more attention to all of us and calling more."[475] Lightfoot's oldest son, Fred, reflected, "In my younger years I didn't see much of Dad, but he's been very supportive of my kids, especially Ben, who's extremely

[473] Nicholas Jennings, *Lightfoot* (Viking, 2017), 238–239.
[474] Ibid., 238-239.
[475] Ibid., 262.

autistic, and comes to visit a lot."[476] Meredith, one of his children from a later marriage observes, "One of the things that I admire about him is that he realizes he has room to grow... He's still learning things about himself."

Ever since he quit drinking, making amends has preoccupied Lightfoot. Sometimes he called it a process of atonement. Later, he took to saying he was in a state of repentance. Again, here's Lightfoot in his own words:

> I've made a few mistakes in my career, I'll admit them. For the last many years, *I've been in a process of atonement.* Honestly, *I try really hard* to please, particularly when it comes to my family. I feel a really strong responsibility to them.[477]

Notice how I italicized statements that reflect Lightfoot's concept of atonement above. It is clear he knows something of repentance— that is, he has changed and done an about-face regarding some of his "sins." When it comes to atonement though, he still has something critically important to learn. Lightfoot views atonement as something he is capable of doing for himself– not something only God can do. To be fair, this view is held by even many religious people. In most religions, the message is focused on what we need to DO to save or atone for ourselves. In Christianity, the message is focused, rather, on the atonement of Christ—what he has DONE on the cross. Herein lies the truth and good news for Gordon Lightfoot or any of us: As we mentioned in chapter three, all—whether prodigal son or elder brother—fall short and need atonement. Yet, none of us can atone for our sins, and salvation is a gift found only in dependence upon the finished sacrifice of Christ:

- "Yet to all who did receive him, to those who believed in his name, he gave the right to become children of God..."[478]
- "But to one who without works trusts him who justifies the

---

[476] Ibid., 265.
[477] Ibid., 240.
[478] John 1:12, NIV.

ungodly, such faith is reckoned as righteousness."[479]

5. The father wound provides a unique opportunity to experience God's love and provision.

Earlier, I shared the Roman Catholic teaching that, "as much as they can, they [children] must give them [parents] material and moral support in old age and in times of illness, loneliness, or distress."[480] Hitting a wall of hopelessness and depression with my own dad's care, I revisited this guidance to think about it more deeply. It's worth noting "as much as they can," does not mean center your lives around or stop caring for yourself or your marriage. And it doesn't mean giving up all the benefits associated with a particular season of life to care for your parent(s) either.

In caring for my dad, I came to recognize that, "as much as you can" included acknowledging the unsustainability of our current situation. And so, in early October, I made a determined shift from trying to sustain what we were currently doing to transitioning him into the best long-term care facility we could find near us. Pam and I chose to divide and conquer. She would prioritize completing all the doctor visits and tests he needed, with the goal of having a good baseline on his health by the end of the month. I would research long-term care facilities near us, pick the top three, and get him on their waiting lists. Not wanting him to worry unnecessarily, the plan was for me to talk to him at the end of the month, once we got him on the waiting lists.

I had no idea how my dad was going to respond to our decision—whether he suspected it, whether he would understand, be upset, sad, or relieved. To give extra emotional space for the conversation, I planned to take a day off work and also asked my mom and several close friends to pray. Two days before the talk was to happen, my dad was unexpectedly admitted to the hospital due to low oxygen and fluid retention. Thankfully, these issues were quickly addressed, but it became clear he could not be left alone going forward. This paved the way for our talk and although he initially felt like, as he put it, "a ping pong ball in a hurricane," he said he totally understood, appreciated all

---

[479] Romans 4:5, NRSV.
[480] Ibid., 535.

we were doing, and trusted us to do what was best.

Providentially, due to the timing of when he went into the hospital and the urgency of his situation, a spot "just happened" to open up in the best of the three options we had identified. God in his mercy answered our prayers and provided for our needs in a way that showed me even more of his heart first-hand: "A bruised reed he will not break, and a dimly burning wick he will not quench; he will faithfully bring forth justice."[481]

6. The father wound can give us laser focus for what is most important in life.

Wounds can give us a heightened sense of what we don't want to do and who we don't want to be. Although my dad did his best to be involved, responsible, and committed up until I was 20, he chose to be only minimally involved in my later life—sadly, even more so in the lives of my children. I was blessed by his early example; yet I and my children were hurt by his later one. But in those wounds, I've experienced God in a way that I might not otherwise have experienced: "When my father and my mother forsake me, then the LORD will take care of me."[482]

To say it another way, I came to experience a unique part of God's loving heart through the cracks in my own. On many occasions, as his light penetrated my bitterness, I repented and grew to new places of understanding, empathy, and forgiveness. Moreover, I also developed rock-solid convictions about the consequential significance of father absence and father involvement. Through research, reflecting on my wounds, and hearing the stories of others, I've come to understand the power parents have—especially fathers—to either damage a child's capacity to receive God's love or be a conduit to it.

As sociologist Christian Smith put it:

> The good news is that, among all possible influences, parents exert far and away the greatest influence on their children's religious outcomes. Stated differently, the bad news is that

---

[481] Isaiah 42:3, NRSV.
[482] Psalm 27:10, KJV.

nearly all human responsibility for the religious trajectories of children's lives falls on their parents' shoulders. The empirical evidence is clear.[483]

As we noted in the conclusion of chapter six, both moms and dads have exceptional value to God in that they partner with Him in turning the hearts of their children toward His ancient paths. Or as Pastor Andy Stanley said, "Your greatest contribution to the kingdom of God may not be something you do but someone you raise."[484] Embracing this vision and calling is a powerful motivator to live life well and with joy.

Carrying the Fire as a Friend of God

In 2003, I attended the National Fatherhood Initiative's Fatherhood Summit and Gala in Philadelphia. While there, I got to mingle with several celebrities, including football star Chris Carter, Frank Abagnale (whose story was told in the 2002 movie *Catch Me if You Can*), James Earl Jones (the voice of Darth Vader), and the late Stephen Covey (a modern day Socrates and author of the book *The Seven Habits of Highly Effective People*). I remember approaching Mr. Covey, whose demeanor was full of wisdom, humility, and gentleness. I said, "Sir, it is great to meet you. I got a lot out of your book." He smiled humbly and said, "Who are you?" I said, "Oh, my name is Greg Austen and I am here to give the invocation tonight. I'm just Roland's pastor." (At that time, Roland was the President of National Fatherhood Initiative.) He paused thoughtfully, then put his hand on my shoulder and said, "You are a lot more than that, Greg. You are a friend of God."

His words penetrated deeply and still whisper to my soul years later: as a Christian and pastor, I am truly a friend of God. The words of John 15:15–16a come to mind:

No longer do I call you servants, for the servant does not know what his master is doing; but I have called you friends, for all

---

483 https://www.firstthings.com/article/2021/05/keeping-the-faith
484 From Session 1 of the 2013 leadership summit called Catalyst West.

that I have heard from my Father I have made known to you. You did not choose me but I chose you and appointed you that you should go and bear fruit and that your fruit should abide.

What a mind-boggling, amazing privilege it is to be a friend of the God of the Universe! God used Mr. Covey's words in a powerful way that night to lift my head and bow my heart at the honor of being one of His pastors, a shepherd of souls. But there is a related and even greater truth: Parents and especially fathers—more than any other people on the planet—are in a strategic position to introduce their children to the possibility of friendship with God!

Could there be any greater privilege? Any more sobering responsibility? Make no mistake, friend, if you're a parent or grandparent, and especially if you're a father, you are the primary conduit for passing on God's heart to your children and grandchildren. Without a doubt, there is no greater calling than enjoying friendship with God, "carrying the fire," and passing on both to the next generation.

All I have in this world
Is fire from above
All I have in this world
Is you

And all the journeys I have walked
I know you've walked them too
All I want is to be faithful
All I want is you

All I have is a love
That set my world on fire
Let it fall, let it burn in me
And oh to be a friend of God is all that I desire
All I want is to be faithful
All I want is you[485]

---

[485] Michael W. Smith, "All I Want" *Healing Rain*, Reunion, 2004.

BONUS TRACK: IRREPLACEABLE: RECOVERING GOD'S HEART FOR DADS PLAYLIST[486]

I created a playlist and continually listened to it during the last two years of this project. It includes many eras and genres of music, but every song inspired, stretched, and helped me feel the gamut of emotions that this book has attempted to speak to. I pray it helps give voice to the deepest parts of you and is a catalyst for creating your own "Irreplaceable" playlist. Admittedly, it's an honest expression of the good, the bad, and the ugly in our stories. It also includes a few songs that may seem out-of-place. In these instances, there was some phrase, verse, or chorus that connected me with my dad. Finally, you'll find that this playlist is heavy on folk and classic rock, and light on country. That's me and I understand if it's not you. As they say, eat the meat and spit out the bones. But above all, enjoy!

"Cat's in the Cradle," Harry Chapin
"The Rub of Love," Chagall Guevara
"Ships," Barry Manilow
"Blessed," Elton John
"The Last Song," Elton John
"The Prodigal Son Suite," Keith Green
"Leader of the Band," Dan Fogelberg

---

[486] An almost complete version of this list except "Circle Game" and "My Buddy" are available on Spotify. Just type in the title of the book. Or if you have trouble, use this link:
https://open.spotify.com/playlist/1nJ2TTE5gCULCKmgKCcPA2?si=755351173 6b34b7d

"Song for My Father," Sarah McLachlan
"Not All Heroes Wear Capes," Owl City
"Watercolor Ponies," Wayne Watson
"Coming Around Again," Remastered, Carly Simon
"Father and Son," Cat Stevens
"Before the Throne of God Above," Shane & Shane
"How Deep the Father's Love," Chelsea Moon & Uncle Daddy
"Oh, the Deep, Deep, Love of Jesus," Audrey Assad, Fernando Ortega
"Hero," David Crosby
"Stay Strong," Newsboys
"Razor Face," Elton John
"Doesn't Have to Be This Way," Alison Krauss & Union Station
"Day is Done," Peter, Paul, and Mary
"The Pony Man," Gordon Lightfoot
"Return to Pooh Corner," Kenny Loggins
"The Best Day," Taylor Swift
"Piece by Piece," Kelly Clarkson
"Papa Was a Rollin' Stone, Single Version," The Temptations
"The Living Years," Mike & the Mechanics
"Sweet Child of Mine," Viggo Mortensen, George Mackay, Samantha Isler, Annalise Basso, Nicholas Hamilton, Kirk Ross, Philip Klein
"Memories Down the Line," Kansas
"Hero," Family of the Year
"The Love of God," Rich Mullins
"Reckless Love," Cory Asbury
"Shoulders," for King & Country
"Run to the Father," Cody Carnes
"Madonna," Oh Father
"Hallowed," Jennifer Knapp
"Heal the World," Michael Jackson
"Everyday Life," Coldplay
"Abba Father," Michael Card
"Forefathers," Dan Fogelberg
"Creed," Rich Mullins
"Dear Theodosia" (feat. Ben Folds), Regina Specktor, Ben Folds

"I Want to Be Just Like You," Phillips, Craig & Dean
"Gracie," Ben Folds
"Kentucky Rose," Michael W. Smith
"First Family," Rich Mullins
"We've Only Just Begun," The Carpenters
"Skyfall," Adele
"Evergreen" (Love Theme from "A Star is Born"), Barbara Streisand
"The Visit," Regina Specktor
"U Can't Touch This," MC Hammer
"Good Good Father," Chris Tomlin
"Pressure Machine," The Killers
"Refiners Fire," The Worship Project, Brian Doerksen, TWP Band
"Messiah, HWV 56, Pt. 1," George Frideric Handel, London
Philharmonic
"Was It Worth It," Lecrae, Derek Minor, Crystal Nicole
"Still Bleeding," Andy Mineo, Co Campbell
"Family Photo," Andy Mineo, Weatherman
"Masterpiece," KB
"Hit You Where You Live," Petra
"David's Song," Steve & Annie Chapman
"Seasons of a Man," Steve & Annie Chapman
"Where the Light Shines Through," Switchfoot
"For Lovin' Me/ Did She Mention My Name," Gordon Lightfoot
"Happy Together," Remastered, The Turtles
"Anthem," Leonard Cohen
"Bird With Broken Wing," Don Francisco
"Desire," U2
"Wedding Song" (There is Love), Paul Stookey
"Women And Wives," Studio Outtake, Paul McCartney
"Bad," Remastered 2009, U2
"Footsteps," Michael W. Smith
"Keep Me In The Moment," Jeremy Camp
"The Flame Passes On," Whiteheart
"Spirit of the Living God," Audrey Assad
"Unless the Lord Builds The House," Keith Green
"Manger Throne" (with Derri Daughterty), Third Day, Derri

Daughterty, Julie Miller

"We Didn't Start the Fire," Billy Joel

"Grow As We Go," (feat. Sara Bareilles), Ben Platt, Sara Bareilles

"Relate" (R3HAB REmix),for King & Country, R3HAB

"A Million Lights," Michael W. Smith

"Conversation," Michael W. Smith

"I'm Still Alive," David C. Clements

"Darling," Halsey

"You're Still The One," Remixed/Remastered, Shania Twain

"Mighty to Save," Newsboys

"Child of Love," We the Kingdom

"The Two Lost Sons" (Luke 15), Caroline Cobb

"Godspeed" (Sweet Dreams), The Chicks

"The Circle Game," Joni Mitchell (no longer on Spotify)

"My Buddy," Halo (only on Youtube)

"All I Want," Michael W. Smith

ACKNOWLEDGEMENTS

First, I want to express my profound appreciation to my editors: Alli Nielsen and Tim Austen. I could not have done this without either of you. Alli, as my friend and favorite contrarian, thank you for making me think deeper, express myself better, and say things in a way that offends less people. Tim, as one of the finest writers I know, thank you for your sacrifice and commitment to this project. Its creative structuring and consistent formatting owe much to your expertise. Our friendship; conversations; and all the perspectives and learnings you continue to share are among the greatest blessings of my life.

Second, I incredibly indebted to the following friends and family for their research, edits, valuable feedback, or encouragement on this project: Pam Austen, Lois Hart, Josh and Emily Ginchereau, Matthew and Kylie Austen, Sarah Austen, Roland Warren, Todd Ramer, Darrell Proctor, Gary Springer, Alex Hettinga, Maurice Wilson, Brian Vare, Kathleen Patterson, Andrew Wood, Tim Shea, Erik Vecere, Rob Denler, Amy Ford, Bob Hershey, Eve Gleason, Vince DiCaro, Tom Loper, and Bob Hershey.

Third, I'm extremely grateful to you, the reader. If there's something specific that encouraged you or any suggestion(s) you have for improvement, I would love to hear from you. Please drop me a note at gregausten7@gmail.com.

Finally, if you've been blessed by the message of this book, here's how you can help get the word out:

- If you bought it on Amazon, please leave a review (you can only do this if you actually bought the book). If you didn't buy the book on Amazon, purchase one as a gift for a friend or

family member and then leave a review.
- Share your endorsement on social media.

Again, thanks so much!

ABOUT THE AUTHOR

Dr. Greg Austen is the Executive Director of Church Outreach & Engagement for Care Net and a part-time church planter with the Evangelical Presbyterian Church (EPC). In his role with Care Net, Greg leads a seven-member team as they equip pregnancy centers and churches to offer compassion, hope, help, and long-term discipleship to women and men facing pregnancy decisions, as well as strengthen fathers and families.

Prior to this, Greg worked at National Fatherhood Initiative for eleven years, and has served as a pastor in New Jersey, Kentucky, and Pennsylvania. A seasoned communicator and community strategist, Greg holds a D.Min. from Westminster Theological Seminary, an M.Div. from Southern Seminary, and a B.S. from Cairn University.

Greg is the author of *How I Became a Christian Despite the Church* and writes a weekly blog at **carpentertheologian.com**. He lives in the Greater Philadelphia area with his wife, Pam, near their three children and seven grandchildren.

A few of Greg's favorite things include exploring new places with Pam; spending time with his kids and grandkids; his black lab, Sydney; quiet mornings writing or with a good book, and a cup of fresh, ground coffee. Greg also loves walks and long bike rides on a beautiful day; bakeries and bookstores; a meal with a friend; spy and mystery thrillers; a good IPA; making playlists; and listening to all kinds of music.

Made in the USA
Middletown, DE
11 November 2022

14700513R00146